MAKING WHOLE
WHAT HAS BEEN SMASHED

John Torpey

Making Whole
What Has Been Smashed

On Reparations Politics

HARVARD UNIVERSITY PRESS

Cambridge, Massachusetts, and London, England   2006

Library of Congress Cataloging-in-Publication Data

Torpey, John C.
    Making whole what has been smashed : on reparations politics / John Torpey.
       p.   cm.
    Includes bibliographical references (p.   ) and index.
    ISBN 0-674-01943-1 (alk. paper)
    1. Reparations for historical injustices—Social aspects.   I. Title.
    KZ6785.T67   2006
    340'.115—dc22   2005052667

A Klee painting named "Angelus Novus" shows an angel looking as though he is about to move away from something he is fixedly contemplating. His eyes are staring, his mouth is open, his wings are spread. This is how one pictures the angel of history. His face is turned toward the past. Where we perceive a chain of events, he sees one single catastrophe which keeps piling wreckage upon wreckage and hurls it in front of his feet. The angel would like to stay, awaken the dead, and make whole what has been smashed. But a storm is blowing from Paradise; it has got caught in his wings with such violence that the angel can no longer close them. This storm irresistibly propels him into the future to which his back is turned, while the pile of debris before him grows skyward. This storm is what we call progress.

Walter Benjamin, "Theses on the Philosophy of History"

Contents

Acknowledgments

The research discussed in this book has been generously supported over the last several years by a number of institutions, to which I would like to record my gratitude: the Peace and Conflict Studies Program at the University of California, Irvine; the University of California Institute for Global Conflict and Cooperation; the University of California Center for German and European Studies; the Center for Research on Immigration and Integration in the Metropolis (RIIM, aka "Metropolis") in Vancouver; the Social Sciences and Humanities Research Council of Canada; and the Hoover Chair in Economic and Social Ethics, Université Catholique de Louvain, Belgium, where I had the great privilege of being a Visiting Fellow in October–November 2003. I also benefited greatly from the discussions that took place at a symposium on "Politics and the Past: On Repairing Historical Injustices" that I organized under the auspices of the Institute for European Studies and the Peter Wall Institute of Advanced Studies at the University of British Columbia in late February 2000.

I have spoken about the issues addressed in the book in numerous venues over the past several years, and I want to thank the many people who participated in those exchanges for their insights. I'm sure that the ideas of many others have found their way into the book, and I hope I have adequately thanked those who helped along the way.

There are a number of people whom I would like to thank more directly, however. I am particularly grateful to the following: Heribert Adam for extensive discussions over the last several years of the issues raised in this book, as well as for our battles on the tennis court; Malcolm Anderson, who gave me a push when I really needed it; Christian Joppke, who offered trenchant comments on an earlier draft; Bob Ratner, for valuable exchanges on these and other issues over the past few years, and for reminding me to watch the occasional hockey game; and Peter Seixas, who has helped sustain my interest in these issues through his Center for the Study of Historical Consciousness at UBC and who has also kept me fit with more tennis. I owe a special debt to Charles Maier, whom I first got to know as a postdoctoral fellow at Harvard's Center for European Studies in connection with work on East Germany; his ideas have been a constant source of inspiration and wisdom on this project. I would also like to thank Jeanne Batalova, Sharon McConnell, and Joseph Tan for their research assistance in the course of this project, and to Rosa Sevy for her efforts in the research and writing of Chapter 3.

This book was finished shortly before the arrival of my daughter, Zoe, and I want to take this opportunity to thank her for her contribution to hastening its completion and for providing me with a welcome alternative to thinking about politics and the past. For her, and for her mother, I hope this book will help make for a more comprehensible present and a better future.

Introduction

In a *New Yorker* cartoon from late 2001, two men are depicted on either side of a desk, one seated and one standing. The man seated appears to be white, whereas the man standing (and speaking) appears to be dark-skinned, though of ambiguous ethnicity. The man standing, presumably the subordinate of the pair, says to the other man, presumably his boss, "Well, if there's not going to be any bonus, how about some reparations?"[1] Soon thereafter, the brilliantly irreverent weekly *The Onion* ran a piece entitled "Four Generations of Americans Demand Sitcom Reparations," poking fun at the notion of payments for past wrongs by suggesting that the major networks should compensate people for having wasted their time with decades of televisual pap.[2]

The cartoon and the satirical item tell us two things: first, that the notion of "reparations" has become sufficiently mainstream that it is assumed to be familiar to the diverse (if rather hip) audiences of *The New Yorker* and *The Onion;* and, second, that the idea of "reparations," usually connected to efforts to redress some past injustice, is sufficiently dubious—sullied, perhaps, by its association with the pursuit of mere lucre—that it may be flippantly compared to a year-end bonus or skewered in satire. In all events, what is worth noting is that the concept of reparations has come to assume a large enough place in the culture that it came to be the subject of such treatments at all.

Writing at the height of what the Nigerian author and Nobel Laureate Wole Soyinka has called "a *fin de millénaire* fever of atonement,"[3] the historian Elazar Barkan argued that the spread of reparations politics is a "neo-Enlightenment" phenomenon reflecting the fact that "liberal Enlightenment principles have become the predominant global ideology at the end of the twentieth century."[4] This enthusiastic embrace of the spread of rep-

1

arations politics reflected the end-of-century ebullience that attended the settlement of claims mounted by Holocaust survivors and slave laborers in the Nazi camps against banks and companies in Switzerland, Germany, Austria, and other countries as well as against the governments of these countries.

These settlements came hot on the heels of the widely touted South African Truth and Reconciliation Commission (TRC), the "mother" of all institutions overseeing what has come to be known, rather awkwardly, as "transitional justice." The charter of the TRC had mandated payment of reparations to the victims of state-sponsored violence, and payments began in late 1998.[5] Talk of reparations for perennially impoverished Africa had been in the air since at least the early 1990s, when the Organization for African Unity organized a panel to discuss the possibility of seeking reparations for past wrongs. Without giving in to the demand for reparations, Bill Clinton at least expressed "regret" for American involvement in the slave trade, the mapping of which the United Nations Educational, Scientific and Cultural Organization (UNESCO) had undertaken in an effort to clarify this disturbingly consequential past. Notwithstanding Clinton's reticence about American involvement in the slave trade, city councils across the United States adopted resolutions calling for reparations for African-Americans; a long-ignored race riot in Tulsa, Oklahoma in the 1920s made national headlines as a commission of inquiry recommended that the state pay reparations to the survivors;[6] and an ad placed by the neoconservative agit-propagandist David Horowitz in campus newspapers across the United States provoked an uproar and a speaking tour in which Horowitz debated the issue with supporters of reparations for black Americans.[7] Even activists seeking reform of the International Monetary Fund and the World Bank had begun to demand "reparations" for the harm allegedly caused by so-called "structural adjustment" policies.[8] In short, reparations seemed to have become the demand *du jour* in progressive circles during the 1990s.

In the meantime, however, the mood surrounding claims for compensation for past injustices has grown more subdued. In part, the attacks of September 11, 2001 undermined the prospects of reparations politics by focusing the world's attention on the all too clear and present danger of terrorism and on the United States' apparently open-ended war against it. Only two months before the attacks, in anticipation of the upcoming United Nations (U.N.) Conference on Racism that took place in late summer 2001 in Durban, South Africa, the prominent nongovernmental organization

Human Rights Watch published a document titled "An Approach to Reparations" that essentially sought to expand the now-traditional framework of compensation for victims of violations of human rights to recompense for older wrongs rooted in slavery. The document called for commissions of inquiry—the equivalent, it said, of truth commissions—to investigate economic inequalities stemming from slavery, the slave trade, and apartheid in the United States, Brazil, and South Africa.[9] This was a remarkable and innovative intervention in the reparations discussion. In the aftermath of 9/11, however, Human Rights Watch has found that its priorities lie elsewhere, and nothing further was heard about the proposal.

Another cause of the relatively becalmed state of reparations politics since the turn of the new millennium is that those seeking compensation for past injustices have significant achievements to their credit. The funds set up by the Swiss, German, and Austrian governments to compensate those whose bank accounts had been improperly held or who had worked as slave or forced labor under the Nazis began payouts to their beneficiaries. The last of the Japanese-descent groups pressing for redress for their internment during World War II, the "Peruvian" or "South American" Japanese, received compensation at the rate of one-quarter of the amount paid to the Japanese-Americans, or $5,000.[10] The World War II–related cases, from which the wave of reparations politics had largely issued, increasingly reached some semblance of "closure."

Demands for reparations for Africa have similarly subsided, though not because they have been achieved; instead, the cause of reparations for Africa foundered at least in part because the quest for reparations was intrinsically problematic. In particular, it was unclear whether reparations were to be for the slave trade or for colonialism, which would have entailed quite different strategies.[11] The lack of clear culpability for slavery—especially the implication of Africans themselves in the slave trade—has surely exacerbated the difficulties associated with claims that Western countries ought to compensate African countries for the wrongs of long ago.[12] Some limited debt relief seems to be all that remains of that campaign, and at least one prominent African—Senegal's president, Abdoulaye Wade—has spoken out against the idea of reparations or even of debt relief, and recommended a bootstrap approach to resolving Africa's economic woes.[13]

Still, the pursuit of reparations is far from dead for a variety of groups. Those who mobilized around atonement for the "rape of Nanking" and many of the surviving World War II sexual slaves of the Japanese army, the "comfort women," remain unrequited. The issue of reparations for African-Americans bubbles along and may yet become a major subject of contention in American politics, although slavery-related lawsuits and even the effort to gain reparations for the Tulsa race riot have encountered major difficulties in the courts.[14] The matter of resolving land and other outstanding claims by Indian groups in North America persists, as Indians on reservations remain among the poorest and most marginalized populations in their nations as well as claimants to self-determination. With the failure of the Australian government to go much beyond a "Sorry Day" commemorating the mistreatment of the continent's indigenous population, the matter of the "stolen generation"—aboriginal children separated, often forcibly, from their families of origin in the interest of turning them into white Australians—continues to stir public controversy. There are also aboriginal land claims to address in Australia. Meanwhile, attorneys and activists concerned with South Africa opened a new phase in the pursuit of reparations for apartheid-era wrongs when, in June 2002, they filed a $50 billion class action suit against Citigroup, UBS, and Credit Suisse in Swiss courts.[15] To complicate the South African picture further, indigenous groups in South Africa—the Griqua, the Khoi, and the San—have also raised land claims going back to the initial settlement of the country rather than merely to the promulgation of apartheid-era laws that dispossessed Africans.

Thus, although the pace and intensity of reparations politics appear to have declined in the new millennium (and particularly since 9/11), the notion remains vibrant and generates political activity among a host of different groups. The idea of reparations has become firmly embedded in our political vocabulary, and a number of campaigns continue, though perhaps less visibly than had been the case previously. Reparations politics, conducted more in the courtroom than in the streets, offer an appealing avenue for activism in a period of progressive paralysis and disarray.

Arguably, however, the slackening of reparations politics derives chiefly from the fact that Holocaust-related claims—the prototype of all reparations politics—have been largely settled, and those who lived through the Holocaust are gradually dying out, taking their claims with them to the grave.[16] The same is true of those of Japanese descent who were interned as "enemy aliens" in the United States and Canada during World War II, whose campaigns for redress also helped provide the model for other reparations claims. In short, the reparations demands arising from World War II–related misdeeds, which did a great deal to stimulate the spread of the notion of reparations, will soon be superannuated, even in the absence of statutes of limitations for the crimes in question.

Meanwhile, the concern in contemporary politics and intellectual life with "coming to terms with the past" has become pervasive.[17] The leading institutional innovation designed to address past wrongdoing, the truth commission, is perhaps the chief expression of this set of concerns. The jacket copy adorning a comprehensive book on the subject—"How Truth Commissions Around the World Are Challenging the Past and Shaping the Future"—suggests the degree of importance that is now widely imputed to rooting out the wrongs of the past and its significance in building a future.[18]

The late-century spike of reparations politics and the routinization of reparations as a political pursuit raise questions about the meaning and desirability of reparations as a way of achieving political aims. Laudable though the concerns with rectifying past wrongs often are, one wonders whether the proliferation of reparations politics is an entirely good thing. Is it more than mere coincidence that the proliferation of reparations politics comes on the heels of the collapse of socialism and extensive doubts about the viability of the nation-state? The global spread of reparations demands and the preoccupation with the past to which it bears witness reflect an unmistakable decline of a more explicitly future-oriented politics.

Indeed, in contrast to the view that reparations politics amounts to the triumph of Enlightenment modes of thinking, I would argue that the phenomenon is a kind of transitional *substitute* for the progressive politics associated with the Enlightenment, cut out for an age of diminished political expectations. The concern with the past, which is often connected with "roots"-oriented politics of various kinds, bears as much affinity to Romantic notions of group belonging as it does to the ethical universalism of the Enlightenment. The advocates of coming to terms with the past typically respond to this charge by insisting that they are fixated not on the past but on the future. In their way, of course, they are; there is also a range of connections between in-group morality and the pursuit of reparations for various pasts. But the contemporary concern to "make whole what has been smashed" in the past, valuable though it may be for many of the formerly victimized and perhaps for forestalling future wrongdoing, cannot replace the elaboration of a new, progressive vision of the human future out of the shards of twentieth-century history.

To the contrary, reparations politics begins from the assumption that *the road to the future runs through the disasters of the past.* This is a circuitous route to a brighter day, but it is one of the few that seems available in a post-utopian, privatizing, business-mad era. The problem is that, unlike a politics that invokes a vision of progress and redemption for all regardless of race, color, or creed, reparations politics is open to impugning because it inevitably provokes the response that it serves only partial, narrow interests. Despite frequent claims that reparations would be good for all concerned, both perpetrators and victims, reparations politics makes claims on behalf of victims and is hence unavoidably partisan. This is not necessarily a damning objection; most politics of any consequence are divisive. The important questions concern what aims reparations seek to achieve, and whether reparations politics are well-tailored to achieve their aims.

This book explores the spread of reparations politics and the attendant efforts to advance human prospects by demanding a reckoning with past wrongs. Chapter 1 explores the larger political context in which reparations politics has emerged with such force. Chapter 2 analyzes the broad array of types of campaigns that have emerged around the world as a result of the growing legitimacy of the notion of reparations. I then proceed to three case studies of reparations politics. In Chapter 3, Rosa Sevy and I examine the "redress" settlements concerning Japanese-Americans and Japanese-Canadians who were "interned" during World War II. The main objective here is to consider the extent to which such arrangements actually achieve the stated aim of "reconciliation" between perpetrators and victims, for it is generally taken for granted—though without much evidence—that reparations do achieve such ends. In addition, it is intriguing that the Japanese-American case has had such a signal impact on other cases of reparations claims-making; typically, in the American context, political innovations among minorities have been initiated by blacks, whose experience has been paradigmatic for other groups.[19] In Chapter 4, I explore the case of reparations for black Americans. I argue that, although it may be true that one can trace to slavery and segregation many of the ills that still beset blacks in American society, the strategy of "reparations" is an unpromising one for attaining significant improvements in blacks' well-being. In Chapter 5, I explore the varieties of reparations politics in contemporary Southern Africa—specifically, in Namibia and South Africa. The Southern African examples demonstrate well the range of "types" that reparations politics may take. Despite the very different kinds of wrongs for which compensation and recognition have been sought, these cases have built on one another in important ways historically. Indeed, it is both the strength and the shortcoming of the notion of "reparations" that it can encompass efforts to come to terms with so many widely differing pasts. I conclude with some reflections on reparations as a mode of political activity.

The chief argument that runs through the book is that reparations politics is precisely that—a form of *politics*, of people mobilizing to frame facts in an effort to achieve or get things in the world. Indeed, it is politics all the way down, so to speak, as Michael Ignatieff has said of human rights activism more generally.[20] Of course, this is not to say there are no moral issues at stake; far from it. In view of the intrinsically painful pasts that are the object of contention, politics and morality are more closely bound up in many of these struggles than in those around other important political issues such as national health insurance or old age insurance schemes. But this affinity tends to suggest that some of the claims raised by these movements lie beyond the scrutiny of critics; such a situation is often a recipe for trouble of its own. It may be best to separate politics and morality, as Max Weber tended to suggest, but it rarely works out that way in real life; the ethic of responsibility enjoins finding the seam where the normatively desirable meets the historically possible.[21] It is the job of the social analyst, it seems to me, to step back and consider what it all means from as unbiased a perspective as possible. That by no means entails that one has no stake in the outcome—only that one is not necessarily guided by the claims of the participants themselves about what they are doing and why they are doing it. In my view, then, the spread of reparations politics is a product of particular historical circumstances—in particular, it is a response to a post-utopian context that differs sharply from the period that preceded it—and seeks to achieve some of the aims of the progressive agenda through a focus on righting the past rather than on the basis of the kind of idealized vision of the human future that drove much that went before it.

CHAPTER 1

The Surfacing
of Subterranean History

The proliferation of demands that states, churches, and private firms be compelled to pay "reparations" to those whom they are said to have wronged in the past, or at least pressured to apologize for such wrongdoing, represents one of the more striking developments in recent international affairs.[1] The term *reparations* was once used exclusively in connection with what were, in effect, fines exacted among states, usually for damages incurred during wartime.[2] The term certainly retains this connotation, but in the meantime it has also come to refer to a host of different activities in which amends are made to nonstate groups and individuals. Yet reparations comprise only the tip of an iceberg of recent efforts to "come to terms with the past." Understood as a complex of concerns, the attention given to coming to terms with the past constitutes a major shift in the way we think and talk about politics. How has this come to pass? What forces are at work?

In this chapter, I discuss the contours of this remarkable situation and the factors that account for the contemporary concern with exorcizing the spirits of the past. I begin with a brief examination of the trajectory of "Western"[3] views concerning standards of justice with regard to past wrongs. I then argue that the defining aspect of our contemporary historical context is its "post"-ness—its quality of being regarded, especially by many intellectual opinion-makers, as "after" other, more future-oriented projects. Above all, I refer to socialism and the democratic nation-state, conceived as a vehicle for creating at least formally equal citizens; these concerns have animated the political energies of large constituencies during the past two centuries. These future-oriented projects have been widely replaced across the intellectual and political landscape by concerns about coming to terms with the past that have extensively supplanted more utopian preoccupations. The concern about coming to terms with many pasts has advanced arm-in-arm with the spread of consciousness about the Holocaust in many parts of the world.[4] Because of its prominence as a model for all politics concerned with coming to terms with the past, the Holocaust has given a major boost to other such projects, helping to make them more successful than they would otherwise have been. In this sense, those who claim that the Holocaust has overshadowed other commemorative projects are mistaken, or at least they are only half right.[5] Far from merely competing with or undermining such efforts, the Holocaust has become the central metaphor for all politics concerned with "making whole what has been smashed."[6]

why?

Repairing the Past: A Brief Intellectual History

The growing recognition of claims for reparations during the past decade or two calls sharply into question the age-old realist idea that was perhaps first articulated by Thucydides: "the strong do what they have the power to do and the weak accept what they have to accept."[7] Although this realist position remains influential in many quarters, it has been eroding since at least the nineteenth century, owing not least to the spread of egalitarian notions flowing from the Enlightenment and the revolutions it inspired. Since that time, we have witnessed a steady shift toward taking the consequences of past misdeeds more seriously, especially those carried out by states, and hence toward a greater sense that "coming to terms with the past" is a matter of considerable moral urgency.[8]

The problem of dealing or not dealing with past wrongs emerged sharply during the French Revolution, as the revolutionaries sought to settle accounts with the past and leap forward into the future (by, for example, creating a new calendar beginning with the Year One). In this connection, it is worth examining Edmund Burke's critique of the French revolutionaries' attitudes toward history and its crimes, for it gives us a convenient yardstick by which to measure the distance we have traveled in the intervening two centuries. Among the many things he disliked about the revolution taking place across the English Channel, Burke excoriated the revolutionaries' inclination to hold their contemporaries accountable for past injustices.

[The revolutionaries] find themselves obliged to rake into the histories of former ages (which they have ransacked with a malignant and profligate industry) for every instance of oppression and persecution . . . After destroying all other genealogies and family distinctions, they invent a sort of pedigree of crimes. It is not very just to chastise men for the offenses of their natural ancestors; but to take the fiction of ancestry in a corporate succession, as a ground for punishing men who have no relation to guilty acts, except in names and general descriptions, is a sort of refinement of injustice belonging to the philosophy of this enlightened age . . . Corporate bodies are immortal for the good of the members, but not for their punishment. Nations themselves are such corporations. As well might we in England think of waging inexpiable war upon all Frenchmen for the evils which they have brought upon us in the several periods of our mutual hostility . . . We do not draw the moral lessons we might from history. On the contrary, without care it may be used to vitiate our minds and to destroy our happiness. In history a great volume is unrolled for our instruction, drawing the materials of future wisdom from the past errors and infirmities of mankind. It may, in the perversion, serve for a magazine, furnishing offensive and defensive weapons for parties in church and state, and supplying the means of keeping alive, or reviving dissensions and animosities, and adding fuel to civil fury.[9]

Although the text is not entirely clear as to which transgressions Burke is objecting to, a more damning view of dredging up old wrongs for political purposes could scarcely be imagined. Yet Burke's view of these matters, like his stance toward the Revolution more generally, would not hold up. With the tremendous spread of historical awareness that accompanied "the age of democratic revolution" and the Romantic reaction that followed, the events of the past were increasingly subjected to a searching and self-conscious scrutiny.

For the revolutionaries of 1789, as later for Karl Marx, the past—replete with injustices as it was—had grown burdensome, a brake on progress that needed to be sloughed off on the road to the promised future. In his reflections on Louis Napoleon's *coup d'état*, Marx famously observed that the past "weighs like a nightmare on the brain of the living" and that this is especially so "just when they seem engaged in revolutionizing themselves and things."[10] History was understood as a succession of injustices, but these injustices were hardly to be dwelt upon or "repaired." Rather, they were

the past = a "brake on progress"

to be recognized, overcome, and left behind (or at least *aufgehoben,* that is, subsumed in the structure of a more advanced epoch). Fantastically, perhaps, the crimes of the past, understood as the changing forms of oppression and exploitation, had paved the way to a better day. With its jaw set resolutely toward the future, Marxism saw in the endless wrongs of yesterday the foundations of a utopian tomorrow.[11] The notion that people had been "traumatized" by the pasts through which they had lived, or that this would have disabled them in some way, was utterly alien to Marx's way of thinking. Instead, he insisted simply that people were exploited and lived under unjust social arrangements; once these arrangements were overthrown, he said, they would enter the realm of freedom and realize their full potential as a species. What cut them off from the achievement of their own essential being was unjust relations in the present, not any uncompleted project of fixing the past. By offering hope to the downtrodden that a new day was just over the horizon, Marxism would succeed—for better and worse—in arraying millions behind its banner over the coming century and more.

Friedrich Nietzsche similarly regarded the past as a burden, but unlike Marx, he found no easy escape into the future. His assessment of the "use and disadvantage of history for life" offered a corrosive condemnation of the outsized cultivation of history that he diagnosed among his contemporaries. This "historical fever" Nietzsche regarded as enervating and enfeebling, contrary to the aims of a protean, heroic "life." Still, in the course of analyzing various possible modes of engagement with the past, Nietzsche recommended a "critical" history that illuminated the degree to which "every past is worthy to be condemned [because] human violence and weakness have always played a mighty role in them." Yet it is not just the past that deserves our condemnation: "For since we are the outcome of earlier generations, we are also the products of their aberrations, passions, and errors, and indeed of their crimes; it is not possible wholly to free oneself from this chain."[12] Rather than leaping out of the past, Nietzsche reminds us here that we cannot escape it and, moreover, that we need to be more attentive to the ways in which the present is the outcome of blunders and cruelty rather than of triumphs and tenderness. Nietzsche was remarkably precocious in advocating this view, which would become the hallmark of a much later age—an era that had experienced more than its share of disaster.

Walter Benjamin's comments on our posture toward history and our responsibility to its victims combined Marx's optimism about the future with Nietzsche's sobriety about the past-in-the-present. In his "Theses on the Philosophy of History," Benjamin describes a Paul Klee painting in which an angel in flight contemplates the wreckage of the past as it piles up at his feet. "The angel would like to stay, awaken the dead, and make whole what has been smashed," but a storm blowing from Paradise drives him backward into the future. "This storm," Benjamin writes laconically, "is what we call progress."[13] Benjamin's aphorism echoes his widely cited pronouncement earlier in the "Theses" that there is no artifact of culture that is not at the same time a product of barbarism.

For all his acknowledgment of the suffering that underlay human cultural achievements, Benjamin is nonetheless prepared to accept the notion that this *is*, or at least is intrinsic in, "progress." However worthy of remembrance these sacrifices surely are, human advance is not conceivable without a certain amount of suffering and gratification forgone. Freud had already suggested as much in his reflections on the "discontent" that human beings experience in civilized society.[14] Like Benjamin, he wanted to minimize the suffering while celebrating the achievements made possible by the sacrifices.

Immediately after World War II, during which human suffering reached appalling new heights, the philosopher Karl Jaspers extended Nietzsche's argument about the inheritance of past crimes to those of the Nazis. In order to do so, however, Jaspers found it necessary to distinguish among types of responsibility for those crimes in an effort to persuade his countrymen to look deeply into their own complicity in Nazi wrongdoing. Seeking to defuse his compatriots' fears that they might face charges of collective guilt despite the fact that they had themselves committed no obviously culpable actions, Jaspers sought to isolate what he denoted as *criminal, political, moral,* and *metaphysical* guilt. Human institutions were relevant only for the first two kinds of guilt, whereas the latter two were purely private and/or theological in character. Jaspers was mainly concerned to promote a conception of guilt that entailed the Germans' *political* responsibility for making reparation to the parties injured by the Nazi regime.[15]

In many of his writings, Jürgen Habermas echoed and reinforced Jaspers's view of these matters. Habermas has frequently reiterated the theme of the fateful continuity of national communities and traditions, and the corresponding need to come to terms with the past, especially in the German case.[16] Although this perspective was met with incomprehension and derision when Jaspers first articulated it, the general posture toward the past that he and Habermas championed eventually became something like the official self-understanding of postwar West Germany with regard to coming to terms with the past. This point of view was not uncontested in the intellectual and political life of the Federal Republic before 1989, but it was prominently articulated by such figures as President Richard von Weizsäcker in his much-noted speech on the occasion of the fortieth anniversary of the end of World War II. The regime in East Germany took a notably different position on this matter, rather incredibly relegating the Nazi past to an outgrowth of capitalism, and hence of the West, with which it purported to have nothing to do.[17]

The shocking brutality of totalitarian regimes in midcentury Europe evoked an even broader response from Jaspers's student Hannah Arendt. In the preface to her classic *Origins of Totalitarianism,* Arendt summarily dispensed with Burke's position that later generations are free to attend only to their past triumphs while blithely ignoring their earlier misdeeds. Sobered by the unprecedented rise of regimes that ruled through naked terror, she insisted that those carefree attitudes toward the past were now gone. "We can no longer afford to take that which was good in the past and simply call it our heritage, to discard the bad and simply think of it as a dead load which by itself time will bury in oblivion," she wrote. "The subterranean stream of Western history has finally come to the surface and usurped the dignity of our tradition. This is the reality in which we live. And this is why all efforts to escape from the grimness of the present into nostalgia for a still intact past, or into the anticipated oblivion of the future, are vain."[18] Arendt's view of our relationship to the past, particularly the notion that the "subterranean" aspects of the Western past have resurfaced after being buried, has arguably become the dominant understanding in our time. This development has been promoted in considerable part by the efforts of "subaltern" groups to claim their place in that history—to emerge, after all, from the obscurity of "the people without history."[19]

The upsurge of interest in coming to terms with the past raises thorny questions, however, about what obligations persons alive today have with regard to wrongs that may have been committed in the past, often very long ago. Some, such as Lukas Meyer, have argued that even "faultless people" may be said to have an obligation, as part of our larger moral duty to create just societies, to provide reparations to those who have suffered wrongs in the past. Meyer says simply: "Surviving victims of past injustices as well as those currently living people who[,] as a consequence of the lasting impact of the past public evil[,] are disadvantaged today have to be compensated."[20] By including both "surviving victims" and "those currently living people who are disadvantaged today," Meyer gets part-way around the knotty question, often raised as an objection to paying reparations (or even just apologizing), "how far back should we go?"[21] In contrast, Jeremy Waldron insists that wrongs done in the past may have been superseded by the passage of time. His major point, however, is that "it is the impulse to justice now that should lead the way in this process [of repairing the wrongs of the past], not the reparation of something whose wrongness is understood primarily in relation to conditions that no longer obtain."[22] This is presumably the spirit of Max Horkheimer's comment that "past injustice is over and done with; the slain are truly slain."[23] The question is: to what extent can past wrongs be said to echo down to the present, and what, as a practical matter, can we do now about rectifying unjust contemporary circumstances rooted in those past injustices?

As Andrew Schaap has pointed out, despite their intimate friendship, Jaspers and Arendt had differing views about what role and consequences past guilt had for politics. Jaspers tended to regard the perpetrators' embrace of guilt and the attendant moral cleansing as essential to renewing a riven moral order. For Jaspers, the overarching theological conception of reparation involved the restoration of a community in need of healing. Yet it is not clear that such a community ever existed to be put back together in the first place. In contrast, Schaap argues, Arendt was inclined toward a more forward-looking approach to dealing with the past that "seeks not to restore an imagined moral order that has been violated but to initiate new relations between members of a polity . . . A reconciliatory moment is not construed as a final shared understanding or convergence of world views, but as a disclosure of a world in common from diverse and possibly irreconcilable perspectives."[24] Arendt's approach to coming to terms with the past avoids the fallacious notion that reparations can restore some mythical political *status quo ante* that in fact never existed, or that we can (or should) ever achieve a past on which everyone agrees. Instead, it invokes the achievement of more satisfying relations among citizens in a future that must be battled out in the public sphere rather than invoked, *ex post facto,* as a restoration of the *status quo ante.* From Arendt's perspective, therefore, it would be impossible to ask, "How do we restore communities that have been fractured by racial violence?"[25] There is no "community" to "restore," her writings suggest, only one to create—in an ever-receding, asymptotic approach to something like the vision of a "beloved community" that animated the early civil rights movement.   *Vision of a "beloved community"*

Over time, however, Arendt's republican approach to dealing with the past has been trumped by Jaspers's more theological conception, as well as by more therapeutic and legalistic, tortlike approaches. With respect to the theological side of things, history is frequently discussed today in redemptory tones. This has indeed been a prominent aspect of the deliberations of the South African Truth and Reconciliation Commission—which, not coincidentally, was headed by Archbishop Desmond Tutu. As Ian Buruma has written, "we deal with history, as with so much in our 'secular' age, in a pseudo-religious manner. The past has become a matter of atonement."[26] As to the therapeutic aspects of coming to terms with the past, the explosion in the use of the notion of trauma to describe collective historical events—and its ubiquitous antidote, "healing"—would scarcely seem to need documenting. Tellingly, however, an International Center for Trauma Studies established at New York University offers discussions of "trauma as a human rights issue."[27] On the legal side, we have witnessed a proliferation of lawsuits designed in one way or another to settle accounts with past injustices—even in the realm of foreign affairs—as well as efforts to forestall or punish state-sponsored wrongdoing, of which the international criminal tribunals for the former Yugoslavia and for Rwanda and the International Criminal Court are the leading examples.[28] Desirable though these efforts may be, they resonate with a decline of the more future-oriented politics that have been characteristic of progressivism for the last two centuries. Against the background of larger social changes, a legalistic, therapeutic, and theological attitude toward coming to terms with the past has tended to supplant the quest of active citizens and mobilized constituencies for an alternative future.

An Avalanche of History

Noble though it is in many respects, the extensive contemporary concern with past injustices represents a striking shift in progressive ways of thinking about politics. It is immediately obvious that the very term *progressive* implies a predominantly future-orientation. The shift from the millenarian striving for a utopian future to the struggle to repair past wrongdoing constitutes a sea change in thinking about politics that flows in part from the impression that the transformative projects of the century just past have left little but brutality and dashed dreams in their wake. What one might call the "lachrymose interpretation of twentieth-century history" (to paraphrase Salo Baron) has fed a shift from the labor movement's former rallying cry of "don't mourn, organize" to a sensibility that insists that we must "organize to mourn." Efforts to rectify past wrongs have thus arisen in part as a substitute for expansive visions of an alternative human future of the kind that animated the socialist movements of the preceding century, which have been overwhelmingly discredited since the fall of the Berlin Wall in 1989.

The spread of reparations politics has thus taken place more or less simultaneously with the diffusion of multiculturalism and identity politics, on the one hand, and with a growing concern about victims and victims' rights, on the other. These relatively new paradigms of public order represent challenges to the idea of undifferentiated mass publics that went hand-in-hand with "Fordist" production processes in midcentury advanced industrial societies. In their stead, reparations politics has raised the banner of the victims of oppression as groups deserving special consideration and concern. Nathan Glazer is correct that "we are all multiculturalists now" in the sense that the kinds of discrimination that undergirded past injustices and the ethnoracial distinctions on which they were often based are no longer regarded as acceptable or publicly defensible in liberal democratic societies.[29] But what one might call the identitarian version of multiculturalism goes beyond this to insist on special recognition for the bearers of particular social characteristics (women, non-whites, homosexuals, etc.). These ideas take issue with the traditional notions of common citizenship and equality before the law.[30]

Indeed, with the related notion of victims' rights, the idea that the law is an instrument of the entire society, rather than one wielded on behalf of particular individuals or groups, is itself called into question. The upgrading of victimhood in contemporary life has been widely remarked, not least by those such as Robert Hughes who regard it as a central element of a larger "culture of complaint."[31] But even less dyspeptic observers agree that something important has taken place in the image and standing of victims in recent years. David Garland, a leading authority on crime and punishment, has thoughtfully described the changing status of the victim in the context of criminal law.

Over the last three decades there has been a remarkable return of the victim to center stage in criminal justice policy. In the [previously dominant] penal-welfare framework, individual victims featured hardly at all, other than as members of the public whose complaints triggered state action. Their interests were subsumed under the general public interest, and certainly not counter-posed to the interests of the offender. *All of this has now changed* . . . The new political imperative is that victims must be protected, their voices must be heard, their memory honoured, their anger expressed, their fears addressed . . . The victim is no longer an unfortunate citizen who has been on the receiving end of a criminal harm, and whose concerns are subsumed within the "public interest" that guides the prosecution and penal decisions of the state. The victim is now, in a certain sense, a much more representative character, whose experience is taken to be common and collective, rather than individual and atypical . . . Paradoxically, this vision of the victim as Everyman has undermined the older notion of the public, which has now been redefined and dis-aggregated. It is no longer sufficient to subsume the individual victim's experience in the notion of the public good: the public good must be individuated, broken down into individual component parts. Specific victims are to have a voice . . . There is, in short, a new cultural theme, a new collective meaning of victimhood.[32]

Garland neatly captures the transformed perception of the victim in contemporary criminal justice and its relationship to the idea of the public. In this context, criminal offenses are increasingly seen as offenses against individuals rather than against the body politic as such. Garland's characterization calls our attention to what one might describe as the privatization of criminal justice, which of course has many other dimensions as well.

Not coincidentally, the developments described by Garland have taken place in a period in which the political left (as opposed to the cultural left) has been in steady retreat and the political right—characterized not least by its persistent advocacy of the privatization of public goods—consistently in the ascendancy. The temporary prevalence in government of nominally social-democratic or liberal parties should not obscure the reality that conservatives have effected a massive shift of the spectrum of respectable political discourse during this period. There is a parallel here to the difference between traveling along the economist's demand-curve and a shift of the curve itself. The names Reagan and Thatcher serve as a kind of shorthand to refer to the transformation in question; their views became the water in which those who came after them must swim. Recall Margaret Thatcher's anti-sociological dictum, "There is no such thing as society,"[33] and Ronald Reagan's credo that government "is not the solution, it's the problem."[34] With that view, Reagan knocked out the underpinnings of the New Deal, which had been motivated by the opposite view. Sealing the shift, it was Bill Clinton, not a conservative Republican, who announced in the mid-1990s that "the era of big government is over." Clinton's famous ability to triangulate involved his attempt to maintain a modicum of the liberal agenda within an utterly refashioned political terrain.[35] Reviewing the conservative triumph since the advent of Reagan, Cass Sunstein put the matter succinctly: "What was then in the center is now on the left; what was then in the far right is now in the center; what was then on the left no longer exists."[36]

Against this increasingly conservative political background, there has emerged a rising attentiveness to the needs and concerns of victims—both the victims of crime in the usual sense and the victims of state-sponsored criminality.[37] The transformation described by Garland with regard to the criminal law context thus has its analog in the realm of human rights abuses by states. Indeed, the victim of political violence has arguably assumed even greater cultural salience than the mere victim of crime, for the crime victim can be seen as having experienced an irrational, unsystematic, pointless kind of suffering; the victim of political violence, in contrast, can be thought of as having suffered the willful mistreatment of the greedy and power-mad. Accordingly, he or she can be seen as especially deserving of attention and even as having a whiff of the saintly—often well deserved—for having survived this maltreatment. These trends have helped stimulate a rising attention to the victims of past wrongs.

For many people, even those who would unblinkingly regard themselves as progressives, the past has extensively replaced the future as the temporal horizon in which to think about politics. This is a remarkable change. Under normal circumstances, the past returns only fleetingly and remains simply part of the stock of ideas on which people draw to make sense of their lives. But it is scarcely the predominant part; ordinarily, people maintain a balance between past, present, and future that allows them to move forward in their everyday lives. An excessive preoccupation with the past is usually a sign that something is amiss—whether in the manner of nostalgia or of failing to let go of past troubles—for individuals as well as for societies.

The balance between past, present, and future seems to have been upset in recent years, and a good part of the explanation for this development lies with the efforts of what I will call—borrowing from the vocabulary of social movement theory and its notion of "political entrepreneurs"—"entrepreneurs of memory" who have sought to make the past more central to us and to our thinking about politics. Since roughly the end of the Cold War, the distance that normally separates us from the past has been strongly challenged in favor of an insistence that the past is constantly, urgently present as part of our everyday experience. To some extent, this is simply the culmination of Freud's revolution in modern thought, which emphasized the ways in which the unmastered past continues to govern our lives and insisted that coming to terms with the individual's past was essential to any genuine human emancipation. Yet any reference to Freud is too general; a satisfactory explanation of recent developments requires reference to sociological factors specific to the age.[38] One such factor is the emergence of an expanding cadre of entrepreneurs of memory, who assert that our ordinary remove from the past does not and indeed should not exist, and that collective unmastered pasts must return to haunt those saddled with them. They may well be correct about these claims in particular cases, of course; the question is why the claim is heard so much more frequently in recent years.

As the sociology of knowledge would predict, the entrepreneurs of memory have stimulated the emergence of discourses about the past that are consistent with the professional outlooks of those who articulate them. In itself, there is nothing surprising or nefarious about this tendency; it simply reflects the expanding political importance in "postindustrial" society of intellectuals and professionals.[39] The use of the term *entrepreneurs* is not intended to be pejorative but merely to indicate that such persons make these kinds of claims more frequently, more insistently, or more publicly than do others. Their ranks are broad; my identification of them is meant simply to identify them as contributors to a trend rather than to cast doubt on the reality of the troubles they address. They include:

- human rights activists concerned to build a better future by putting an end to a so-called "culture of impunity" in offending states;[40]
- theologians who see history in redemptory terms and who promote a religiously defined conception of reconciliation as the remedy for past wrongs;[41]

- therapists who specialize in dealing with the "traumas" of the past and who view history in therapeutic terms governed by the aims of "healing" and "closure"[42];
- attorneys, especially those specializing in class-action suits, who see the past as a series of potentially justiciable offenses;
- historians, who have frequently come to play an important role as consultants and expert witnesses in political and legal efforts to come to terms with the past;[43]
- educators with a political agenda regarding the presentation of the past to younger people, who see history as redolent with lessons for the present;
- and, finally, what one might call the activist injured, who are often associated with ethnic organizations and who seek to gain recognition or compensation for those of their kind (and sometimes for others) who have suffered injustices in the past.

With regard to this last category, it is perfectly natural that some of those wronged in the past would adopt this experience as their chief mission in life. But it should be recalled that such persons are not necessarily representative of their (putative) group. Erving Goffman noted in his discussion of those mobilized around "stigma" that "representatives are not representative, for representation can hardly come from those who give no attention to their stigma."[44] The "activist injured" are unrepresentative in precisely the same sense, for they have identified strongly and durably with their one-time victimization, though this need not be and for others is not the case. Some injured persons, but by no means all, make a cause—one might even say a calling—of their past injury. Needless to say, such persons often do a great deal of work oriented to coming to terms with the past. Others, however, prefer to eschew such endeavors; for example, the first person approached to be the director of the United States Holocaust Memorial Museum in Washington, D.C., then-president of Orion Films Arthur Krim, declined the offer, saying, "I prefer to work for something for the future rather than for the past."[45]

In his discussion of the politics of stigma, Goffman goes on to say that the informal community and the organizations that grow up around particular stigmata will define an individual who shares a stigmatized condition "as someone who should take pride in his illness and not seek to get well."[46] Stigmatization, in other words, may be used to produce a sense of self, camaraderie, political purpose. Likewise, the activist injured seek to encourage such solidarity and to rally around their flag others similarly situated.

Although not even all survivors join or participate in the organizations designed to seek amends for the wrongs once done them, it turns out that identification with past injury may comprise the touchstone of group belonging even for the *descendants* of those injured. A group that understands itself as the "Second-Generation Survivors of the Holocaust" exemplifies this phenomenon.[47] More generally, nationalists everywhere often nurture ageless grievances as the basis of claims for separation or statehood for those of their flock. Presumably such later-generation "survivors" are as doubtfully representative of their group as the activist injured themselves, even if the claim that inequities currently facing a group are rooted in past wrongs may be perfectly plausible. For example, although not all black Americans whose ancestry is traceable to slavery days would view themselves above all as the descendants of slaves, the pursuit of reparations for slavery and legal segregation depends in part on sustaining the notion that today's black Americans are to be understood in those terms. This view is plausible enough. Indeed, if ameliorative policies are to be defended at all, it is necessary that Americans regard blacks in the first instance as the descendants of slaves, and not primarily as beneficiaries of the Civil War, the civil rights movement, or affirmative action.[48] The point is that the shared consciousness of past suffering may be and often is deployed to stimulate group self-understanding and political involvement. Like all such notions, however, these self-conceptions are not "natural" or given a priori but the product of political and symbolic effort.

In connection with the activities of the entrepreneurs of memory, in recent years we have witnessed the emergence of a veritable memory industry that preoccupies large numbers of academics and political activists. A growing catalog of groups and organizations devote themselves to one or another aspect of the project of coming to terms with the past—with trauma, memory, healing, transitional justice, reconciliation. Special lectures, journals (e.g., *History & Memory*), conferences, and nongovernmental organizations addressing these subjects abound; leading foundations pour money into undertakings devoted to examining these issues both in theory and in practice. These activities may make important contributions to resolving contemporary conflicts, but the extent of the concern with coming to terms is nonetheless strikingly novel and problematic. Memory emerges with such force on the academic and public agenda today, according to one insightful critic, "precisely because it figures as a therapeutic alternative to historical discourse."[49]

The growing significance of coming to terms with the past is neatly suggested by the changing character of the institutional innovations that arise during periods of major social change. Compared to the period before 1989, truth commissions—of which more than twenty have been instituted during the last two decades—have come to be the most characteristic institutional novelty associated with countries undergoing a transition from authoritarianism to (it is hoped) some more democratic form of governance, whether by revolutionary or less dramatic means. Confirming this trend, the Ford Foundation and other philanthropists have bankrolled the International Center for Transitional Justice, a nongovernmental organization with deep roots in previous efforts to come to terms with the past.[50] Yet, as Deborah Posel and Graeme Simpson have pointed out, the recent proliferation of truth commissions is rather ironic when set against the background of postmodern doubts about the very possibility of truth.[51]

In part through the efforts of the various entrepreneurs of memory, we have been faced in recent years with an avalanche of history—but a history conceived as far different from the heroic, forward-looking tales that for two centuries underpinned the idea of progress. Instead of illuminated manuscripts decorated by latter-day monks for the edification of the faithful, which had characterized history-writing under the sign of Hegel, we are presented with ugly narratives of injustice, plunder, and dispossession. These critical histories, very often closer than their naively mythopoeic predecessors to the real story of how we got where we are now, have helped promote extensive efforts to "repair" what has been damaged en route to the present. In consequence, many countries—especially the more prosperous, and especially the more privileged groups within those countries—are confronted today with the task of digging themselves out from under the accumulated burdens of their history.

Yet the rising of concern with the past overlaps so directly with the decline of more explicitly future-oriented politics that it is hard to avoid the conclusion that this is more than mere coincidence. The intensive and often censorious attention to the past is a response to the "collapse of the future"—the decline of the bold, progressive political visions that had been embodied in the socialist movement and, in a larger sense, in the project of the nation-state understood as a community of equal citizens.[52] The fervent pursuit of the past during the last decade or two partakes of a larger sense that, as the noted critic George Steiner has deftly put it, "the dishes are being cleared" on that epoch of Western culture that can be understood as a tale of hope and progress.[53] Deprived of these narratives of *Bildung*, of reaching out toward a better future for all, our era is marked by a pervasive mood of "enlightened bewilderment,"[54] lacking any firm direction adumbrated in a vision of a society better than the really existing variant. We live with the (presumably temporary) abeyance of what *New York Times* columnist Thomas Friedman has called "big idea politics"—that is, we lack a political vision capable of energizing large numbers of people on its behalf.

Under these circumstances, a preoccupation with the rights of culturally defined groups has extensively replaced the collective visions that animated the Fordist class politics of the twentieth century, which, at their admittedly all-too-infrequent best, suppressed ethnic and racial divisions in favor of "one big union." Identification with one's putative group, defined in terms of sociological criteria of identity, shoulders aside the civil rights movement's goal of equal rights (and jobs) for all in a "beloved community." These various shifts in political self-understanding have their positive sides. They rightly seek to rectify the inattention to non-whites, women, and other ignored groups that could often be found in the labor/socialist and civil rights movements. But these different kinds of politics go hand-in-hand with a decline in the commonality politics that had long been the staple of progressive thought.[55]

The concern with memory and coming to terms with the past must therefore be understood in part as a defensive response to the disorientation induced by the collapse of an invigorating conception of a common destiny. In the absence of a horizon for which to aim, the excavation of memory and its mysteries compensates for those shortcomings of the present about which their opponents can do little, politically speaking. Perhaps never before has so much intellectual and political firepower been trained on history as a battleground of political struggle and a field of scholarly exploration. Who today, ensnared in the riddles of the past or crushed under its bulk, could imagine the exhortation of the Russian Futurists to "burn down all libraries so as to emancipate the senile spirit from the dead weight of the past"?[56]

My point is not to recommend either nostalgia for bygone enthusiasms or the ahistorical rumination of the cow described in Nietzsche's discussion of the pros and cons of contemplating history: Nietzsche's blissful bovine is untroubled by the remembrance of things past and thus is able to live vigorously in the present. It is, rather, simply to recognize that something profound has taken place in our ways of thinking about possible human futures; Nietzsche's trepidation about the debilitating effects of a surfeit of history is entirely apposite to our situation.[57] When the future collapses, the past rushes in.

The Collapse of the Future I: Socialism

We live in an era whose mental and political parameters are shaped by the end of Communism and of the attendant international rivalries of the Cold War. Despite its moments of high drama, the Cold War tended to reduce ideological conflict to the matter of endorsing one of two mutually exclusive alternatives—capitalism or communism, anti-Fascism or anti-Communism.[58] This Manichaean thinking led to extensive blindness toward the faults of each side's respective partners in international affairs. Such thinking helped to smother attention to past misdeeds on both sides of the Cold War divide—those of Germany and Japan as they were transformed after the war from fascist enemies into allies of the "Free World," on the one hand, and those of the Soviet Union, which quickly transmogrified from ally to enemy, on the other. *Realpolitik* argued against airing out these old wounds, and heroic images of a prosperous capitalist or an egalitarian communist tomorrow helped keep eyes fixed firmly on the future. The dynamics of the Cold War thus banished much discussion of what meanwhile have come to be known as the crimes of the past to the murky twilight of the struggle between Communism and the Free World.

That struggle paired two countries that embodied divergent but quasi-messianic projects for the future of the world. One was a former colony, born of revolution, that had been a role model for many people struggling for freedom from one or another imperial yoke (including at one time even Ho Chi Minh, whose nationalism eventually came to partake too much of that un-American brew, Communism). The other was a newly influential Eurasian power that asserted a claim to bearing the mantle of progressive humanity after World War II. Between them, they had been seen as the vanguard of the global future at least since Alexis de Tocqueville's famous prediction that they would one day divide the world between them.[59] After World War II, the Soviet Union inherited the anti-colonialist banner from the United States, which in turn had stepped in to replace a declining Old World as global hegemon.

From the point of view of the broad masses outside Europe, the Soviets' (enormous) contribution to the defeat of Nazism and their espousal of the anti-colonial cause after World War II were thus of a piece. After all, as Marx had noted in his discussion of "primitive accumulation," the extermination and enslavement of the indigenous populations of the Americas, the "looting" of the East Indies, and the massive stimulation and expansion of the slave trade in Africa had heralded "the rosy dawn of the era of capitalist production."[60] Race and racial domination have been at the heart of the modern capitalist enterprise since its inception,[61] and the Soviets' stance on these issues appeared to be considerably more compelling than that of the racially retrograde United States or a Europe hanging on, often brutally, to "a dying colonialism."[62] Accordingly, W. E. B. Du Bois, who at midcentury had become the leading voice of pan-Africanism after his disillusionment with the prospects of racial equality in the United States, admonished his readers that if an "ultimate democracy, reaching across the color line and abolishing race discrimination" could be achieved "by means other than Communism, [then] Communism need not be feared"; otherwise, there was no alternative for the darker peoples of the earth to "the method laid down by Karl Marx."[63]

In the minds of the world's non-white populations, much of the West was tainted for its rapaciousness and savagery in the course of creating the white-dominated modern world. (Recall Gandhi's quip in response to the question of what he thought of Western civilization: "I think it would be a good idea.") The Allies' shortcomings in the arena of race relations generated considerable hand-wringing among Western opinion-makers about the political advantages this situation might give to the Soviets after the war. Whether or not ideologically close to the Soviet Union, communists had frequently been among the most engaged participants in the freedom struggles of blacks in the United States, South Africa, and elsewhere. This fact gave Marxism a considerable base of support among black Americans during much of the twentieth century.[64] Ultimately, the challenge posed to the self-described Free World by the very existence of the Soviet Union, and of socialist movements more generally, was critical to achieving national self-determination for the formerly colonized and to transforming racist practices in the United States. The effect was perhaps more indirect in the United States, but socialist support for anti-colonial and anti-racist movements helped to create a favorable political context for the black freedom movement.[65]

With the decline of a vibrant socialist movement following the end of the Bretton Woods system in the early 1970s, and of the USSR itself in the early 1990s, progress in global race relations has in certain respects stagnated.[66] Africa has been largely reduced to a backwater of foreign policy concern, though movements such as the Jubilee 2000 campaign for debt relief (with high-profile support from U2 lead singer and activist Bono) have had some limited success in obtaining relief from the crushing debt facing many Third World countries.[67] Similarly, some of the wealthier countries have been persuaded to make available cheaper medicines for treating AIDS in some of the world's poorest nations. But these measures hardly amount to a major redistribution of wealth and power to the predominantly non-white Third World. Meanwhile, the momentum toward racial equality in the United States has stalled with a backlash against affirmative action that led to the first major Supreme Court challenge to using that policy in higher education admissions since its affirmation in *Bakke*. Nearly four decades after the "second Reconstruction" which the civil rights movement forced upon the American government, the picture regarding the welfare of the black population remains mixed and is a matter of continued sharp controversy.[68]

More broadly, the challenge of socialism was arguably decisive in pushing the capitalist democracies to institute welfare and other policies that blunted the sharpest edges of the market economy. In the aftermath of the Great Depression, welfare states came to be the norm in the more industrialized countries. In part this was an indigenous reaction to the devastation that economic collapse wreaked on the populations of these countries; this was the social self-defense side of the "double-movement" that Polanyi argued would be generated by what he called "the great transformation"— the commodification of the means of life and, indeed, of life itself.[69] But the institution of national welfare states was also a response to the perception that the Soviets, who had notably abolished capitalism, did not seem to suffer the same shocks from the global economy during the 1930s. In addition, socialist and communist parties throughout the West pushed for policies that softened the blows of capitalism's "creative destruction."[70]

The waning of the early, interracial (and, under the tutelage of Bayard Rustin, socialist-inflected) civil rights movement and the collapse of socialism have resulted in widespread disorientation among the forces that had once been allied with the future, so to speak, about how to understand themselves in the post-Communist age. Some of them have been among those mobilizing against globalization. Yet it remains unclear what anti-globalization movements stand *for*. In any case, they have not yet developed the organizational stability necessary to replace the old socialist and communist parties as a major source of pressure for social change. This stability may well be difficult to achieve because some of these movements insist that Robert Michels's "iron law of oligarchy" is an illusion, and so they seek to undermine it as much as possible. This disposition, in turn, cuts them off from the advantages of the "organizational weapon."[71] The old is dying, and the new is still struggling to be born.

Others from the once-socialist fold—particularly those most strongly charmed by Communist promises of a redeemed humanity that were betrayed by the Soviets and their minions—have issued feverish *postmortem* diatribes against the seductions of Communist utopianism and the disastrous realities of its Soviet incarnation.[72] Their aim in the battle over the past is to nail irretrievably shut both the coffin of Communism and, more broadly, the revolutionary tradition stemming from the French Revolution. This counterrevolutionary thrust, advanced with rapier intellect by François Furet, has developed closely with a strong revival of both Tocqueville and totalitarianism theory, the approach that sees Communism and Nazism as two species of that deformed genus, twentieth-century mass politics. Totalitarianism theory was of course first adumbrated by Hannah Arendt, herself to some extent a theoretical descendant of Tocqueville.

Yet, for all their shared enthusiasm for the idea of totalitarianism, Arendt and the "young Tocquevilleans" differ sharply in their attitude toward the revolutionary heritage in modern political culture. The excesses of Communism did not vitiate the idea of revolution for Arendt, who lionized the American version in which she found refuge from Nazism, whereas they did so for Furet, who—like Tocqueville before him—found lamentable the consequences of its French variant for his own *patrie*. In contrast to Arendt's loving invocation of "the revolutionary tradition and its lost treasure," Furet and his followers seek to squelch the chronic instability produced by the shimmer of revolution and by the other abstractions promulgated by intellectuals—in the French tradition, *maitre-penseurs* with a privileged insight into political truth. Herein, according to Furet and his epigones, lies the error of those led astray by the Communist illusion, just as Tocqueville had seen the French revolutionaries' penchant for abstraction as the key to their excesses.[73]

For her part, Arendt remained committed, in a Jeffersonian vein, to the revolutionary tradition as an affirmation of (Arendt's term) "man's" ability to escape the stagnation of unfreedom and of the quintessentially human capacity to "start something new." Indeed, one form of that revolutionary creativity was the soviets or councils (*Räte*), which, Arendt noted in the 1960s, "were to make their appearance in every genuine revolution throughout the nineteenth and twentieth centuries." She regarded these "spontaneous organs of the people" as having created "a new public space for freedom which was constituted and organized during the course of the revolution itself," beyond and even against the designs of the leaders of the revolution.[74] In the "catching-up revolutions" of 1989, the so-called round-tables briefly played an analogous role, bringing together various parties with a voice in the funeral arrangements for Soviet-style socialism and in planning the outlines of the new regime.[75] Since then, constitution-writing has vied with efforts to come to terms with past wrongdoing as the central activities associated with changes of regime.

The problem is that, for fairly obvious reasons, a preoccupation with the past has generally been the terrain of conservatives. Edmund Burke's political philosophy is perhaps the leading example of the sensibility in question. Because the present always and inevitably remains one of unnecessary suffering and unjustifiable inequality, to be superseded in a coming better day, the future is of necessity the temporal horizon of earthly improvement in human circumstances. "The meek shall inherit the earth"; "the workers have nothing to lose but their chains, and a world to win." But the lowly need the future in order to realize those hopes, which is the best they have in the still-unjust present. It is no coincidence that George Steiner's concern about the "problematic" status of hope in our day stems from a view that the twin progeny of prophetic Judaism—Christianity and its secular sibling, Marxism—have atrophied.[76] Each was—is—concerned with bringing nearer its own vision of paradise, the one in heaven, the other on earth.

The Collapse of the Future II: The Nation-State

It is not only Communism that has proven to be an illusion, however. The idea of the nation-state, too, has been widely discredited in intellectual and progressive circles. It is now often seen more in its historical role as the platform for delusions of grandeur leading to tragedy than as a structure in which disparate groups might achieve formally equal citizenship. As the paradigmatic case of nationalism gone disastrously wrong, the Holocaust and its reception in opinion-making circles have done much to undermine confidence in the nation-state as a political form in the Euro-Atlantic world. The human rights "revolution" with which the international community responded to World War II–era atrocities has promoted a deep skepticism about the nation-state as a force for good in the world. The more sophisticated advocates of human rights recognize the force of Freud's argument that, whatever distress the need for an agency capable of enforcing the rule of law (that is, a state) may cause us, we cannot do without it—for otherwise there would be no "rights" other than those of the stronger.[77] Yet among many of those who understand themselves as progressive, the nation-state today is regarded as guilty until proven otherwise of the many charges now leveled against it. This is an enormous change of sensibility since the heyday of the nation-state in the early twentieth century.

In his discussion of "The Nation," Max Weber noted that the phenomenon was usually related to the notion of the superiority or irreplaceability of a particular group's cultural achievements.[78] This view of the nation, especially insofar as it privileges one *culture* over others, is now routinely condemned in enlightened circles as a grotesque form of hubris likely to have been at the root of, or to issue in, self-aggrandizing violence. The principal exception to this proposition involves those cases of national strivings tied to efforts to escape from some sort of imperialist or quasi-imperialist overlord. In other words, nationalists seeking to achieve the norm of self-determination that underlay the French Revolution and that was reaffirmed at the international level in Woodrow Wilson's "Fourteen Points" after World War I still have a legitimate cause. This helps to account for the support many on the left give to "indigenous" nationalism; "indigenes" are nationalists with human rights on their side.[79] We are to look askance, however, at national feeling among the already powerful.

Against this background, it is difficult today to relate to, or almost even to conceive of, Hannah Arendt's view that "the decline of the nation-state"—that is, "the conquest of the state by the nation"—had led to "the end of the rights of man."[80] Arendt disputed the natural law notion that we were born equal, insisting instead that we only became so as a result of laws that treat everyone the same. Hence, for Arendt the preferential treatment of nationals over other persons that spread during the late nineteenth century and after represented a betrayal of the Bill of Rights and the Declaration of the Rights of Man and Citizen, the legal universalism of which articulated the true vocation of the nation-state. Inasmuch as she was a refugee from Nazi racism herself, her rejection of differential legal treatment on racial grounds was equally damning, if theoretically complex.[81]

Also largely forgotten is the fact that a sense of common membership was a crucial concomitant of the extension of welfare benefits designed to furnish their recipients with a minimum of security in the face of capitalism's systemic inequities. Taking the goal of common citizenship for granted, T. H. Marshall was profoundly uninterested in the particularities of the groups that would benefit from the kinds of rights he analyzed in his classic essay, "Citizenship and Social Class." Marshall's Olympian insouciance about the "identity" of the bearers of rights is all the more remarkable since the essay was written on the very eve of Britain's massive ethnoracial transformation which would result from large-scale immigration from its former colonial possessions.[82]

As nation-states have been downgraded as a source of identification, at least among leftish intellectual elites, they have come to be regarded by many progressives today as illegitimate entities, mere brute victors in a sordid saga of "internal colonialism." Such nation-states are seen (not entirely inappropriately) as having been created on the strength of injustices against others including expropriation, murder, rape, and the destruction of once-vibrant cultures. The rights of minorities—particularly though by no means exclusively those deemed "indigenous"—to "their" cultures have thus been one of the most widely discussed extensions of the norm of self-determination in recent years.[83] Under these circumstances, the authority of the nation-state to mold its populace in the image of elite defenders of the national mythology—once essentially untrammeled—has largely evaporated. Programs like the "Americanization" schemes of the early twentieth century are quite unthinkable today, for they would violate the reigning norm of multiculturalism.

Among the more educated strata in the world today, national(ist) histories—once the pedagogical forge of imagined national communities—have fallen under the suspicion of uncritically celebrating the narcissism of small differences. Such histories, once the mother's milk of national feeling, are seen as the inappropriate glorification of the crimes perpetrated on the road to the present arrangements of cultural, ethnic, and state power. An excellent example of this transformation in thinking about the history of the nation can be found in the ongoing controversies over the content of school history textbooks and museum exhibitions in Germany, Japan, and the United States.[84] Similarly, post-apartheid South Africa is caught up in a vigorous debate about the way the country's history should be represented to its schoolchildren. Arrayed against the traditionalists are those who want a history that bends over backwards to make up for the "standardized falsifications" of the past and that involves oral traditions and indigenous modes of knowledge rather than merely "the old-fashioned pursuit of objective historical truth through texts."[85] In short, historical consciousness in enlightened circles worldwide is now more likely to be bound up with a search for perpetrators and with the *ex post facto* recognition of victims than it is to be the heroic foundation myth of a striving *Volk*.

Another result of the declining persuasiveness of national narratives is the growing inclination among many people to regard themselves as members of a "diaspora." The implication is that they are really from someplace else and that that place or its putative people are the chief group to whom loyalty is owed. Ethnic activists in supposed diasporas have played a crucial role in foregrounding experiences of historical injustice in the Euro-Atlantic world in recent years. The activism of Jews in the United States and elsewhere with respect to reparations for Nazi crimes is too well known to require much elaboration here. But it is worth noting that Iris Chang, author of *The Rape of Nanking*, was the daughter of Chinese immigrants to the United States; moreover, she became involved in publicizing the atrocities committed by the Japanese during World War II as a result of her involvement with Chinese-American activists devoted to cultivating the memory of those events.[86] Similarly, the Armenian communities in Europe and the United States have played a decisive role in promoting the official recognition of the 1915 massacres as a genocide.[87] Also important has been the African diaspora in the Americas. Those who call attention to the connections between colonialism, the slave trade, slavery itself, and the continuing discrimination against those of African descent in the United States and elsewhere have done so in part by insisting that there exists a community of identity and interests among the inhabitants of Africa and African-descended peoples elsewhere.[88]

The weakening of national feeling—a trend interrupted in the United States by the attacks of September 11, 2001—seems in many ways unstoppable. Pervasive talk of a "globalizing" world, entailing the heightened geographic mobility of far-flung populations, suggests that the developed world has become a more or less open vessel taking in hitherto unfamiliar peoples from around the globe. A mere glance at the faces of those walking the streets of Berlin, London, Paris, New York, Sydney, and Toronto indicates that there is much to this view. Yet the images of multicolored, multiethnic populations have also helped stimulate a concern about identity and roots among both those in motion and those receiving them. This sense of transformation and drift could scarcely fail to promote a concern about who one "really" is, especially as politics in the world's powerful countries since Reagan and Thatcher seems increasingly oriented to scaling back the scope and range of government activities. If the nation-state offers its citizens less and demands less of them (e.g., the shift away from conscript armies, the erosion of public services and benefits), it is hardly surprising that they would look elsewhere for the sources of their self-understanding.

The intensified search for the moorings of the self is precisely the response to contemporary developments that one might expect on the basis of Marx's previously quoted remark concerning the resurgence of the past at times of major social change. The presence of the past *is* enhanced when people are in the process of "revolutionizing themselves and things," as they appear to be doing today. The vision of citizenship as equality before the law has been shaken by the many failures to live up to that standard in the treatment of various groups. In the past, those failures tended to lead those who were discriminated against to attempt to redeem the claim of equal treatment. Now, however, there is a growing inclination simply to abandon the ship as not worth salvaging or to demand reparations for the earlier breach of faith. This is yet another illustration of Albert Hirschman's argument about the choice between "exit" and "voice."[89]

The Past after the Future

The discrediting of the twin forces that dominated twentieth-century history—namely, nationalism and socialism/communism—has gone hand-in-hand with a pervasive consciousness of man-made catastrophe in our post-Holocaust, post-gulag era. This consciousness of humanly ordained catastrophe so prominent in the current era is deeply intertwined with our perception of twentieth-century European history as an epoch of unprecedented cruelty and disaster. This interpretation is strengthened by views of the century as a "short" one, bracketed by the rise and demise of the system created by the Bolsheviks and marked by a nearly century-long conflict between liberalism and totalitarianism that took the form of a "European" or indeed "world civil war." These prominent views, advanced by such redoubtable historians as Eric Hobsbawm, François Furet, and Ernst Nolte, properly point to two of the most decisive watersheds of the era—the Russian Revolution and the end of the Cold War—as well as to the gruesome toll exacted by Nazism, Communism, and their various imitators.[90]

Interpretations of the history of the twentieth century cannot fail to point to its staggering capacity for generating mass death, which unquestionably surpassed that of all its predecessors. Yet the emphasis on the "short" century's bookends also tends to overshadow its critical turning point—namely, the Allied powers' defeat of fascism and Japanese imperialism—and the opening it created for humanistic and emancipatory projects that have profoundly shaped subsequent history and politics. As Jürgen Habermas has noted, the portrayal of the century just concluded in catastrophic colors obscures the decisive achievement that issued from the end of World War II: "At that time, the rug was pulled out from under all claims to legitimacy that did not at least rhetorically embrace the universalistic spirit of the political Enlightenment."[91] Decolonization in Africa and Asia was one important consequence, and the consolidation of the notion of human rights as a demand that could be raised against abuses of state power was another. Those who stress the disastrous features of the era typically underplay the new opportunities for the just and peaceful organization of human affairs that were achieved as a result of the defeat of fascism and imperialism. Contemporary campaigns to make whole what has been smashed would be unthinkable without these victories.

The catastrophic interpretation of the twentieth century accords with recent historiographical trends that see the Nazis' chief misdeed as that of having perpetrated upon white/Christian/European populations the same outrages they had routinely carried out against non-white/non-Christian/non-European colonial populations with relatively little outcry from Europeans. In other words, Nazism is seen as continuous with "classical" European colonialism.[92] For example, in his recent history of twentieth-century Europe, *Dark Continent*, Mark Mazower has argued that the German assertion of racial superiority was a rude awakening for smug Europeans because Nazism "turn[ed] imperialism on its head and treat[ed] Europeans as Africans."[93] This claim, which fits in nicely with the "dark continent" theme enunciated in the book's title, surely has a superficial plausibility. It certainly was a shock to many Europeans, accustomed to viewing themselves as the avatars of civilization, to find themselves confronted with a party that was prepared to implement against one group of people a project of extermination on a scale unprecedented in their experience.

Yet the equation of Nazism with European colonial domination is deeply problematic. The racist policies of the Nazis and their collaborators may indeed have made Europeans aware of the centrality of "race" in parts of the world whose exploitation made possible many of the comfortable illusions of white European society. Still, the parallels between the Nazi project and the colonial one are sharply limited. This assertion can be clarified by a brief consideration of one of the most frequently cited quotations in recent discussions of imperialism—namely, Joseph Conrad's characterization of that state of affairs in *Heart of Darkness:* "The conquest of the earth, which mostly means the taking it away from those who have a different complexion or slightly flatter noses than ourselves, is not a pretty thing when you look into it too much. What redeems it is the idea only. An idea at the back of it; not a sentimental pretence but an idea; and an unselfish belief in the idea—something you can set up, and bow down before, and offer a sacrifice to."[94]

To contemporary sensibility, the passage reads like an ironic observation skewering imperialist hypocrisy. It harmonizes well with the postmodern inclination to see the knowledge and cultural products of the "oppressors" as threadbare veils for the exercise of power—ideas as mere fig-leafs covering egregious designs. The ideas that Europeans set up and bowed down before were, of course, those of the "white man's burden," the *mission civilisatrice,* and other self-congratulatory clap trap about the backwardness of those racial others whom states and private companies sought to exploit for their own gain.

But just as it must be admitted that the notion of a civilizing mission was to a considerable extent a mask for plunder and brutality, that notion also decisively distinguishes colonialism from Nazism, which had no such mission. European missionaries to the colonies—and even some employees of the governments and companies engaged in the plunder of overseas territories and peoples—were often aghast at the depravities committed in the name of civilizing and other less uplifting missions. This point receives considerable emphasis in Adam Hochschild's widely praised exorcism of *King Leopold's Ghost.* Much as they may deserve to be remembered and perhaps even recompensed, extensive atrocities and brutal exploitation on a large scale do not transform colonial plunder into genocide; the systematic extermination of the Africans of the Congo à la the Holocaust was not on the agenda, even if gross wastage of human life surely was. Thus, despite Hochschild's inclination to draw parallels between the Holocaust and what King Leopold did to the Africans of the Congo Basin, he eventually concedes that "the killing in the Congo . . . was not, strictly speaking, a genocide" because "the Congo state was not deliberately trying to eliminate one particular ethnic group from the face of the earth."[95] In contrast, the Nazis were relatively forthright about their plans to subject those deemed *lebensunwertes Leben* ("life unworthy of life") to a future of murderously unremitting toil, if not immediate death. They had no intention of "civilizing" those they considered subhuman *Untermenschen,* and they did not send missionaries with their soldiers when they sallied forth to colonize their heathen.

The vagaries of the definition of genocide have led to ever-widening use of the term in ordinary parlance and in political controversy over past injustices. For example, those seeking reparations for the children of the "stolen generation" in Australia have invoked the last clause of the Genocide Convention ("forcibly transferring children") to argue that the Australian government (and churches) involved in the removal of these children from their homes through the middle of the twentieth century had engaged in genocide.[96] The spread of reparations as a means of coming to terms with the past may have created incentives for certain groups to have the past wrongs done to them declared a "genocide" because of the possible compensation that may follow. For example, some Armenian activists have suggested that if Turkey can be forced to recognize that what happened in 1915 was genocide, their next step might be to claim reparations or demand the return of land once owned by Armenians.[97]

In sobering contrast to the rhetorical competition to acquire the appellation of genocide to describe certain *past* atrocities, the practical impact of the 1948 Genocide Convention in halting state-sponsored mass killing in the present has been distinctly limited. To be sure, numerous participants in the massacres in Bosnia and Rwanda have been or are being tried on charges of genocide. Such a development may give pause to future dictators and barbarians—especially before they book flights out of their blood-soaked countries. Yet despite the appearance of numerous contenders that fulfill the criteria for genocide as these are laid out in the Convention, the

United Nations has never invoked the procedure for translating that agree-ment into action while mass killings are actually in progress.[98] According to the terms of the Convention, the invocation of that instrument could trigger concrete measures to halt the killings, a contingency that most states have preferred to forgo. Here we run head-on into the *Realpolitik* that con-tinues to guide much statecraft, despite the remarkable expansion of non-governmental participation in foreign policy-making and widespread changes in attitudes toward state-sponsored atrocities. We thus confront the paradoxical situation that the incentives for claiming to have been the (de-scendants of the) victims of past genocide that have been created by the spreading attention to reparations demands are more effective than the mechanism designed to stop genocide in the present.[99]

In sum, we find ourselves in a post-utopian "age of genocide" which, skeptical of new blueprints for a heaven on earth, instead fixes its gaze firmly on the horrors and injustices of the past. In the conclusion of his magisterial autopsy of twentieth-century Communism, *The Passing of an Illusion*, Furet writes: "The idea of *another* society has become almost im-possible to conceive of, and no one in the world today is offering any advice on the subject or even trying to formulate a new concept. Here we are, condemned to live in the world as it is."[100] This assessment underestimates the unfamiliarity of market capitalism to many of the societies that have been exposed to it since the Communist collapse—not to mention the amount of advice promoting that new kind of society that has been dis-pensed by the Economics Departments of many leading American univer-sities. Unsurprisingly, however, given the real object of his ire, Furet saw only socialism as "another" society. But even the creation of capitalism in societies that have not previously encountered it is a novel experience, if not a new idea.[101]

Still, Furet's diagnosis of the lack of alternative visions of society is very much on the mark. The unmistakable mood of post-totalitarian caution was neatly reflected in the comments of a participant at the 2002 Pôrto Alegre alternative "summit" on globalization, held to coincide with the annual conclave of the world's leading capitalists, the World Economic Forum in Davos.[102] The organizers had adopted the motto "Another world is pos-sible." Yet when a journalist asked why the group seemed to have come up with so little in the way of plans for an alternative future, the Brazilian novelist Moacyr Scliar explained the absence of any grand vision of the future emanating from the meeting as follows: "The political horrors of the twentieth century taught us that it's better we don't leave here with a magic formula."[103]

In the absence of a plausible overarching vision of a more humane future society, the significance of the past and of people's recollections of it become magnified; righting past wrongs tends to supplant the search for a vision of a better tomorrow. The reckoning with abominable pasts becomes, in fact, the idiom in which the future is sought. We might call this the *involution* of the progressive impulse that has animated much of modern history— the deflection of what was once regarded as the forward march of progress and its turning inward upon itself in a climate of conservative dominance. Where can one now find analogs of those venerable early twentieth-century expressions of optimism in the future conveyed in the Italian socialists' *Avanti!* or the German Social Democrats' *Vorwärts?* Not since the Romantics has so much energy been spent on digging up the past, sifting through the broken shards, and pondering what people think about them. This situation has everything to do with the enshrinement, over the past two decades or so, of the Holocaust as the "true emblem" of our age.[104]

The Holocaust as Standard and Model

Far from a merely local event of little relevance to those outside the Euro-Atlantic world, the Holocaust has emerged as the principal legacy of the twentieth century with respect to the way our contemporaries think about the past. The perfidy of the Nazi assault on European Jewry has emerged as a kind of "gold standard" against which to judge other cases of injustice and to which advocates seek to assimilate those instances of human cruelty and oppression for which they seek a reckoning. Those who regard the Holocaust as a sponge of historical memory that sucks the juices out of alternative projects for coming to terms with past wrongs are thus only half right. The Holocaust has not only absorbed an enormous amount of attention among those wanting to come to terms with the past; it has also facilitated attention to the catastrophic past more generally.

For example, in its effort to call attention to the crimes of Communist regimes around the world in the course of the twentieth century, *The Black Book of Communism* made this point in the very act of insisting that Communist crimes were more atrocious and hence more deserving of recompense than those of the Holocaust. The book, which was first published in France in 1997 to intense controversy that was repeated when German and

Italian editions appeared soon thereafter, took its title from an eponymous volume compiled by Ilya Ehrenburg and Vassily Grossmann in 1981 that documented the atrocities that would later be known as "the Holocaust."[105] In the provocative introduction to what otherwise were relatively sober (if macabre) country-by-country analyses of Communist atrocities, editor Stéphane Courtois asserted that "in contrast to the Jewish Holocaust, which the international Jewish community has actively commemorated, it has been impossible for victims of Communism and their legal advocates to keep the memory of the tragedy alive, and any requests for commemoration or demands for reparations are brushed aside . . . [A] single-minded focus on the Jewish genocide in an attempt to characterize the Holocaust as a unique atrocity has also prevented an assessment of other episodes of comparable magnitude in the Communist world."[106] This extraordinary outburst led some of the contributors to *The Black Book* to distance themselves publicly from Courtois's introduction.[107]

Recent controversies over the "uniqueness" of the Holocaust, and over whether the Nazis' crimes were more damnable than those of the Communists, should sound familiar to those who have followed these matters during the past couple of decades. In effect, these disputes over the way in which we think about the history of the twentieth century reprise the central arguments of the *Historikerstreit* ("historians' debate") of the mid-1980s. The renewal of competition over whether the Nazis or the Communists were responsible for greater evil, in which *The Black Book of Communism* has been perhaps the most inflammatory intervention, thus seems something of a rearguard action, with relatively little prospect of transforming our perception of the larger meaning of the twentieth century. Dan Diner has suggested one important reason for this outcome: terrible though the gulag was, the "knowledge" associated with our grasp of the "liquidation of the kulaks as a class" or of other Communist brutality cannot constitute the basis of an ethnic self-understanding because most of the relevant groups do not persist through historical time.[108] Ethnic and racial conceptions of groups are more likely to have perceptible, ongoing referents than classes. That fact undermines the likelihood that class-related injustices will capture the imagination of the successors of those who suffered them and make them the focus of campaigns for commemoration and reparations.

The Black Book's strenuous efforts to demonstrate the extent to which Communist oppression had ethnoracial dimensions bear unintentional witness to the validity of Diner's insight. Thus, in the book's chapter on Cambodia, Jean-Louis Margolin writes: "[F]or the Khmer Rouge, as for the Chinese Communists, some social groups were criminal by nature, and this criminality was seen as transmittable from husband to wife, as well as an inherited trait . . . We can speak of the *racialization* of social groups, and the crime of genocide therefore can be applied to their physical elimination."[109] Margolin is pointing to a crucial feature of the interpretation of the crime of genocide as it has come to be understood since the Holocaust assumed its dominant role in contemporary historical consciousness: namely, that the notion of genocide has mainly come to be applied to groups defined in ethnoracial terms, despite the Genocide Convention's inclusion of national and religious groups as possible victims of that crime. Diner's observation about the difficulties of constructing an "actionable" historical memory out of the experiences of economically defined groups is thus very much to the point.

Despite the contrasting political implications, both those seeking greater recognition of Communist misdeeds and those such as Peter Novick who observe with misgivings the steady growth of the Holocaust in American public discourse argue that the Shoah has attained such overriding prominence in our mental landscape that it may be difficult to give other human catastrophes the attention they deserve.[110] In contrast to those seeking to gain greater attention for other past crimes, however, Novick's critique comes from the future, so to speak. He wishes us to view the Holocaust as a cautionary tale leading us to work harder to forestall any repetition of its horrors, not as an episode redolent with "lessons" about the shadow side of human nature and certainly not as an event on which to focus our political endeavors today. The convergence of views between the two camps regarding the Holocaust's predominant position in current discussions of historical injustices is nonetheless striking and bespeaks the towering significance of that episode in contemporary Euro-American historical consciousness.[111]

Yet those in—or at least from—the Third World are intensely aware of the extent to which the Holocaust and its legal and financial consequences may be relevant to their own situation as well. Thus, for example, the Nobel Prize–winning Nigerian novelist Wole Soyinka, addressing efforts to gain reparations for past misdeeds suffered by Africans, has written that "it is not possible to ignore the example of the Jews and the obsessed commitment of survivors of the Holocaust, and their descendants, to recover both their material patrimony and the humanity of which they were brutally deprived."[112] In a further instance of this African appropriation of the Holocaust and its consequences, the report of the International Panel of Eminent Personalities to Investigate the 1994 Genocide in Rwanda and the Surrounding Events notes in its recommendations concerning reparations that "the case of Germany after World War Two is pertinent here."[113] Such references to the exemplary character of the response to the Shoah for those who have suffered violence and degradation elsewhere demonstrate that, far from obscuring their suffering, the paradigmatic status of the Jewish catastrophe for our time has helped others who have been subjected to state-sponsored mass atrocities to gain attention for those calamities—though hardly all of them, to be sure.

Our world is thus populated by "one, two, many Holocausts," to paraphrase a slogan from the Vietnam era. The "victory" that went to those who defended the uniqueness of the Holocaust in the *Historikerstreit* of the mid-1980s has since been overtaken by the efforts of those seeking attention to various historical injustices and who, in so doing, find "holocausts" of many kinds in the historical inheritance of our age. The proliferation of holocausts inflates the term and undermines the notion of the uniqueness of the Nazi genocide, but—given the Holocaust's paradigmatic role in the contemporary "consciousness of catastrophe"—it does encourage attention to other catastrophic pasts.[114] Indeed, the recent appearance in Germany of a volume titled *The Red Holocaust and the Germans* bespeaks the crumbling of a taboo in that country on comparisons with the genocide perpetrated by the Nazis, and the growing acceptability of applying that term to other historical experiences. The publication of such a title by a reputable scholarly institution would have been almost inconceivable only a few years ago. That the volume bears witness to a stark shift in mentalities seems all the more certain in that the collection was edited by the director of the renowned Institute for Contemporary History, a quasi-official institution long dedicated to making sense of the Nazi past.[115]

The consolidation of the Holocaust as a standard for historical injustice has stimulated a vigorous competition for recognition of various historical injustices as "Holocaust-like" or "worse than the Holocaust." Commentators and activists concerned with the horrors of Communism, the legacies of the African slave trade, and the fate of non-white indigenous populations at the hands of European colonizers have been in the forefront of these efforts.[116] The result is an often unseemly contest for the status of worst-victimized. Thus the African scholar Ali Mazrui has written bluntly: "Twelve years of Jewish hell—against several centuries of black enslavement."[117] It is difficult to avoid the conclusion that the Holocaust has emerged as the model for other historical disasters in part because it has facilitated demands for reparations by other groups that have suffered tragic histories. Yet it could not have done so without the development of a broader sense that the twentieth century, and European domination particularly, were catastrophic wrong turns in world history.

The various developments outlined in this chapter have fed a major shift in much progressive thinking from a focus on the future as the proving ground of social change to a preoccupation with the past as the arena in which to seek improvements in the human condition. Against this background, demands for reparations have proliferated in various settings around the world. We now turn to an exploration of the global dynamics of reparations politics.

CHAPTER 2

An Anatomy
of Reparations Politics

The preoccupation with past crimes and atrocities mirrors the eclipse of more visionary modes of imagining the future. At the same time, it promotes attention to the once-neglected suffering of victims and bears witness to an enhancement of their status vis-à-vis the official or quasi-official perpetrators of injustices. In this chapter, I offer a framework for understanding the worldwide spread of reparations politics at the dawning of the new millennium. I emphasize reparations in the narrow sense as a response to past injustices, while viewing reparations politics as a broader field encompassing such phenomena as transitional justice, apologies, and efforts at reconciliation as well.

Defining Reparations

Let us begin by defining some terms. Perhaps the most frequently used single term connected with many of the efforts to come to terms with the past is that of *reparations*. Generally speaking, the term has come to refer to compensation, usually of a material kind and often specifically monetary, for some past wrong. The prominence of this term derives from the signal importance in recent history of Holocaust-related reparations in stimulating the concern to come to terms with past injustices elsewhere. Claims for reparations have spread parallel with the diffusion of Holocaust consciousness, at least among political and intellectual elites, in precincts far distant from the mainly European sites of the Jewish Shoah. A widespread Holocaust consciousness, in turn, has been the water in which reparations activists have swum, defining much of the discourse they use to pursue their aims.

Yet the late-twentieth-century spread of interest in the notion of reparations cannot be understood apart from the semantic meanings of the term itself. The term is one of the "re-words" that Charles Maier has identified as the object of rising consideration among various groups in recent years.[1] The first thing that must be said is that sometime after World War II the word came to be transformed from its original connotation of war reparations into something much broader. Before World War II, the use of "war" as a modifier here would have been nearly redundant; in that era, it went without saying that reparations were an outgrowth of war. Perhaps the paradigmatic case of reparations was that mandated by the Versailles Treaty which ended World War I and imposed heavy obligations on the Germans to compensate the Allies for their wartime losses. In such cases, the term was synonymous with "indemnities"; again, the use of "war" to modify the main term would have been largely superfluous. It went without saying—in English at least—that reparations was an exaction imposed by the winners of a war on the losers, who were said to have been responsible for the damage caused by the conflict. This meaning of the term *reparations* is the *only* one employed in the European history textbook that I used as an undergraduate in the late 1970s, Robert Paxton's *Europe in the Twentieth Century;* the current, broader usage was simply not yet a widely accepted part of the lexicon.[2]

There was not a little "victor's justice" in the formula underlying reparations, and the party on whom the indemnity fell was keenly aware of this fact. As a member of the negotiating delegation at Versailles, Max Weber opposed the imposition of heavy reparations obligations on Germany. He rightly feared that the obligation would be resented and would lead to subsequent German hostility.[3] The burden of German reparations that came out of Versailles has almost universally been seen as contributing greatly to the resentments that gave rise to the Nazis and hence led to the outbreak of World War II. The Germans may have had particular reasons for resentment; according to Paxton, the commonplace practice of imposing reparations was exacerbated after World War I by a novel element of moral recrimination that may have marked a significant signpost on the way to future usage.[4]

After World War II, in the most prominent early effort by a German to deal with the legacy of Nazi rule, the philosopher and "inner émigré" Karl Jaspers wrote in *The Question of German Guilt* of the need for the German populace to atone for the wrongdoing carried out in its name. Jaspers argued that it was incumbent upon the Germans to make amends for the atrocities committed by the Nazi regime, claiming that "everyone really affected by the guilt he shares will wish to help anyone wronged by the arbitrary despotism of the lawless régime." Jaspers used the term *Wieder-gutmachung*, translated variously as "reparations" or "reparation." *Wieder-gutmachung* would entail "tightening our belts so that part of their destruc-tion can be made up to the nations attacked by Hitler Germany."[5] Jaspers's emphasis was on reconstruction, the restoration of what had been de-stroyed by German actions.

Jaspers also noted that there are two motivations for aiding those in need and that the two were not to be confused: "the first calls on us to help wherever there is distress, no matter what the cause—simply because it is near and calls for help. The second requires us to grant a special right to those deported, robbed, pillaged, tortured and exiled by the Hitler regime." In making this distinction, Jaspers averred, "both demands are fully justi-fied, but there is a difference in motivation. Where guilt is not felt, all distress is immediately leveled on the same plane. If I want to make up for what I, too, was guilty of, I must differentiate between the groups afflicted by distress."[6] In the overall context of Jaspers's argument about the "way of purification" that he regarded as essential to a viable postwar German society, the meaning of the passage is somewhat obscure insofar as his concern was to persuade the German population as a whole of its respon-sibility to make amends for the devastation wrought by their country. The burden of Jaspers's text is precisely that *all* Germans must regard them-selves as sharing this responsibility.

Whatever his intentions in *The Question of German Guilt*, Jaspers's distinc-tion reflects two very different senses of the notion of "reparations." In the first set of circumstances to which Jaspers refers, the phenomenon to which a response is necessary might be characterized as a sort of *generalized* dis-tress. One need not possess any *personal* responsibility for the difficulty in which someone might find himself in order to feel an obligation to assist him. One might argue that this is the challenge of modern citizenship as an institution oriented to achieving equality among the members of a state in the face of an economic system that systematically produces inequality.[7]

In the second sense, however, the circumstances in question concern actions for which "I, too, was guilty." The question of one's responsibility for the actions of one's government may be disputed. But Jaspers clearly believed that all Germans were responsible for the atrocities committed at the behest of the Third Reich in a way that he would presumably not have claimed was true for, let us say, the heirs of the system of racial slavery in the United States. "Reparations" in the first sense relates to rectifying injustices whether or not one had any hand in the commission of the wrongs in question, whereas guilt—at least in the sense of temporal and political propinquity—is intrinsic to the second meaning. In the past couple of decades, the second meaning has become extensively equated with the first, at least by those seeking to make claims about righting past wrongs. In other words, the category of *beneficiary* has in some respects been assimilated into that of *perpetrator*. The result has been a proliferation of efforts to claim reparations for wrongs done more or less long ago, but for which at least a plausible case can be made that (1) gross violations of human rights occurred in the past and (2) the effects of those wrongs persist into the present. Clearly, all of this is a long way from the notion of "war reparations."

Despite the more or less equivalent meaning of reparations and reparation in the translation of Jaspers's text, the two terms have come to connote rather different things. The singular "reparation" has come to suggest a panoply of different responses to atrocities and wrongdoing, including "restitution, compensation, rehabilitation, satisfaction [measures to acknowledge the violations] and guarantees of non-repetition."[8] Reparation thus involves a variety of actions and activities that seek to restore the *status quo ante*. With the possible exception of "guarantees of non-repetition," which are predominantly political and legislative in nature, the activities that comprise reparation are notably legalistic in character and may or may not involve transfers of money. In contemporary usage, the notion of reparation thus hews closer than its sibling reparations to the terms' roots in the idea of "repair." That is, reparation is more akin to the idea of restoration of the state of affairs before the violation occurred. By contrast, reparations has come to be used almost synonymously with compensation—that is, with money transfers of a relatively direct kind. One *makes* reparation, in short, but one *pays* reparations. Paradoxically, the singular of the term connotes a multiplicity of activities, whereas the plural tends to entail only one.

This usage is reflected in the United Nations' "Basic Principles and Guidelines on the Right to a Remedy and Reparation for Victims of Violations of International Human Rights and Humanitarian Law." This document is perhaps the most important expression of the contemporary desire to ensure that victims of human rights violations have a solid foundation for making claims against those who have wronged them. The document, the drafting of which began in the late 1980s, seeks to lay out the bases on which such claims can be made, by whom, against whom, for what offenses, and with what aims. The language of the text and the prominence in its drafting of two leading international human rights lawyers—Theo van Boven and Cherif Bassiouni—make it clear that the document is primarily a product of legal thinkers and concerns. Indeed, the reparative measures it outlines would be perfectly familiar to anyone with a basic knowledge of Western legal systems of torts and damages.

In this sense, the Basic Principles and Guidelines reflect the expansion to the international realm of legal concepts that have long been common coin in domestic contexts. That is, the law of nations—in which the relevant parties were states—has been slowly mutating into a different kind of system in which individuals are legitimate actors as well. This development is connected to the general erosion of the supremacy of the notion of sovereignty and the contemporaneous burgeoning of the human rights paradigm in response to the carnage of World War II.[9] Since that time, individuals and subnational groups have effectively been endowed with standing in international law in a series of U.N. documents and international covenants. This shift arose in part because, in addition to making war on other countries, the Nazis also made a separate, undeclared war on defenseless Jews as well as on other groups (e.g., the handicapped, homosexuals, and Gypsies). As a result, and despite longstanding debate about whether Jews constitute a nation, the assault on the Jews eventually gave them a kind of legal standing in international law (quite apart from the existence of Israel), setting an important precedent for other groups to lay claim to a similar status.

During roughly the same period that the United Nations has been working on the "Basic Principles," the notion of reparations (plural) has gained considerable momentum as a rubric under which to make claims in a variety of different contexts around the globe. However, one of the most prominent and significant campaigns concerning historical injustices—one that, indeed, set major precedents for what was to come—usually went under the term *redress*. I refer to the campaign mounted by activists seeking action regarding the internment of Japanese-Americans and Japanese-Canadians during World War II. This may have been an effort to understate the monetary dimension of the claims, which were not necessarily terribly important to the actors involved—except in symbolic terms. In the end, of course, the reparations of approximately $20,000 per person that were paid to the Japanese-Americans and Japanese-Canadians were not especially large, even if they were not entirely insignificant either. Although this campaign was more about official acknowledgment of past wrongdoing than it was about the money involved, redress activists wanted to ensure that the amount paid was at least significant enough to be symbolically meaningful. Still, it seems reasonably clear that Japanese-American redress was "not about the money."[10] The U.S. Congress, for its part, was intent on ensuring that the case would not be seen as a precedent for other cases, especially claims by American blacks. These intentions and the term *redress* notwithstanding, the case in fact did much to promote the idea of reparations as a way of dealing with various kinds of injustices.

Despite (or possibly because of) the fact that the plural version of the term *reparations* now largely means one thing—money—it has become the central idea structuring a variety of campaigns around the world for addressing various wrongs. These efforts include a movement for reparations for forced and slave laborers exploited by the Nazis during World War II, for blacks in the United States (although there is some division over the question of whether these reparations would be for slavery, for Jim Crow legislation, or for specific cases of atrocities such as took place in Rosewood, Florida or Tulsa, Oklahoma), for apartheid in South Africa, for the depredations of the Germans in pre–World War I Southwest Africa (now Namibia), for the so-called comfort women sexually exploited by the Japanese army during World War II, and others. While these cases involve very different kinds of wrongs, they tend to have one factor in common: namely, the violation took place across and to a large extent on the basis of an ethnoracial distinction. The only example in which this kind of distinction is not the most salient is the case of the comfort women, where gender was the chief basis of exploitation. Still, even the comfort women were chosen largely on the basis of their ethnoracial distinctness from the Japanese (although some were Japanese as well). In any case, it is striking that so many different groups have mobilized around the idea of reparations for past injustices suffered by people in the past—often, though by no means always, by those whom these activists regard as "their" group (or its ancestors).

Some people use the term *reparations* synonymously with *restitution*. Like reparations, restitution can be interpreted expansively to include a variety of ways of making amends.[11] The two terms should not be used interchangeably, however. Even if the dictionary permits a broad interpretation, the term *restitution* typically suggests a more narrow concern with the return of specific items of real or personal property. In contrast, the term *reparations* has come to suggest broader and more variegated meanings. It is telling, for example, that studies of the problems connected with the return of land to blacks in South Africa and to Indians in the northeastern United States both speak of "restitution" rather than "reparations."[12] The distinction between restitution and reparations is captured nicely by certain remarks in the study that underlay the Civil Liberties Act of 1988, which sought to recompense Japanese-Americans for their "internment" in the United States during World War II. That study, *Personal Justice Denied*, noted that the Japanese American Evacuation Claims Act of 1948 "attempted to compensate for the [internees'] losses of real and personal property" but made no attempt to compensate for the stigma, deprivation of liberty, or psychological impact of exclusion and relocation.[13]

It is an important feature of contemporary reparations politics that they give much greater weight to psychic harms and trauma than was the case in the period up to and immediately following World War II.[14] This shift reflects the "triumph of the therapeutic" in realms far removed from individual psychology.[15] It also points to the transformation of the concept of trauma from a purely physical to a predominantly mental construction—a process that, according to Ian Hacking, arose from late-nineteenth-century interpretations of railway accidents.[16]

In contrast to restitution, then, the notion of reparations suggests attempts to make up for egregiously and unjustly violated selves and for squandered life chances, rather than attempts to compel the return of goods per se. The spread of human rights ideas in the post–World War II era has fueled the sense that such wrongs, no matter how acceptable they may have been deemed at the time they were committed, may now be said to have been illegitimate and must be compensated or redressed accordingly. Because it now covers responses to this broad class of wrongs, the term *reparations* has emerged as the most widely used term relating to coming to terms with past injustices.

The human rights instruments promulgated by the United Nations after World War II were drafted in order to ensure that human beings would not, in the future, exercise their barbarous impulses on others without the victim having a juridical leg to stand on—especially when the perpetrator was the victim's own government. Human rights talk, the curtailment of the strong "Westphalian" notion of sovereignty, and the rising status of the individual as a subject of international law have gone together. In turn, reparations have been an essential complement to the spread of human rights ideas. Reparations help to make the notion of human rights seem real and enforceable in the absence of a global police force empowered to back rights claims with armed might.

Mapping Reparations Politics

Connected as it is etymologically to the word "repair," the term *reparations* now suggests activities oriented to repairing frayed or torn relations handed down from the past. As was suggested in the previous chapter, the theological and legal ways of thinking about repair have become predominant, yet the modalities of repair are manifold. The repair of shattered social relations may involve trials of perpetrators, purges, truth commissions, rehabilitation of those wrongly convicted of crimes, monetary compensation, social policies designed to rectify inequalities rooted in unjust past social arrangements, memorials, changes in school history curricula, and more.[17] Following Pierre Bourdieu, we may find it useful to conceptualize the various phenomena connected with reparations politics not as a mélange of isolated cases but as a *field* of interrelated activities.[18] As has already been noted, the term *reparations* is used to discuss claims for mending past wrongs that are themselves extremely varied, running the gamut from human rights abuses against individuals such as unjust imprisonment and torture to such diverse social systems as plantation slavery, apartheid, and colonialism. Yet viewing reparations politics as a field helps us to grasp the ways in which, far from each of the groups in question pursuing purely their own narrow concerns, the various kinds of reparations politics share a common language and outlook concerning the importance of the past for moving forward in the present.

As Figure 1 suggests, the broad field of reparations politics can be regarded as a series of concentric circles. These circles progress from a "core" of what has come to be known as transitional justice (typically involving legal and quasilegal mechanisms such as criminal trials, political purges, and truth commissions), through compensation and restitution of a material kind, to apologies and statements of regret, and finally to a concern with reshaping collective memory that one might refer to as the pursuit of a communicative history—that is, history-writing that emerges from consultation and agreement among the various parties to a particular past, on the

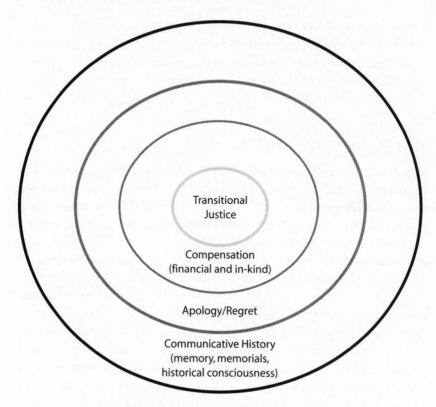

Figure 1. The field of reparations politics

basis of the notion that they are the ones (most) directly affected by the history in question. This conceptualization distinguishes among ideal types of activities germane to coming to terms with the past that may, in practice, be found lumped together in any given case. As one moves from the center of the map to its periphery, the stress in the types of activity tends to move from a focus on the perpetrators to a concern with the victims or their descendants.

At the core of the field are those activities associated with transitional justice in what might be called its classic sense. Here the perpetrators of the injustices in question comprise a more or less identifiable group, and they are, generally speaking, still alive. Punishment of misdeeds or at least illumination of the circumstances of their commission—rather than compensation for the victims—is the focus of the activity of repair. In contrast, reparations in the narrow sense of material compensation steers concern away from evildoers and, instead, in the direction of *victims* as well as of *beneficiaries* rather than perpetrators per se. Whether or not those who suffered the alleged wrongs are still alive becomes a major bone of contention in the struggle for reparations. The further removed in time one gets from the commission of the acts for which compensation is sought, the thornier the problems of repair become. Even if they are dead, however, there may be beneficiaries in the present who may be said to owe reparations to the heirs of the one-time victims of the injustice. Apologies and statements of regret involve exchanges between perpetrators and victims, whether the interaction takes place between surviving members of either group or their descendants.[19] Apologies may or may not be accompanied by material compensation. They are a more purely symbolic exercise, even if it is also often true that monetary payments are chiefly symbolic in nature. Finally, efforts to commemorate past suffering and to get the history straight are increasingly contentious, despite having arguably the least momentous impact on public policy. This aspect of reparations politics, the search for a communicative history, involves scrutiny and revision of school textbooks, the erection of commemorative plaques and memorials, and the search for a past about which all the (putative) participants can agree. Let us now examine each of these types of activities in greater detail.

Transitional Justice

The notion of transitional justice gained currency in connection with the demise of military dictatorships in Latin America and Southern Europe in the 1970s and after. Hard on the heels of the departing generals, the collapse of Communist regimes in the Soviet Union and Eastern Europe and of the apartheid regime in South Africa further strengthened this approach to thinking about politics.[20] The writings in this genre have sought to make sense of the global trend toward democratization that swept far-flung parts of the world in the closing third of the twentieth century.[21] The chief activities associated with transitional justice have been trials and purges of perpetrators and collaborators, bans of people from holding certain kinds of offices ("lustration"), and the instauration of truth commissions.[22] As a general rule, the misdeeds for which a reckoning is sought in processes of transitional justice are atrocities and wrongs committed by agents of the state against individuals, usually for political apostasy and principally in the form of what the United Nations has codified in recent years under the heading of "gross violations of human rights."[23]

Underlying what is sometimes called transitology is a generic transition to democracy (or at least one "from authoritarianism"). Yet the particular type of rule that is being left behind, and the variety of paths away from undemocratic rule, make a very big difference in determining what kind of transitional justice will occur.[24] For example, one of the most insightful analysts of the legacy of Communism in the Eastern bloc, Tina Rosenberg, has noted that the transitions in the former Soviet bloc and those in Latin America had both important similarities and major differences. Rosenberg distinguished between the "criminal regimes" that had ruled the Communist countries and the "regimes of criminals" that held sway under the generals in Latin America. Her analysis of Communist regimes owed much to the view of those such as Vaclav Havel who maintained that everyone in the Communist countries bore their share of complicity in the persistence of the political order. Accordingly, Rosenberg suggested that it was more difficult to envision trials of "collaborators" in such countries than it would be in the case of brutal regimes run by relatively small groups of *responsables*.[25]

Yet such trials were blocked, at least initially, in those cases where the transition from violent rule was a bargain negotiated among political elites. The leaders of the old regime were not likely to lay down their guns if they would soon find themselves facing criminal trials; hence, amnesty was the order of the day.[26] The subsequent efforts to prosecute former Chilean strongman Augusto Pinochet revealed that not everyone accepted these bargains, which were hammered out by elites in the waning days of their rule. Still, coming to terms with the past in Latin American and East European societies has chiefly involved a sort of collective agreement to move on, either because that was the deal that permitted the transition to more democratic forms of rule or because there was no obvious way to prosecute any but a few "big fish." As Sharon Lean has pointed out, demands for and payments of monetary reparations have been relatively limited in the Latin American cases.[27] However, small programs have been designed to compensate the victims of torture in Chile and Argentina.[28] There has also been what Jon Elster calls a "second wave" of prosecutions in recent years.[29]

Against the background of the spreading worldwide preoccupation with righting historical injustices, however, the main difficulty with the transitional justice paradigm has been its foreshortened time horizons, its tendency to view the past as having begun only the day before yesterday, so to speak. Since this approach has been dominated by lawyers, political scientists, and human rights activists, whose concerns tend to be legalistic and oriented to the character of present-day political institutions, the disproportionate attention to regime changes of the very recent past is perhaps not surprising.

In contrast to the historical shallowness of the transitional justice paradigm, many of the historical injustices for which repair and reckoning have been demanded in recent times involve wrongs that occurred or had their origins relatively far back in the past, and in societies with apparently venerable liberal credentials. These demands for repair of the subterranean past concern heinous regimes and actions that may stretch back hundreds of years, or they may impugn political and social orders whose flaws for particular groups have only recently grown politically salient. Demands for repair of the legacies of these pasts recall the important lesson, once taught us by Barrington Moore, that even liberal democratic societies were born in fire and blood.[30] Campaigns for attention to and repair of these past wrongs also highlight the fact that for some groups even in liberal democratic societies of long standing, dispossession was the rule and the liberal promise of equal treatment was chimerical until only yesterday—or, indeed, it remains so into the present day.

The theoretical premises underlying the transitional justice model thus distort our understanding both of authoritarianism and of liberal democracy. The model takes the self-characterization of liberal societies too literally to accommodate the insistence of various groups that they have been denied the equality that such societies claim to afford their citizens. As Aristide Zolberg has pointed out, "Despite the usage popularized by Washington-area political scientists, authoritarianism should not be thought of as a distinct regime type but, rather, as an element of political process shared by many different systems of rule and associated with a variety of socioeconomic formations."[31] Thus it is not only in recently authoritarian regimes that a reckoning with the past is sought, as the transitional justice literature tends to imply. Like recently dictatorial regimes, liberal democracies also face demands for repair arising from instances of past abrogation of the universalistic ideas on the basis of which they claim legitimacy. At the same time, compared to regimes based more on force than on persuasion, such efforts at repair demonstrate the liberal democracies' greater inclination and ability to respond to demands to mend a torn social and political fabric.

Reparations

Generally speaking, there are three principal sources of claims for reparations, understood in the narrow sense of monetary compensation. First are those cases arising from acts of injustice perpetrated during the course of World War II. These include claims arising from state-sponsored mass killing, forced labor, and sexual exploitation perpetrated by the Axis powers (Germany and Japan, but also Austria), as well as from the unjust wartime incarceration of those of Japanese descent in Allied countries (the United States and Canada, although some of those "interned" as enemy aliens in the United States actually came from Latin America, especially Peru) and from economic or other kinds of collaboration in Nazi crimes by putatively neutral countries (Switzerland, France, the Netherlands). These claims have proven paradigmatic for others seeking reparations for the injustices done them or their kind.

Second are those claims that were made in the aftermath of the transition to democracy to rectify state terrorism and other authoritarian practices. Such cases have been prominent aspects of political life in Latin America, Eastern Europe, and South Africa in recent years. These cases, however, have been more notable for generating truth commissions, debates over past complicity with the old regime, and purges of collaborators than they have been for demands for monetary compensation as such, though restitution and privatization of property have been major issues in post-Communist countries.[32] Coming to terms with the past in these countries has primarily involved clarifying the circumstances under which victims of the regime suffered, in accordance with the transitional justice approach, but monetary compensation has played a small role nevertheless. As we shall see later in the discussion of reparations politics in Southern Africa, the South African case is a mixed one, combining aspects of this second source with the third—namely, campaigns for reparations stemming from colonialism.

Demands for reparations arising from colonialism can be broken down further, depending on whether we are referring to the "classical" European version of colonialism, one or another variant of "internal colonialism" (e.g., slavery, Jim Crow, apartheid),[33] or more recent neocolonial structures and institutions. With respect to claims emerging from the aftermath of classical European colonialism, claims for reparations have been mounted both by the formerly colonized, especially in Africa, and by a variety of indigenous groups against states dominated by the descendants of their European conquerors. More recently, demands for reparations have been raised against international lending agencies whose policies some regard as the cause of, rather than the cure for, Third World poverty and environmental destruction. During the protests against the World Bank and the International Monetary Fund in April 2000 in Washington, D.C., for example, activists insisted that the World Bank should pay reparations for its funding of dams that have allegedly displaced over 10 million people from their homes and land, caused severe environmental damage, and driven impoverished borrowers further into debt.[34]

Largely because of the publicity given to the Truth and Reconciliation Commission (TRC), the transition from apartheid to nonracialism in South Africa has bulked very large in recent discussions of coming to terms with the past. Yet despite sharing certain characteristics of the other transitions, the case of South Africa is different from them in a manner that highlights some of the complexities of material reparations. As in some of the Latin American cases, the TRC was also empowered through its Committee on Reparation and Rehabilitation to provide limited compensation to the victims of human rights abuses perpetrated by state security forces.[35]

But here the similarities with the Latin American and East European countries end. The apartheid regime was not simply another brutal regime but a species of the genus colonialism. As Mahmood Mamdani has pointed out, "Where the focus is on perpetrators, victims are necessarily defined as the minority of political activists; for the victimhood of the majority to be recognized, the focus has to shift from perpetrators to beneficiaries. The difference is this: whereas the focus on perpetrators fuels the demand for justice as criminal justice, that on beneficiaries shifts the focus to a notion of justice as social justice."[36] In other words, the TRC neglected "the link between conquest and dispossession, between racialised power and racialised privilege, between perpetrator and beneficiary"[37]—in a word, the enduring legacy of inequality that the apartheid system and its predecessors had left in its wake. Along with violations of human rights in violent regimes, colonial conquest and expropriation have come to constitute major sources of demands for reparations. Mamdani's analysis of the South African case suggests how the language of reparations has broadened out from the paradigm case of reparations for the Jewish (and other) victims of the Nazis into a rhetoric available for groups that have suffered very different kinds of historical injustices.

In an earlier essay on this theme, I argued that there were two principal types of reparations claims, paralleling the variants suggested by Mamdani.[38] I called these two types of reparations claims commemorative and anti-systemic, reflecting the difference between specific abuses committed against individual persons who are still alive today, on the one hand, and systemic abuses in the past that can be said to be the cause of group-based inequalities in the present, on the other. The decisive issue in this distinction is the extent to which *economic disadvantage in the present* is relevant to the claim for reparations. In other words, even if current economic circumstances are taken into account in the design of a reparations program, economic inequality is not at the core of commemorative reparations claims.[39] In contrast, such inequality *is* at the heart of the matter for those demanding anti-systemic reparations. To put the matter another way, commemorative reparations are important for what they *say*, whereas anti-systemic reparations are important for what they *do*.[40] The distinction has a corollary in the political orientations of those who pursue them. Commemorative reparations may well be the end of the matter for many who seek or receive them, whereas those making anti-systemic reparations claims are more likely to be connected to broader movements for egalitarian social change. For them, the pursuit of reparations tends to be but one strategy in a larger project designed to promote equality. Broadly speaking, the difference is between those oriented toward *identity* politics and those oriented toward *commonality* politics.[41]

Building on the earlier distinction between types of reparations claims, one might characterize reparations politics along the lines suggested in Figure 2, which is intended to be suggestive, not comprehensive. Rather than being mutually exclusive, as the earlier distinction between two types of reparations politics may have suggested, reparations campaigns should in fact be regarded as poles along a continuum. Many who seek reparations of the commemorative sort also see what they are doing as helping to ensure the growth and survival of democracy and the rule of law, or perhaps as part of the struggle to end sexual violence, torture, and impunity. In that sense, they are operating in an anti-systemic fashion. Still, economic inequality remains less central to their concerns than are human rights (in the sense of liberal autonomy). The continuum relating commemorative

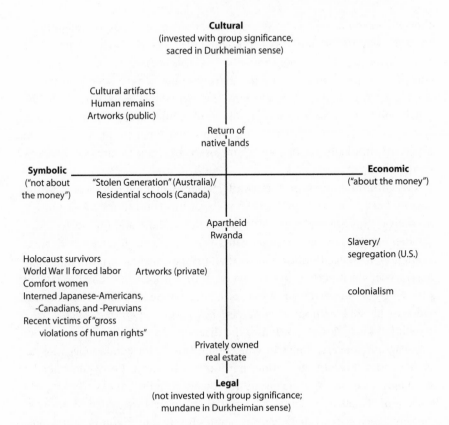

Figure 2. The "meaning of money" in reparations claims-making

and anti-systemic reparations claims is indicated by the "east-west" axis in Figure 2. The distinction has been rephrased, however, according to the "meaning" various reparations claims assign to money (to the extent that it plays a role at all). Reflecting this distinction in meaning, the endpoints on the continuum are now designated as "symbolic" and "economic." At the symbolic end, the meaning of money chiefly or exclusively concerns the seriousness of an apology for, or recognition of, previous wrongdoing. The meaning of money at the other end is straightforwardly "economic." In other words, although an apology may not be irrelevant to the acceptability of the financial compensation on the part of the recipients, that compensation really *is* "about the money."

In addition to clarifying the relation between commemorative/symbolic and anti-systemic/economic reparations claims, the diagram suggests a further dimension according to which reparations claims may be categorized. Here the key consideration concerns the extent to which claimants regard past injustices as having contributed to *the destruction of "a culture,"* and the role of reparations in repairing the damages said to have been inflicted on a culture. This aspect of reparations claims-making bears witness to the heightened significance in recent politics of culture generally. More specifically, the notion of rights to one's culture has emerged as an important aspect of multicultural discourse and its recognition of previously disregarded groups.[42]

This cultural dimension of reparations claims-making is indicated by the "north-south" axis in Figure 2. The poles of this continuum run from reparations claims arising from the expropriation of land and objects regarded by their previous owners or inhabitants as having deep cultural significance, at the top, to alleged unjust takings that are specifiable in a more mundane legal sense, albeit perhaps retroactively so. In short, groups may or may not care much about particular objects or lands; if a piece of land or an artifact were to be sold without anyone else being very interested, such a case would fall in the lower portion of the diagram. Cases in the top portion of the diagram concern things in what Emile Durkheim would label "the sacred" realm; those in the bottom portion involve what he would call "the mundane." Let me now explicate the diagram, which seeks to capture a variety of reparations claims currently afoot around the globe, if not necessarily every conceivable claim. It might also be said that different people might regard each case differently; this diagram attempts to capture how most people would regard each of the different cases.

As indicated in the lower left of Figure 2, symbolic reparations are those given to or sought by those groups who were victimized and forced to perform forced labor by the Axis powers during World War II; those of Japanese ethnicity unjustly interned in North America during that war; and recent victims of "gross violations of human rights." The claims are in many ways analogous to the sorts of civil liabilities that might routinely be brought against firms accused of wrongdoing, except that the responsible parties are often states or churches as well as private firms. (The fund recently created by the German government to compensate World War II–era forced and slave laborers was a joint government–industry undertaking prompted by lawsuits against companies, but the terms were largely hammered out under official government auspices.) The claims are not generally justified in terms of any alleged cultural destruction, however, but simply in terms of the direct suffering sustained by the victims. (Interestingly, despite the notion that the Holocaust amounted to the "destruction of European Jewry," one has little sense that "Judaism" suffered greatly, perhaps because Jewish history is so extensively bound up with stories of persecution and persistence.) The harms for which compensation is sought are chiefly psychological rather than physical, although physical injuries and the infirmities of old age may underlie the claims as well.[43] Or the money is simply a way of lending greater seriousness to the apology or recognition of wrongdoing, which is the more important matter.

The restitution of artworks to private owners falls near to these kinds of harms, in the sense that their expropriation may have been unjust but the objects lacked great spiritual value to a national or religious community, a "culture." The return of such artworks is often largely a symbolic matter, as the person(s) reclaiming them may simply give them (back) to a museum for public display rather than profiting from their re-acquisition or even just holding them privately.[44] When the artworks in question came not from private hands but from state-run institutions, however, the problem becomes a knottier one, and perceptions of injustices by one country or community toward another—claims of national honor, so to speak—come into play. The inflammation of national feelings shapes decisions about what is just with regard to artworks plundered during wartime.[45] Thus, in late 1998 Russia announced that it would return some of the artworks it acquired as booty during World War II, but only to individuals, particularly those who were "victims of the Holocaust." In contrast, the offer of restitution "did not extend to so-called trophy art, the works taken by Soviet troops from Germany and Eastern Europe that the Russians consider to be reparations for the wartime ravages their country suffered."[46] In short, claims for restitution of artworks stolen from public institutions tend to be evaluated more in cultural than in purely legal terms; this explains the location of these kinds of claim in the "northwest" quadrant of Figure 2.

Restitution of real property lies further toward the "economic" end of the continuum concerning the meaning of money because such properties are more likely to have a use value and/or a market value that can be reappropriated by the owners of wrongly expropriated property or their heirs. However, Charles Maier has noted that, as with artworks, "many private owners ask only for nominal recognition of earlier ownership and donate the property for public uses."[47] In any case, precisely because of its mundaneness, real estate expropriated by a nefarious regime is less likely to excite the passions associated with the illegitimate taking of artifacts understood in primarily cultural terms. It is thus located at the "legal" end of the continuum concerning the importance of cultural restoration in reparations politics.

Let us now move to the opposite (upper) end of this continuum. Cultural artifacts, along with human remains, have long been housed in museums of anthropology and natural history. They have been widely seen as essential for the pursuit of scientific knowledge or the advancement of public understanding of the groups from which they were taken (or, perhaps, by which they were given). Museologists Ruth Phillips and Elizabeth Johnson have noted that such artifacts often were collected by those most sympathetic to the peoples with whom Europeans came into contact, and that such collectors often sought to defend these peoples from obliteration by encroaching outsiders.[48] Yet the perception has spread in recent years that even such sympathetic views had a paternalistic quality about them, and that in any case the basic relationship involved was one of racial domination and exploitation rather than any fair negotiation between equals.

The result has been an accelerating shift toward negotiating new relationships between museums and the communities from which originated the artifacts and remains that museums display or house. One prominent legislative effort to regulate these new relationships was the 1990 Native American Graves Protection and Repatriation Act (NAGPRA) in the United States. With that act, "mainstream respect for the dead was formally extended to Indians," an outcome that took cognizance of the traditional American respect for freedom of religion and its abrogation with regard to native populations.[49] Despite following a less litigious and more political route to this destination, Canada followed the NAGPRA precedent in 1992 when a "Task Force on Museums" issued guidelines regulating the disposition of cultural objects held in the country's museums.[50] The trend toward the protection and "repatriation" of native artifacts and human remains has raised concerns among those troubled by the tendency to declare certain objects, however unclear their "paternity," the property of certain groups and hence off-limits to science.[51] One also imagines that it was easier for legislators to pass a law providing for the return of Indian remains than for the return of Indian lands.

The identity-driven politics of recent years has tended to draw the divide between conqueror and aborigine more sharply.[52] This is perhaps understandable insofar as the path to redress of historical injustices rooted in race and ethnicity involves the reassertion, as the grounding of claims for such redress, of precisely those categories of difference on the basis of which the earlier wrongs were perpetrated. The assimilationist ideals of yesteryear have been tarnished as the "subterranean" history of relations between indigene and invader have been brought to light. Some of the intruders upheld an ideal of common citizenship consistent with liberal principles, which require the deemphasis of difference in favor of what people share in common.[53] Yet others argue that the assimilationist policies toward aboriginals in the settler states of North America and Australia were ultimately designed to eliminate the indigenous population in order to make their land available for appropriation by white settlers.[54] The assimilation and acculturation of indigenes, which presuppose conquest by outsiders, is a fundamentally different matter from that of incorporating immigrants, who can reasonably be expected to give up at least some of the old ways and to accept those of the receiving country. The extent to which entry into the dominant society was voluntary leads to different kinds of rights and expectations on the part of those incorporated.[55] Although some aboriginals may choose to assimilate into the dominant society, it is unreasonable to expect them to do so, or to give up their claims to traditional lands.[56]

Despite the prevalence of land claims in many other parts of the world, the movement for reparations in Australia has tended to stress assaults on aboriginal culture rather than land claims. Those pursuing reparations in Australia have focused chiefly on the "stolen generation"—aboriginal children who were forcibly removed from their families and placed in the homes of white Europeans in an effort to transform them into Euro-Australians. As Chris Cunneen has pointed out, in addition to the physical and emotional harms that were inflicted, much of what was deemed to have been wrong about the removal of aboriginal children concerned the loss of cultural rights and opportunities.[57] Relatively little is said about aboriginal rights or claims to land.

The situation in Canada with regard to residential schools for aboriginal children is quite similar. It was the comparable practice of forcibly introducing indigenous children into state- and church-run schools that provoked the Canadian national effort to make amends for past mistreatment of indigenes (known as First Nations in Canadian parlance). That effort is outlined in the 1998 report *Gathering Strength: Canada's Aboriginal Action Plan*, which is "designed to renew the relationship [of the federal government] with the Aboriginal people of Canada."[58] The Action Plan follows up on the recommendations of the report of the Royal Commission on Aboriginal Peoples (RCAP).[59] Its "Statement of Reconciliation: Learning from the Past," calls special attention to the cultural distinctiveness of indigenous populations: "Diverse, vibrant Aboriginal nations had ways of life rooted in fundamental values concerning their relationships to the Creator, the environment, and each other, in the role of Elders as the living memory of their ancestors, and in their responsibilities as custodians of the lands, waters and resources of their homelands." The claims for reparations by aboriginal peoples in Australia and Canada are heavily grounded in the cultural damage they have sustained under these policies of forced assimilation. Hence, both are located closer to the "cultural" end of the "north-south" axis in Figure 2, though not as high as land claims, which tend to carry a heavier burden of cultural loss.

Yet both culture and economics were involved in the encounter between indigene and European settler, and both, according to *Gathering Strength,* had often been ignored in the past: "The assistance and spiritual values of the Aboriginal peoples who welcomed the newcomers to this continent too often have been forgotten."[60] The cultural dimension of the demand for the return of traditional lands is connected to the claim that those lands involve territories that were inhabited by the groups in question for long periods before the arrival of European settlers and that those spaces have a special spiritual significance as repositories of both ancient ancestors and traditional wisdom.[61] Groups thought to be connected to an immemorial past have acquired an enormous symbolic authority among many people in rootless, cosmopolitan societies caught up in the modern capitalist whirlwind of "creative destruction," of which today's so-called globalization is merely the latest wave.[62]

Despite the frequent invocation in these cases of claims that the real estate in question is "sacred ground," another important motivation behind the demands for the restitution of native lands has to do with the economic viability of aboriginal communities and their right to control their own resources. This is the significance, for example, of a recent agreement between the Canadian province of Quebec and the Cree Nation, which "gives Indians management of their natural resources [and] recognizes their full autonomy as a native nation."[63] Demands for the return of lands are a prominent element of politics in North America and the antipodes, but they can be found in less obvious places as well. As we shall see later in this book, a number of groups in Southern Africa have recently launched a campaign for the restitution of lands to indigenous groups in South Africa, Namibia, and Zimbabwe.[64] Claims to control over land, as well as to fishing rights and other rights of usufruct in natural resources, are at the heart of these discussions. Hence, these claims are located in the diagram closer to the "economic" end of the continuum concerning the meaning of money than are the reparations sought in connection with the stolen generation, the inmates of residential schools, and the like.

R. S. Ratner and his colleagues advance an unusual and innovative perspective in the debate over the land claims advanced by indigenes against the majority in settler societies.[65] The authors are sympathetic to the aboriginals' demand for the return of the lands taken from them by European interlopers in the process of white settler colonization. In comparison to the situation in the United States and in most of eastern Canada, however, relations in British Columbia between First Nations and the majority are complicated by the lack of any treaty basis for the earlier expropriations, to which recourse might now be had to help sort out claims of ownership.[66] The prevailing doctrine that the lands were *terra nullius* ("empty land") may have made the confiscation of land easier at the time, but that legal theory (also deployed in the British colonization of Australia) has led to a situation in which new arrangements must be negotiated against the backdrop of a worldwide movement of "indigenous" peoples with considerably greater power than would have been the case, say, before 1960. Around that date colonialism in traditional form, whether external or internal, became less and less defensible, violating as it did the norms of national autonomy that European political development had done so much to promote.[67]

Some observers have objected to these land claims because of the aboriginal governments' record of corruption, nepotism, and undemocratic practices.[68] In a realist vein, however, Ratner et al. accept the idea that the First Nations' control over land and other resources may lead not to the restoration of putatively indigenous ways of doing things, but rather to the creation of exploitive "comprador bourgeoisies" (analogous to those that had emerged from independence in the post-colonial Third World) that are prone to corruption and abuse of power. Given the similarity between process and outcome in these two post-colonial contexts, Ratner et al. argue that such corruption has little to do with the predispositions of Indians per se and is, instead, a phenomenon that arises with all elites who are not subject to appropriate accountability. Ratner et al. see no plausible moral alternative to the return of native lands in British Columbia and elsewhere.

Yet they also appreciate that this may not be the road to nirvana because, in the absence of the necessary constraints, control over such resources may enable indigenous elites to exploit their newly privileged positions to the advantage of their families and friends. This does not mean that British Columbia—or any substantial swath of societies once settled by overseas Europeans—is going to be returned to the native populations lock, stock, and barrel, of course; only a negotiated solution involving all of the concerned parties is plausible or feasible. The surfacing of the subterranean past has given those defined and recognized as "aboriginals" a major advantage in their dealings with nonindigenous majorities. Still, as in all reparations politics, a deal must ultimately be struck between the various parties to the dispute.

Part of the rationale for returning lands to indigenes in Canada arises from the fact that, generally speaking, First Nations populations—like aboriginal groups subordinated to European-derived societies elsewhere—define the bottom rung of the racial order. Their condition constitutes the most glaring violation in Canadian society of the norm of equal citizenship.[69] The indignities and inequalities suffered by natives in Canada occupy a place on the public agenda analogous to that of blacks in the United States. The two groups share the historical condition of having been forcibly subjected to white European domination, but here the similarities end. Whereas indigenes were subordinated as a result of conquest on their home turf, blacks were subjugated through forced migration and enslavement on lands far distant from their origins.

These variations in the process of subordination generate different kinds of reparations politics in the present. Just as the differences in the degree of voluntariness in the incorporation of immigrant and indigene lead to different rights and expectations, those between aboriginal and slave yield divergent concerns and demands. Whereas Indians and other indigenes can lay claim to "their" original homelands, whether as sacred or as economically essential to their well-being, black Americans cannot pursue this course. Instead, they must have recourse primarily to redress for the ways in which their treatment has violated—and, of critical importance, continues to violate—self-proclaimed American norms of freedom and autonomy. Although small numbers returned to Africa in the early nineteenth century (with the creation of Liberia), blacks today also cannot lay claim to the territories from which they originated. Those areas are now sovereign nations, and—some Afrocentric rhetoric notwithstanding—few American blacks would be likely to return to them now. In pursuing reparations, black Americans must rely on the prospect that greater awareness of the fore-shortened opportunities historically made available to them will pique the conscience of the broader American populace and spur more vigorous efforts to achieve racial equality, as occurred during the civil rights movement. But then this may not help improve the blacks' situation in the United States. There is much merit in the view that such progress as occurs tends to be a reward of sorts for blacks' contribution to American wars.[70]

In the case of reparations for black Americans, the material dimension of reparations is manifestly paramount. At this point, it is not possible to claim that reparations will help those directly subjected to enslavement, the historical crucible out of which the diminished status of blacks in American society is generally said to have developed.[71] As a result of this historical distance from the "scene of the crime," so to speak, some argue that it is better to assert that the inequalities suffered by blacks today are a product of the more recent history of legal segregation ("Jim Crow"), through which many people still alive actually lived. Yet the main concern of all of these commentators and groups is with the economic inequalities suffered by blacks in contemporary America. Hence, this claim is located near the extreme economic end of the axis concerning the meaning of money in reparations claims. Indeed, the case of reparations for black Americans is virtually the paradigm case of anti-systemic reparations, where the central problem is the alleviation of economic inequalities said to be rooted in a past system of domination.

Whereas economic disadvantage is central to this claim, there is nonetheless a cultural dimension of the demand for reparations. For this reason I have located the case of reparations for black Americans nearer to the middle along the "north-south" axis. In his prominent book on the subject of reparations, *The Debt: What America Owes to Blacks*, Randall Robinson, a leading advocate of reparations for black Americans, bases a considerable portion of his argument on the notion that the experience of enslavement deprived blacks of their African cultural heritage.[72] This element also plays a prominent role in the reparations demands of black nationalist groups. Despite its potential contribution to galvanizing blacks behind a reparations agenda, however, insistence on the cultural dimension of reparations arguably makes the goal more difficult to reach. Emphasizing the cultural separateness of blacks seems likely to send the campaign for reparations down a political blind alley. To the extent that the wrongs for which redress is sought are chiefly economic, and to the extent that material improvement in the lives of black Americans is the primary aim of those who support the movement for reparations, it may be best for those advocating the cause of reparations to focus on economic harms in mounting their case.[73] We will explore the campaign for reparations for blacks in greater detail in Chapter 4.

As in the cases of "internal colonialism" in the United States and South Africa, although cultural loss plays a part in demands for reparations for classical "overseas" colonialism, the economic gains to be had from reparations are clearly the central consideration. Most such demands have emanated from Africa. This is in part because some other regions of the formerly colonized world, especially Latin America, attained their independence long ago and thus have weaker grounds for claiming that European colonizers are the source of their problems. A number of Latin American countries, especially Brazil, were also major beneficiaries of the slave trade, weakening the region's claims that it was a mere victim of colonialism. Meanwhile, Asia was colonized by Japan as well as by predatory European states, muddying the historical-political waters (and generating claims against the Japanese themselves, especially with regard to the "Rape of Nanking" and the "comfort women"). Moreover, the perception of (sub-Saharan) Africa as "black" helps sharpen the apparent divide between perpetrators (Europe) and victims (Africans). Thus, contemporary Africa alone can be said to have suffered both from a colonial rule that ended only recently and from having been turned "into a warren for the commercial hunting of black skins" during the colonial past.[74]

Finally, as a result of decolonization, the colonizers have been largely driven from the continent or were subordinated to large non-white majorities in the transition to independent rule in the middle third of the twentieth century. Hence, there are relatively few outstanding land claims as such, although pressure on whites to return the valuable lands they own and farm has been a major issue in recent Zimbabwean politics and plays a role in contemporary South African life as well. Thus, Africans have made demands for reparations, but those demands have had relatively little to do with land claims per se except where settler colonialism is still a significant element of the social configuration.

The pursuit of reparations for Africa took wing in the early 1990s. First, an international Conference on Reparations was held in Lagos, Nigeria in December 1990. Thereafter, the Organization for African Unity (which has since been replaced by the African Union) empaneled a so-called Group of Eminent Persons "to explore the modalities and strategies of an African campaign for restitution similar to the compensation paid by Germany to Israel and to survivors of the Nazi Holocaust."[75] A second conference was held in Abuja, the capital of Nigeria, in June 1993 to explore the possibilities of mounting a campaign for reparations. The group's work bore little fruit, in part because it was closely tied to the career of the then-president of Nigeria, Moshood Abiola, who was subsequently arrested by his successor, Sani Abacha, and died under mysterious circumstances in a Nigerian prison soon thereafter. Heeding the conference's call to create nationally based reparations movements, black Labour MP Bernie Grant headed an initiative in London called the Africa Reparations Movement "to obtain Reparations for the enslavement and colonisation of African people in Africa and in the African Diaspora." Grant died in 2000, and the movement subsequently atrophied.[76]

The discussions at the 1993 meeting were also complicated by the fact that the participants could not decide whether the chief wrong to be rectified was to be slavery or colonialism, which the Africa Reparations Movement's statement suggests is unproblematic. One participant in the gathering, the prominent author and historian Ali Mazrui, focused primarily on slavery in his later written remarks about the campaign. Mazrui acknowledged the role of Africans in the slave trade but argued that the chief beneficiaries were Americans and Europeans, who therefore had a responsibility to compensate Africans for the damage done them. In particular, he proposed a massive program of black education and training designed to make up for "what may well be the most devastating consequence of Black enslavement and African colonization—the enormous damage to Black and African capacities for self-improvement as compared with other societies."[77] This proposal suggested a way around the knotty problem of the form that reparations should take, avoiding any hint that it would come in direct monetary form.

The presence at the Abuja meeting of a participant from Tunisia pointedly raised the difficulty, however, concerning the major cause of action underlying a potential campaign for reparations for Africa. Should reparations be sought for the ravages to the continent caused by slavery or, as the Tunisian delegate proposed, for the damage caused by European colonialism? As Wole Soyinka has remarked in his discussion of the episode, a campaign directed against colonialism would "dilute the original cause and require a totally different orientation and strategy, [and] would expand to embrace the indigenes of both North and South America, Australia, and New Zealand."[78] Clearly, this approach was not the appropriate one for those wanting to make good on the depredations of the Atlantic slave trade in sub-Saharan Africa, as opposed to redressing the consequences of colonialism.

Even assuming that colonialism would be the principal cause of action, however, Rhoda Howard-Hassmann has raised substantial doubts that such reparations can properly be said to be owed.[79] From the vantage point of one who has written about economic development in Ghana, she explores the claim, originally advanced by the Caribbean scholar Walter Rodney, that "Europe underdeveloped Africa" and finds it wanting—not least on logical grounds.[80] Howard-Hassmann argues that there could be many reasons for the impoverished condition of contemporary Africa, and that there is no way to determine with certainty that colonialism (or slavery) was the main cause of this state of affairs. Nonetheless, Howard-Hassmann agrees with the proponents of reparations that the West must assume some responsibility for the continent's disastrous economic situation.[81] Such measures could include "debt relief, a special development fund, and improvement of access to international markets," as proposed at the recent U.N. Conference on Racism in Durban, South Africa.[82] The proposal to open markets to African goods has been a leading objective of the New Economic Program for African Development (NEPAD), whose implementation the recently founded African Union has adopted as one of its chief aims. But these endeavors by the wealthy parts of the world are more in the nature of Jaspers's responses to generalized distress than to those that arise out of the guilt of a perpetrator.

The objective of the Jubilee 2000 movement for debt relief for the world's poor countries is to have the international community—which is to say its wealthiest and most powerful members—assume greater responsibility for the plight of Africa and the Third World. As we shall see in Chapter 5, the movement's South African branch, in collaboration with nongovernmental organization (NGOs) and local South African political organizations, has launched a campaign to demand reparations from European companies and banks that profited from apartheid, especially those in Switzerland.[83] We thus come full circle: the model of commemorative claims pioneered by the victims of the Holocaust, and the language and strategies it generated, are being deployed by activists seeking reparations for the consequences of the internal colonialism of the apartheid regime. Nothing could better demonstrate the fundamental coherence of the reparations claims being raised around the world today, regardless of differences in their locales and in the types of injustices for which they seek recompense.

Finally, in addition to broader demands for reparations for the damage done by slavery and colonialism, such claims have been raised in response to the role of the more powerful countries and institutions of the world in connection with the 1994 genocide in Rwanda. As the OAU put it in its special report assessing the genocide in Rwanda, "The international community must be made to understand the need for reparations for its complicity in the calamities of the past decade."[84] The question of Western responsibility for the killings in Rwanda has become the subject of heated debate, frequently tied to the figure of Canadian general Romeo Dallaire and his unheeded calls for reinforcements in the critical hour. A striking feature of this discussion is the extent to which the West is held responsible for the killings that, after all, were committed by Rwandans.[85] The authors of the OAU report recognize this fact, but they nonetheless regard the West as bearing a heavy burden of responsibility, going back to the origins of European colonialism.

The discussion of responsibility for the genocide thus seems oddly to reprise the colonialist perception that Africans lack independent agency. Yet in contrast to the cases of colonialism and slavery, the sufferings of the Rwandans were largely self-inflicted, however much European colonial regimes may have prepared the ground for this tragedy. The case for reparations from the international community seems correspondingly shakier. Still, there is precedent for holding persons and (by extension) countries accountable for acts of *omission* rather than those of commission. As the historian of Japan John Dower has noted, the Tokyo Tribunal sentenced General Matsui Iwane to death for his failure to prevent atrocities by his troops at Nanking in 1937.[86] Moreover, as Daniel Levy and Natan Sznaider have pointed out, in the current period, the central role of the Holocaust in collective memory means that we are all responsible for ensuring that "Auschwitz" happens "never again."[87]

The campaign for reparations from other countries and international institutions has had relatively meager results in part because the Rwandans must be cautious about antagonizing many of their biggest donors. Nonetheless, extensive efforts have been made to come to terms with the past within Rwanda itself. These efforts are hampered, however, by the large number of victims and the paltry means available to compensate them. Demands for reparations in the Rwandan case present many perplexities stemming from the fact that both the so-called *genocidaires* and the ultimately victorious Rwandan Patriotic Front, which now holds power in the country, committed human rights abuses for which the United Nations has mandated a formal right to reparation. Similarly, the dilemma of whether reparations should be directed toward individuals or toward the reconstruction of Rwandan society and infrastructure plagues efforts to meet the desperate needs of a society that has undergone a tremendous catastrophe. To make matters worse, the large number of perpetrators has overwhelmed the judicial system, despite the recourse that has been had to traditional (*"gacaca"* or "front-porch") forms of justice. Meanwhile, the International Criminal Tribunal for Rwanda (ICTR) seems a rather distant reality for most Rwandans.[88] The perception that the ICTR could not, therefore, do its work as a form of political education led subsequently to pressures to ensure that Saddam Hussein would be tried inside Iraq—as well as by the Iraqis themselves in order to provide the desired political lessons.

In sum, it is difficult to locate Rwanda on the grid in Figure 2 because money has both symbolic and economic meanings for those who receive it. What is clear is that cultural loss plays little role in the claim, primarily because the genocide was essentially an indigenous phenomenon—even if it might have been prevented or stanched by bystanders who did nothing.

Apology and Regret

Perhaps the best the Rwandans can expect is some sort of apology for being left by the world's most powerful to twist in the wind. Samantha Power has noted that Bill Clinton offered an apology—or, more accurately, a "carefully hedged acknowledgment"—for the West's failure to stop the massacres in Rwanda in 1994.[89] Power's qualification of the Clinton apology points to the high importance that may be accorded not only to the precise wording of statements of apology and regret in contemporary reparations politics, but also to the ways in which "talk is cheap." Indeed, without some sort of monetary compensation to go along with an apology, many will be inclined not to take such apologies very seriously.

At the same time, compensation without apology is likely to be dismissed on the grounds that "it's not about the money," and any suggestion that it *is* about the money may be regarded as demeaning the suffering of the individuals in question, which are said to be beyond price.[90] This is very much the situation in the case of the so-called comfort women, or military sexual slaves used by the Japanese government during World War II.[91] The apologies of the Japanese government have generally been less than full-throated, and the compensation offered has been made available mainly through the Asian Women's Fund, a private institution. Without an un-varnished statement of apology in conjunction with putting a sum of money where its mouth is, the Japanese government is unlikely to satisfy the demands of the comfort women.[92] As Roy Brooks has noted, corpora-tions settle claims against them every day by means of monetary compen-sation without any corresponding admission of wrongdoing. These deals are designed to "make this go away," but they skirt the issue of culpability in favor of more rapid—if perhaps less satisfying—closure. But these are settlements, not reparations, which of necessity entail some statement of regret.[93] Mere payment without acknowledgment of wrongdoing is not likely to redress the harm done.

Before the *"fin de millenaire* fever of atonement," Nicholas Tavuchis de-veloped the most nuanced and insightful analysis of the social alchemy worked by apologies. He argues that profound differences exist between apologies at the individual level and those at the collective level, and that there can be no assumption that the collective level works in the same way as the individual. This is in part because "an authentic apology cannot be delegated, consigned, exacted, or assumed by the principals, without totally altering its meaning and vitiating its moral force."[94] Whether apologies are important to the individuals who are members of groups that have been wronged in the past is likely to vary from person to person. As noted in the previous chapter, the activist injured, who are more likely to seek re-dress than others of their kind, are unrepresentative in their desire for such redress; some people just want to move on and leave the past behind. Different people relate to these pasts differently.

Apologies have grown so important in recent years, however, that Jeffrey Olick and Brenda Coughlin claim that the "politics of regret" is the signature of our age. They argue that the rise of regret is a product of "the transfor-mation of temporality and historicity that is tied up with the decline . . . of the nation-state" and its project of integrating and assimilating disparate groups.[95] That is, although it may once have gone without saying that the state could and should turn "peasants into Frenchman," whatever the costs to "their culture," states can no longer ignore the "subterranean" histories of the many groups who are submerged or oppressed in the nation-building process and who now seek apologies and reparations for their forcible incorporation into the nation and/or the modern world-system. Olick and Coughlin's discussion of the politics of regret thus links up directly with the changes taking place in historiography and in historical representations of "the nation."

Toward a Consensual Past

Debates over representations of history—and especially over whose voices constitute "the past"—have been a major aspect of history-writing since the 1960s, when labor and social historians began to insist on a new "history from below." In a programmatic statement, the English Marxist E. P. Thompson wrote that he was "seeking to rescue the poor stockinger, the Luddite cropper, the 'obsolete' hand-loom weaver, the 'utopian' artisan, and even the deluded follower of Joanna Southcott, from the enormous condescension of posterity."[96] The historians of "post-colonialism" pushed this agenda forward by posing the question, now intended to speak to racial and cultural "others" as well as working-class people, "Can the Subaltern Speak?"[97] The trend recently culminated with an impulse toward *Provincializing Europe*—that is, locating it in a position more appropriate to its proportionate size in a world in which non-European peoples are both numerically dominant and increasingly accorded the respect of comprising a genuine portion of humanity rather than some eternally inferior "Other."[98] Much of this historiography has promoted the surfacing of subterranean elements in the once-cozy national and Western narratives of uplift to which Arendt had called critical attention.

Yet the diversity of groups whose pasts have been resurrected has also helped fragment the traditional objects of history, paralleling a broader shift in the social imaginary from masses to small groups and individuals. This shift was reflected in the turn toward network theories of society, which mirrored the world of computers on which the very ideas were banged out.[99] The trends also echoed the transformation of one big audience for mass media into a minutely divided series of market niches. The political theorist Susan Buck-Morss has captured succinctly the general outlines of this situation: "[T]he mass-democratic myth of industrial modernity—the belief that the industrial reshaping of the world is capable of bringing about the good society by providing material happiness for the masses—has been profoundly challenged by the disintegration of European socialism, the demands of capitalist restructuring, and the most fundamental ecological constraints. In its place, an appeal to differences that splinter the masses into fragments now structures political rhetoric and marketing strategies alike."[100] Buck-Morss zeroes in on the fundamental transformation that has occurred; the idea of well-being for the undifferentiated "masses" has been replaced by the goal of satisfying the wants, often defined in cultural terms, of minutely nuanced population segments. Mass utopia, whether capitalist or socialist in coloration, is thus out; group self-expression and group self-esteem are in. These various currents, along with the creeping delegitimation of the nation-state as a site for realizing egalitarian aspirations, have fueled a shift in history-writing from a *Marxisant* focus on state and class to a preoccupation with a plethora of sociological categories (race, class, gender, sexuality, disability status, etc.) as the cornerstones of a new understanding of the world. In the process, "one-nation" ideologies and the corresponding idea of assimilation have become increasingly suspected of being a form only of "ethnic cleansing," not of potential inclusion.

These tendencies are also reflected in the transformation of official commemorative practices. In contrast to the era following World War I in the North Atlantic world, at least, the commemorative acts of governments today have little to do with heroic myths of national sacrifice and greatness.[101] Far from celebrating conquest, triumph, and uplift, monuments must acknowledge the forgotten, the mistreated, the enslaved, the murdered. The Holocaust museums and memorials in Washington, D.C., Berlin, and many other places are only the tip of an iceberg that now memorialize the unjustly slain, rather than those who have fallen in the wars that comprise the *via dolorosa* of the nation. At the same time, observers have noted a shift, especially since Maya Lin's Vietnam War Memorial, from the commemoration *en masse* of the national "myth of the war experience" to the memorialization of the individual who dies, futilely, in war.[102]

As a result of the swelling attention to the subterranean past that has followed from these various changes, historians have more frequently been asked to leave the quiet of their studies to play an unwonted (though often rather lucrative) role as expert witnesses and members of commissions of inquiry into potentially actionable pasts.[103] Needless to say, this has raised alarm bells among those intent on upholding the boundary between truth-seeking and partisan advocacy, and hackles among those excluded from the largesse and unprecedented archival access offered the chosen few by some of the companies that find themselves under intensified public scrutiny. Gerald Feldman, one of those asked to investigate the history of German companies potentially implicated in past activities that might now generate claims for reparations, defends the employment of scholarly experts in these situations. He argues that there is no reason that historians should not be paid for their work just as other professional experts are.[104]

Inevitably, however, the beneficiaries of such opportunities are likely to be regarded with some envy by those who do not share in them. It is hardly surprising that the historians so employed have found themselves under attack for allegedly forfeiting their independence. The matter of scholarly independence in such cases is a genuine concern that cannot be dismissed out of hand. Can one be expected to judge dispassionately the activities of those who are paying one's fees? Equally important, however, is the threat that historians, as a consequence of their professional commitment to unending revisionism, may pose to commemorative projects.[105] Analysts who suggest that "the victims of an inhuman regime might have lost some of their humanity on the road to perdition," for example, are not likely to be welcomed by the entrepreneurs of memory who are vital to many reparations efforts. This is so even if the community of historians might agree that such efforts make a contribution to historical "truth."[106]

Yet not all historians have been comfortable assuming this extra-academic role—not because it means leaving the familiar confines of the ivory tower, but because they question what purposes the partisan pursuit of the past might serve. For example, the prosecution of a very elderly Maurice Papon for helping to deport French Jews arose against the background of changing perceptions of France's role in World War II and a greater understanding of and attention to the complicity of the Vichy regime in the persecution of the Jews.[107] Henry Rousso, a leading analyst of French attitudes toward the Vichy past, has shown that the prosecution of Papon represents a remarkable shift from attention to crimes defined and prosecuted by the state to a focus on crimes against Jews that have been initiated above all by private parties, such as the Nazi-hunter Serge Klarsfeld. Thus, recent judicial actions concerning World War II perpetrators "did not occur because of a *raison d'état*, but because of a will to render justice to the victims, in the name of a 'duty to memory' whose objective was the perpetuation of memory against all forms of forgetting, considered in this perspective as a new crime." According to Rousso, the trial bore witness to a troubling "desacralization of state authority and of traditional French national sentiment" in favor of strengthened group identities "in a country that has always in large part denied them."[108] The pressure to come to terms with the pasts of particular groups reflects a rising attentiveness to the concerns of victims as they define themselves, rather than to offenses understood to have been committed against the citizenry as a whole.

Rousso is skeptical about the attendant commingling of judicial and scholarly purposes, arguing that the issue is unclean. In contrast, Charles Maier has argued that the roles of historian and judge share important similarities. Both must ultimately arrive at plausible narratives based on the motivations of actors, though the judge must ultimately decide and, perhaps, punish. Despite the prosecutorial tone of much of the relevant historiography, he argues that the drift in recent years has been toward much greater attentiveness to the voices of the previously voiceless. Maier thus shares Alan Cairns's view regarding the desirability of the formerly "subterranean" emerging into the light.[109]

Ultimately, Maier states, "the projects of reparation, remembering, and reconciliation involve the right to tell histories and have them listened to respectfully." This has led to efforts by various interested parties that have sought to repair deep-rooted international rifts by drafting histories that can attain the assent of "both sides" in past conflicts. For example, Polish and German historians and history teachers have tried to develop textbooks telling the story of their twentieth-century relations "in mutually acceptable accounts."[110] Indeed, the contents of history textbooks have become a major focus of both public controversy and scholarly inquiry worldwide.[111] The ongoing fracas regarding the degree of recognition and contrition for World War II atrocities in Japanese school history texts is an excellent case in point. The development of mutually agreeable accounts is thought to promote reconciliation, a term that is widely used in discussions of coming to terms with the past generally. According to one analyst of the problem of reconciliation, such mutually satisfactory narratives are perhaps the best that previously divided groups can hope for, opening the way to a common future.[112] With luck, what they do with that future will be a matter of bargaining, negotiation, and compromise—the mundane business of politics.

In the meanwhile, the teaching of history, the contours of "collective memory," and the character of "historical consciousness" have become major subjects of concern among certain segments of academia and the wider public.[113] These concerns are fueled in part by demands from legislators for new "standards" in history education that often appear to be veiled orders to reinstitute a more celebratory historiography now long since beyond retrieval. Yet these are also the concerns of specialists who pursue the past—or at least the memory of it—as a sort of glue under-girding collective identities. Under these circumstances, as Peter Novick has argued, the past comes to serve the purposes of group cohesion.[114]

Yet the critical historiography that Nietzsche recommended to us must remain open to contestation and thus cannot well serve the interests of those in need of a particular image of the past that remains frozen for future generations—however much "agreed upon" by the putative participants or their heirs. The scholarly pursuit of the past can be *political* and hence con-tribute to revealing the subterranean aspects of the past, but it fails if it becomes *politicized*, subservient to narrowly partisan interests.[115] The best that history can do to serve the future is to make certain statements im-possible by documenting beyond the shadow of a doubt that *this* actually happened.[116]

In the end, what matters is the horizon in which the past is viewed: how forward-looking is the preoccupation with representations of the past? The question is one of balance, and of how to draw inspiration from the past in the face of the sobering recovery of its uglier, previously subterranean features. There will be continued cause for controversy over the facts of past history and over their relation to current inequalities and injustices. For now and for the foreseeable future, however, efforts to repair historical injustices form an important part of the search for justice in the present. A major catalyst for this set of concerns was the redress settlements reached by the U.S. and Canadian governments with regard to the Japanese-descent populations incarcerated as "enemy aliens" during World War II. These set-tlements, now some years old, offer an unusual opportunity to explore the results of reparations claims-making.

As we explore the varieties of reparations politics, the various possible modes of repair laid out above—transitional justice, compensation, apolo-gies, and efforts to construct a communicative history—should be kept in mind as possibilities in each case. Yet the focus will be on compensation—reparations in financial form—primarily, because it is around money that many of these campaigns crystallize. The extent to which it is "about the money" will in each case prove a key variable for understanding the larger stakes. Cases in which money plays a chiefly "symbolic" role—such as the case of reparations for interned Japanese-Americans and Japanese-

Canadians, and for victims of human rights violations generally—will be contrasted with those cases in which the "meaning of money" is primarily "economic"—that is, reparations for systems of domination such as slavery, apartheid, and colonial genocide. We will also consider the extent to which "culture" plays a role in these claims, for this factor shapes the nature of different kinds of reparations politics.

CHAPTER 3

Commemoration, Redress, and Reconciliation: The Cases of Japanese-Americans and Japanese-Canadians

WITH ROSA SEVY

Amid all the talk in recent years of coming to terms with the past, there has been much emphasis on the healing and reconciliation that are expected to flow from reparations processes. Despite the widespread assumption that these eminently desirable outcomes will result, little research has been done demonstrating that healing and reconciliation actually do arise from efforts, whether chiefly symbolic or mainly monetary, to come to terms with the past. Lily Gardner Feldman has argued that considerable reconciliation has been achieved between Germany and a number of other countries, especially Israel, as a result of German diplomatic efforts in the postwar era.[1] Yet the cases Feldman examined are matters of foreign affairs, whereas many of the cases of reparations claims-making involve wrongdoing against populations internal to the perpetrator-states. Thus, in her comprehensive recent study of truth commissions, one of the chief institutions of transitional justice, Priscilla Hayner has noted that "there has been no study to date of the psychological impact of truth commissions on survivors."[2] Similarly, Heribert Adam has argued that, whatever the benefits of the South African Truth and Reconciliation Commission (TRC), it did not lead to reconciliation between the majority black and minority white populations in post-apartheid South Africa.[3]

These findings raise questions about the consequences of efforts to redress past injustices generally. Do such efforts result in reconciliation, as their advocates claim? If so, for whom do they do so—all members of the putative "community" in question? For only some? And if they do lead to reconciliation, how so? What does that mean? In short, although there is much talk of reconciliation among those concerned with righting the injustices of the past, there is scant (if any) empirical research assessing the *consequences* of reparations arrangements. This chapter seeks to begin to plug that large gap in our knowledge about reparations politics.

In contrast to the outpouring of scholarship on the causes of the internment of Japanese-Americans and Japanese-Canadians and on the quest for redress in these two cases, little research has yet addressed the question of whether reparations "works"—that is, whether reparations arrangements actually achieved the aim of giving these previously wronged groups a fuller sense of membership in the societies of which they are a part and from which they were once so egregiously segregated. Whereas others are still pursuing various forms of redress for the wrongs they insist have been done them, the Japanese-descent populations in these two countries have already obtained "redress" in the form of official apologies as well as compensation in the amount of approximately $20,000 for each person incarcerated by his or her respective governments as potential threats during World War II.

In order to explore the extent to which reconciliation actually results from reparations efforts, in this chapter we examine the existing literature and consider evidence from interviews with a number of former internees and redress activists. In addition, we examine the representations of internment and redress in several museums devoted to commemorating the history in question. Concern about the possible sequestration of specific ethnoracial groups in times of crisis has arisen once again, and this "post–9/11" context informed the questions we posed. We sought to understand whether and how the initiatives grouped under the rubric of reparations politics actually contribute to the greater integration into the larger society of previously mistreated groups. Given that the black experience has tended to be paradigmatic for political innovations concerning minorities in the United States, the centrality of Japanese-American redress to subsequent reparations politics is particularly intriguing. Moreover, exploring the cases of Japanese-descent persons in North America comparatively, this research may shed light on efforts to come to terms with the past elsewhere as well.

Background: The Internment Experience

Soon after the Japanese attack on Pearl Harbor in December 1941, Japanese-Americans and Japanese-Canadians on the West Coast of their respective countries came under the intense scrutiny of their governments as an alleged national security threat. Each government forced its Japanese-descent community to undergo mass evacuation and removal from coastal regions to temporary detention centers, from which they were soon moved to internment camps and other areas deemed less militarily sensitive that were scattered throughout the western half of their respective countries.[4] In Canada, British Columbia's provincial cabinet passed Order in Council P.C. 1486, according to which, under the blanket powers of the federal-level War Measures Act, some 22,000 Japanese-Canadians were relocated from the coastal "protected area" and sent to internment camps in the interior of the province as well as to sugar beet farms in southern Alberta and Manitoba.[5] In the United States, meanwhile, on February 19, 1942, President Franklin D. Roosevelt signed Executive Order 9066, allowing governmental authorities to designate restricted zones and to determine which people, if any, should be removed from those zones. Although the order mentioned no specific racial or ethnic group, it was in fact directed at and came to focus on the Japanese-American community and soon resulted in their mass removal from these areas. In the event, nearly 120,000 Japanese-Americans were moved to detention camps.[6]

After the end of the war, the majority of Japanese-Americans returned to the West Coast. Although some stayed behind or even went (or, in some cases, went *back*) to Japan, by 1950 the Japanese-American populations of Los Angeles and San Francisco had returned to their prewar levels. In contrast, it took another decade for the Japanese-American population of the Seattle area to be restored to its prewar strength.[7]

In contrast to their American counterparts, Japanese-Canadians generally did not return to the West Coast after their release from internment. First, Japanese-Canadians were not allowed to travel freely until 1949, when the War Measures Act and the last of the wartime restrictions were lifted.[8] Once they were free to leave their places of confinement, the Japanese-Canadians were not allowed to concentrate in major urban areas; the Canadian government used its regulatory powers to keep them dispersed, restricting their numbers and distribution in cities such as Winnipeg, Toronto, and Montreal. As a result of these measures, of the total of 22,000 who were removed from the West Coast under the War Measures Act, some 13,000 Japanese-Canadians remained in the provinces east of Alberta after the end of restrictions. As of 1947, only 6,776 Japanese-Canadians remained in British Columbia, less than one-third of the 1942 population.[9]

Contrary to their American counterparts, by the time the Japanese-Canadians were allowed to return to the West Coast, it was "too late for reconstruction."[10] The very foundations of the community had disappeared, and so most Japanese-Canadians had no choice but to rebuild their lives in the places to which they had been dispersed. Unlike their American counterparts, the Japanese-Canadians had to rebuild their lives after having been not only uprooted and stripped of their property, but also scattered across Canada.

For many years after the end of the war, the internment experiences of the Japanese-descent populations were relatively neglected as political concerns were frequently downplayed or avoided, even (indeed especially) by those who had endured them. Instead, like Holocaust survivors, those who had undergone the internment generally sought to "get along by going along," channeling their energies into rebuilding their forcibly interrupted lives. In the 1970s, in the wake of the U.S. civil rights movement and the subsequent rise of various movements devoted to the empowerment of ethnic minorities, second- and third-generation Japanese immigrants to the United States (also known as the Nisei and the Sansei, respectively) increasingly began to demand "redress" for the internment.[11] As a result of this pressure, the goals of securing an official government apology, payment of reparations to individual survivors, and creation of a public education fund were broadly debated within the Japanese-descent communities in both the United States and Canada.

These efforts culminated in 1988 with legislation in both countries that was designed to make amends for the earlier wrongs. In the United States, on August 10, 1988, President Ronald Reagan signed into law the strategically named Civil Liberties Act of 1988. The bill mandated that the surviving internees should receive individual payments of $20,000 and an apology from the president of the United States acknowledging the injustice of the internment. Shortly thereafter, on September 22, 1998, Canadian prime minister Brian Mulroney offered a formal apology in the House of Commons to Japanese-Canadians who had been interned, and announced that each of the survivors would be eligible for compensation in the amount of $21,000. The extra $1000 in the Canadian case was, according to redress activist and leading scholar of Japanese-Canadian life Art Miki, intended to reflect the greater severity of Canadian mistreatment of its Japanese-descent minority by comparison to their treatment in the United States.[12]

Reparations and Reconciliation

The Japanese-American and Japanese-Canadian redress movements exemplify and in important respects helped to stimulate the spread of reparations politics in recent years. The core principle behind reparations derives
from a compensatory theory of justice, which affirms that injuries must be
compensated and wrongdoers should pay victims for losses.[13] Yet reparations are at one level an impossible challenge, as Charles Maier has noted,
for they can never make up for what has been lost: possibilities for personal
and professional development, personal relationships, physical health and
well-being. Material reparations by themselves do not generally suffice to
make good on past wrongs, but they try to shift the losses from the terrain
of the irrecoverable and to place them in "the realm of the politically negotiated." Such negotiations indicate that communications between perpetrators and victims are being resumed. By rejuvenating a political dialogue, the hitherto antagonistic parties engage in a process that may allow
them to live together and to resume political, commercial, and cultural
interaction.[14]

Moreover, not only are material reparations incapable of "making whole
what has been smashed," but monetary compensation in the absence of an
apology is likely to be dismissed by at least some of the potential recipients
on the ground that their claims are "not about the money." The wrongdoers, or at least their putative heirs, must offer some statement of apology
for wrongdoing as well; otherwise, the recipients may well view financial
compensation as mere "blood money." An official governmental apology to
the victimized group explicitly acknowledges the wrongdoing, and this is
normally an important aspect of the process of coming to terms with the
past. In his trenchant study of the social characteristics of apologies, Nicholas Tavuchis argues that "to apologize is to declare voluntarily that one
has no excuse, defense, justification, or explanation for an action that has
insulted, failed, injured, or wronged another."[15] According to Tavuchis, the
essence of apology lies in the wrongdoer's acknowledgment of the fact of
violation, the acceptance of responsibility for the wrong, and the implicit
or explicit promise that similar acts will not be repeated in the future.

The ultimate goal of reparations and apologies concerning official misdeeds would be to achieve what Maier calls "political reconciliation."[16] In
these contexts, reconciliation is not merely a desirable outcome, but is
rather the primary objective of efforts to come to terms with the past. In

contrast to apologies among private parties, where publicity could vitiate the whole effort to accept personal responsibility for wrongdoing and to make amends to the specific person or persons in question, political reconciliation necessarily implies *public* acknowledgment, *public* recognition of harm, and *public* accountability. The public acknowledgment and acceptance of responsibility for past injustices is regarded as essential if the parties involved are to move forward in the future. In addition to its public dimension, reconciliation requires a structural and institutional dimension, a framework of rights and justice. As Judy Balint has argued, reconciliation entails institutional change that will ensure a durable reconciliation and guarantees of nonrepetition of the previous wrongdoing.[17]

Beyond these considerations, the term *reconciliation* involves the wrongdoer's recognition that the past actions in question were indeed wrong, as well as a sense on both sides that some basis exists for moving ahead without excessive or persistent rancor and without constantly resurrecting the painful past as a point of contention in the present. In general, to the extent that those once wronged remain present in the country in question, reconciliation should involve a fuller sense of membership in the society, for it was precisely equal membership of which they were previously deprived. Alas, the larger society may or may not take much notice of the process designed to achieve reconciliation. Yet the official efforts to make amends for past injustices are frequently—though not always—an important concern for persons who share the "racial" or phenotypical characteristics on the basis of which members of the reparations-seeking group were once wronged. In short, reconciliation is about moving on, and hence it is more about the future than it is about the past.[18] In order to explore whether redress or reparations leads to reconciliation in these and similar cases of past injustices, we have sought answers to the following questions:

- To what extent did the redress arrangements for Japanese-Americans and Japanese-Canadians actually lead to a sense of reconciliation, understood in the above terms, among those once wronged?
- What place do the past wrong—in this case, the internment experience—and the redress arrangements occupy in the self-understanding of these groups today?
- How is the internment experience represented in museums, and do the representations of this experience in museum exhibitions bespeak a sense of reconciliation?

- To what extent have events since "9/11" revivified remembrance of the internment experience and perhaps undermined the sense of reconciliation among Japanese-descent persons in the United States and Canada?

In order to address these questions, we interviewed a number of leading figures in the redress movement as well as others less prominent in order to get a sense of their perspective on the outcome of the redress agreements. As a complement to these interviews, which reflect "elite" rather than "ordinary" perspectives among the relevant populations—that is, the perspectives of "entrepreneurs of memory"—we visited museums in the United States and Canada in order to examine their representations of the internment and redress experiences. These persons and institutions are perhaps the most demanding when it comes to the achievement of "reconciliation," and they are likely to be the most critical of what they regard as shortcomings in the process of coming to terms with the past. Although their views are not representative of Japanese-Americans and Japanese-Canadians across the board, they reflect the opinions of those who have most actively sought to come to terms with the World War II past. Combining this data with other research findings on the consequences of redress offers an opportunity to assess the extent to which reparations processes lead to reconciliation in cases of historical injustices.

The Redress Movement and Its Consequences

The struggle of the once-wronged Japanese-Americans and Japanese-Canadians for redress reflected a search for public acknowledgment of the injustice inflicted upon them by their governments. But the success of redress depended on a specific set of conditions. According to Roy Brooks, successful redress movements have been able to reach "the hearts and minds of lawmakers and citizens alike."[19] Yet Brooks also emphasizes that the success of any redress movement depends above all on the degree of political pressure exercised by the claimants and their supporters. As we shall discuss below, strong political pressure was indeed crucial to the success of the redress campaigns of Japanese-Americans and Japanese-Canadians.

The Redress Movement in the United States

Whereas those consigned to the internment camps were mainly Issei and Nisei (first- and second-generation immigrants), the redress movement in the United States was primarily due to the Sansei (third-generation immigrants) and their emergence as a political force. Unlike some other non-white minority groups in American society, Japanese-Americans were able to break through the political barriers and to achieve a measure of political representation at the highest levels of government, including the federal government. According to John Tateishi, now a prominent leader within the Japanese-American community and a major architect of the Japanese-American redress campaign of the 1970s and 1980s, the Japanese-Americans' willingness to abandon their traditional ways and to assimilate into American society played a major role in this development. In his view, only through assimilation can ethnic groups in American society overcome the obstacles they face in gaining political influence. He emphasized that, in order to become American, Japanese-Americans had to give up their culture of origin: "Assimilation was one of the key factors for us. It was one of the prices we were willing to pay to become American."[20] This is an intriguing insight and one that is rather at odds with the multiculturalist tenet that the cultivation of distinctiveness is the route to social recognition.[21]

The legislative success of the redress campaign was largely the result of the Japanese-American community's ability to provide economic, political, and community support for the redress movement, which in turn depended on its relatively successful assimilation into the larger society subsequent to the internments. In this respect, the achievement of Japanese-American redress legislation mirrors that of the Jewish community in calling attention to the injustices suffered by Jews during World War II. Like the Japanese-Americans, Jews at first tended to avoid any focus on their suffering. Only later, after they had become assimilated into and prosperous in postwar American society, did they seek to call attention to the Holocaust.[22] To a certain extent, therefore, when it comes to commemoration of and compensation for past wrongs, "the rich get richer," whereas less powerful and less well-funded groups have greater difficulty generating notice for the injustices once done to them. Still—and to a considerable degree on the basis of the successes of these two groups—reparations politics has become a much more widespread phenomenon in recent years, providing a frame for activism from groups calling attention to past wrongs and to their claims.

Yet ethnic assimilation has had an ambiguous relationship with political involvement in the United States. "Assimilation" into American political life, with its ever-declining levels of active participation, might well be a negative outcome. Indeed, what we might call apathetic assimilation would be the political equivalent of Alejandro Portes and Rubén Rumbaut's notion of downward assimilation, whereby "the learning of new cultural patterns and entry into American social circles does not lead . . . to upward mobility but to exactly the opposite."[23] At the same time, contrary to those who worry about the fragmenting characteristics of identity politics, engagement in ethnic group-oriented activity may not necessarily promote division. According to Stephen Fugita and David O'Brien, for example, involvement in ethnic community organizations helps integrate individuals into the larger political system. Rather than competing with involvement in the mainstream, in other words, participation in an ethnic community may also act as a conduit to political involvement in the broader polity. That is, Japanese-American cultural traditions and historical experiences seem to have both encouraged their members' involvement in ethnic voluntary organizations *and* led to a high degree of political participation.[24] This finding helps to explain the high level of participation in the redress movement that has been reported by several authors.[25]

Despite the Japanese-Americans' extensive assimilation into American society, a number of those we interviewed also agreed that the rise of the redress movement reflected the view that, after years of reticence and an emphasis on assimilation into the mainstream society, they could no longer remain silent about the internment and the injustices they had experienced. Several interviewees stressed that the civil rights movement had strongly encouraged Japanese-Americans' pursuit of redress. Though heavily focused on the black-white divide in American life, the civil rights movement had made them realize that they had to "force their voice on the public," as one person put it, if their concerns were to be noticed. In other words, the civil rights movement taught them that they had to stand up for their rights. Many of those with whom we spoke suggested that this was a departure from traditional Japanese attitudes of deference. Indeed, one Japanese-American redress activist indicated that it was precisely by speaking up about the injustices done them that the Japanese-Americans became more genuinely American.[26]

As in the civil rights movement, the architects of the movement for Japanese-American redress believed that it was strategically important to frame their demands in terms of constitutional violations—transgressions against the rule of law itself—rather than in terms of the wrong inflicted on a particular group. Instead, they stressed that, as a violation of the Constitution, it was a wrong done to the entire country. As John Tateishi put it, the position was, "don't emphasize your own pain, because no one cares about the pain of the Japanese-Americans. You have to emphasize the pain and wrong to the country."[27] Another attributed the widespread support for the movement to this framing of the internment as a violation of the U.S. Constitution, which enjoys a remarkable reverence among many Americans, rather than as a wrong against the Japanese-Americans as such. This strategic appropriation of "constitutional patriotism"[28] is reflected in a sign at the Japanese American National Museum in Los Angeles that reads, "Even though the United States Constitution guarantees all citizens equal protection, it failed to protect Japanese Americans. This failure affects all Americans." This approach to the campaign was also reflected in the legislation that made redress a reality, the Civil Liberties Act of 1988, whose title made no mention of Japanese-Americans at all.

The Redress Movement in Canada

The Canadian redress movement was different from its American counterpart. In contrast to the situation in the United States, where Japanese-Americans had come to hold important political positions, the Japanese-Canadians had no representation among the country's power elite; at the time of the campaign, there were no Japanese-Canadian judges, senators, or politicians to influence the state apparatus. In this regard, Art Miki, a prominent leader in the Japanese-Canadian redress campaign, stated that "the advantage in the United States is that Japanese-Americans had important political positions, [whereas] the Japanese-Canadians had none. We had to work with the Prime Minister, engage in public dialogue, and have press coverage" in order to succeed in their quest.[29]

Whereas the Japanese-American campaign relied crucially on support from high government officials but was largely restricted to Japanese-Americans and a few non-Japanese-American supporters, the redress campaign in Canada was forced by circumstances to look for allies outside the small and fragmented Japanese-Canadian community. Movement leaders thus devoted themselves to building morale among the community and to creating a national coalition involving most of the country's ethnic groups, churches, unions, and human rights organizations.[30] Moreover, according to Tomoko Makabe, unlike the American Sansei, the third-generation immigrants in Canada have not been especially active politically. In her book, *The Canadian Sansei,* Makabe reports that the majority of the Sansei she interviewed were not active in any formal organization—a striking contrast with their American counterparts. At the time of the redress movement, Makabe argues, the Canadian Sansei had successfully established themselves among the Canadian middle classes. The redress campaign was not an important issue for many of them, she argues, and they could not see its relevance to the contemporary Japanese-Canadian community. "From the beginning to the end," she writes, "the involvement of Japanese Canadians as a whole in the redress movement was limited to a very small segment of the population."[31]

This claim contradicts the view of some leaders of the Canadian redress movement, however. For example, Audrey Kobayashi, a leading movement activist and academic, claimed that "Japanese-Canadians were much more invested in the redress movement [compared with their American counterparts]; it was seen as the responsibility of everyone."[32] Japanese-Canadian leader Art Miki shared this view, arguing that the community played a very active part in implementing the redress settlement and that a proportionately large number of Japanese-Canadians were employed in national, regional, and local offices involved in carrying out the agreement.[33] In part as a result of the relatively small size of the Japanese-Canadian population, there may well have been proportionately high participation of its older generations in the redress movement.

Yet interviews and visits to several Japanese-Canadian organizations and cultural sites left the distinct impression that the younger generations have a declining interest in specifically Japanese-Canadian ethnic, cultural, and historical activities. Art Miki himself confirmed this impression; he claimed that the people who attend the events organized by Japanese-Canadian cultural organizations are mainly from among the older generation.[34] In contrast, Nagata found that approximately 71 percent of all the Sansei respondents in her study reported membership in organizations consisting primarily of Japanese-Americans.[35] Despite the assimilation experienced by the younger generation of Japanese-Americans, according to Fugita and O'Brien, a high level of involvement in and psychological identification with their ethnic community persists. Meanwhile, according to sociologist Larry Shinagawa, the intermarriage rate of Japanese-Americans is 50 percent (for men) and 60 percent for women,[36] yet in Canada the rate is even higher, between 75 and 80 percent.[37] Partially because of sheer numerical considerations, the Japanese-Canadian community appears to face much more significant challenges to its cohesiveness than its counterpart south of the border.

Younger Japanese-Canadians may lack community participation in part because after the end of the internment period, circumstances compelled them to retreat from ethnic group consciousness and to assimilate into the wider society. In Canada, leaders with whom we spoke were much more concerned than their Japanese-American counterparts about the community "dying out" as a result of their integration into the broader society and the weakening of ethnic consciousness. Although the Japanese-Canadian redress campaign ultimately appears to have done relatively little to sustain the group's ethnic consciousness in Canada, the Japanese-American preoccupation with past injustices to the group may have helped, paradoxically, *both* to sustain ethnic consciousness *and* to stimulate a sense that Japanese-Americans are nonetheless full members of American society.

As in the Japanese-American case, it was strategically important that the Japanese-Canadian redress campaign framed its demands in terms of a universal principle rather than of wrongs done to a minority. Internment was described as a matter of a human rights violation. Similarly, making amends for that mistreatment was portrayed as a matter of living up to a peculiarly Canadian sense of "fairness" that concerned all Canadian citizens, not just a specific group. Audrey Kobayashi has argued that the redress settlement must be understood as reflecting a transformation of the whole society, and not just the concern of the Japanese-Canadians. As she put it, "It's an agreement for all Canadians, both because it establishes an important precedent, procedurally and in principle, for recognizing and righting official wrongs of the past and because, by including legislative change and especially a provision for a Canadian Race Relations Foundation, it has potentially shifted the ground for human rights provision in Canada and for overcoming the effects of racism."[38] These are precisely the kinds of measures that fit the criteria for durable reconciliation outlined above, and the appeal to the broader Canadian citizenry echoes the terms of the Japanese-American redress settlement.

Yet the settlement-mandated creation of a Canadian Race Relations

Foundation intended to address questions of racial discrimination against *any* group signals another contrast with the American experience. Although the 1988 Civil Liberties Act set aside funds for education about racial injustice, the terms of the legislation were designed specifically to avoid any generalization of the Japanese-American internment experience to that of "race" generally in United States history. Members of the U.S. Congress involved in drafting the legislation were aware that such loose talk might stimulate claims from American blacks.[39] Such claims posed a much more costly and more divisive threat than the relatively modest redress payments to 80,000 Japanese-Americans.[40] Instead of a foundation to study race relations, then, the redress legislation in the United States mandated the creation of a Civil Liberties Public Education Fund. The diffuseness of the name of the redress law, the Civil Liberties Act of 1988, was a strategic strength in pursuing redress for the wrong done to a specific ethnoracial group. Yet the name of the law had the vice of its virtue. It failed to signal that the wrong in question was rooted in racial discrimination, arguably an ongoing problem requiring further attention. The Fund closed its doors in November 1998 and is no longer in operation.[41] In contrast, the Canadian Race Relations Foundation only began operation in late 1997 and continues to the present day.[42]

The Impact of Redress

We may now ask: what effect did the legislation—and the accompanying apology and compensation—have on Japanese-Americans and Japanese-Canadians? Did it enhance their sense of reconciliation with the country that had once wronged them? Given the limited evidentiary basis on which we can draw, our inferences will be circumscribed. But they offer some sense of the impact that the redress settlements had on those to whom they were chiefly directed.

For many Japanese-Americans, achieving redress legislation enhanced their sense of belonging to the larger social and political body of Americans. The redress arrangements reinforced—or perhaps gave them for the first time—a sense that they were integrated into the country and that they were full citizens of it. One respondent, long active in a more liberal Japanese-American group called the National Coalition for Redress and Reparations (NCRR), indicated that redress permitted recognition of his status as a citizen equal to all other citizens. He said: "To me, the critical issue was whether they'd see me as a first-class citizen," adding, "I don't care if you like me, just treat me as equal. If they weren't willing to treat me as equal, there'd be no reconciliation."[43]

At least some Japanese-Americans viewed the redress campaign as a means of restoring lost honor, which remained a widely held concern among Japanese-Americans despite its perceived "Japanese-ness."[44] For these people, redress represented vindication. According to John Tateishi, "Honor is a guiding motive for the Japanese-American, and the camp experience dishonored the Issei and Nissei." He added: "Redress was a way to restore our sense of honor, be part of America and feel vindicated. If redress hadn't happened, it [the wrong involved in the internment] would always fester."[45] Despite Tateishi's view that the redress agreement put a stop to the "festering," Haru Kuromiya of the NCRR stated that "It didn't achieve any closure, there will never be that."[46]

Many Japanese-Canadians experienced similar feelings of vindication and reintegration following redress. Some Japanese-Canadians read the Canadian government's official acknowledgment of the past injustice as a way of saying that they genuinely belonged to the country. According to Art Miki, once the legislation was adopted, some of them said, "I finally feel as though I'm a real Canadian."[47] Another interviewee explained, "Nissei felt like they were Canadian as a result of redress."[48] Similarly, as one of them said, "The redress was a milestone for the Japanese-Canadians because many of us felt like second-class citizens before it."[49] For others, however, acknowledging their membership in the society also enhanced their sense of ethnicity, stimulating pride in their Japanese heritage. Art Miki stressed that "many community members had lived with the feeling that it was negative being Japanese." He explained that for other Japanese-Canadians, redress lifted a feeling of guilt from them because some of them had felt that the internment had somehow been their own fault. For others, the official acknowledgment confirmed their sense that "we knew the government was wrong, [and] it was time they apologized."[50] Similarly, Maryka Omatsu noted that for the first time in their lives, the settlement made many people feel proud of being Japanese-Canadians.[51]

In general terms, activists agreed on the "healing" quality of the redress experience. Keiko Miki, president of the National Association of Japanese Canadians, summarized this point when she said, "Generally the whole process was a healing process."[52] According to Omatsu, the long years of discussion regarding redress became part of a healing process. The members of the community underwent a psychological transformation, for as a result of the redress campaign they started to talk and discuss the internment after years of having avoided it. "By bringing a shameful past into the open, and more importantly, by demanding and fighting for its rights," she wrote, "the community became engaged in an important healing process."[53]

This emphasis on the "healing" character of the redress experience reflects the extensive use of therapeutic language and thinking in connection with processes of coming to terms with the past.[54] As with psychotherapy in general, however, it is not entirely clear what "healing" might mean in these contexts. It is doubtless true that many people experience improvements in their psychological well-being as a result of redress efforts. Still, the metaphor of "healing" suggests the axiom "forgive and forget." However, those engaged in reparations politics are typically more inclined to the view that people should "forgive and remember." The "healing" of wounds inflicted by historical injustices would entail a kind of forgetting that is at odds with the project of the "anamnestic" redemption of past suffering adumbrated by Walter Benjamin.[55] "Healing" and "closure" thus have the vice of their virtues, so to speak. By neutralizing a once-painful past, they also anaesthetize it and "put it behind us" in a manner that may be at once salutary and narcotizing.

Monetary Reparations

The reactions of Japanese-Americans and Japanese-Canadians to the financial aspects of the redress settlement point to the symbolic meanings of money in reparations politics, as outlined in the diagram in the preceding chapter. The monetary payments governments offered to the survivors of the internment were intended to substitute symbolically for the loss of time, freedom, dignity, privacy, and equality arising from the internment experience, even though "no amount of money can fully compensate the excluded people for their losses and sufferings."[56] As many people have noted, "Even as an ideal, and certainly in practice, [monetary] reparations fall short of repairing victims."[57] Money matters in these contexts, but it is not always clear in what way.

The issue of financial compensation was a source of much dispute within the Japanese-descent communities in both the United States and Canada. John Tateishi, one of the principal architects of the redress campaign in the United States, was initially uninterested in any apology; on the basis of the notion that "talk is cheap," he had wanted to demand monetary compensation above all else.[58] In contrast, in reparations politics it is frequently maintained that not all the money in the world can compensate people for what they have lost as a result of previous injustices, and this is of course unavoidably true. In the words of Frank Kitamoto, a dentist and president of the Bainbridge Island (WA) Japanese American Community, "The $20,000 we got can't repay the humiliation we went through."[59] Even if money plays a role in many of these processes, cases of commemorative compensation for gross violations of human rights—in contrast to those designed to rectify economic disparities—are not really about the money.[60] The meaning of money in these cases is symbolic rather than strictly economic.

On the other hand, an exchange of valued goods—in the modern world, usually money—is often all that can be done, as a practical matter, to make amends for the wrongs of the past. Thus, despite his insistence that the $20,000 was insufficient to compensate for what was done to the Japanese-Americans, Kitamoto quickly added: "It's easy to say you're sorry, but not without money to make it seem more serious." John Tateishi regarded the monetary compensation as appropriate, arguing that "the jurisprudence system in the US says: 'You violate someone's rights, you pay'."[61] Although the quest for financial reparations is frequently dismissed as a peculiarly "American" malady, others also see monetary compensation as a means—however inadequate—of making amends. Japanese-Canadian redress activist Art Miki stated: "Monetary compensation was symbolic of the seriousness of what happened, yet you can never equate it with the losses." He added that monetary compensation is important even though it does not adequately reflect the material losses that people sustained; "the claim for money was for the loss of basic rights."[62] As politics grows more "juridified" generally, a tort model for dealing with past wrongs grows ever more widespread.[63]

Still, like others involved in reparations politics, those we interviewed tended to say that redress was not really about the money. Rather, it was the apology issued by the government that made the redress settlement truly meaningful. According to Art Miki, "Money was not so important. At one point, money didn't matter so much because a lot of people never expected it."[64] The government's acknowledgment of wrongdoing and its acceptance of responsibility became the paramount issue for many members of both communities. As John Tateishi observed, "The money had no impact (for me), but the letter from [then-President of the United States] George Bush was very meaningful."[65] These varied views of the importance of money in reparations politics reflect a broader issue in these processes. Whereas "it's not about the money," money may be crucial for any successful attempt to come to terms with the past because it demonstrates the perpetrator's seriousness in assuming a responsibility to repair past damage—a commitment, that is, that goes beyond mere words.

Reparations may enhance the government's standing in the eyes of those citizens concerned with their country's capacity to rectify past injustices. According to Yasuko Takezawa, the redress legislation enhanced the U.S. government's legitimacy for many Japanese-Americans whose trust in the government had been deeply shaken by the internment experience.[66] One interviewee confirmed this view, however grudgingly. Although he prefaced his remark with the caveat that racism remains rife in American society, he said, "I think this is a more impressive country for [having done] redress."[67] In an "age of apology," a society's capacity to face up to its past injustices may do much to enhance its legitimacy, both in world opinion and in the eyes of its own members.[68]

Despite the different meanings that the redress legislation had for different individuals, it does seem to have provided some measure of reconciliation—a sense of closure, of vindication, of restoration of lost honor, and of membership in the larger society. Still, one must bear in mind that responses to redress within the Japanese-descent *community* in each country varied from person to person. Indeed, one must always be cautious in using the term "community" at all, for despite the importance of ideas of common descent, shared culture, and physical characteristics (aka "ethnicity"), not all individuals saw the issues in the same way. In interviews among Japanese-descent persons in the United States, despite their limited scope, we encountered a rather sharp divergence of views among those affiliated with different ethnic organizations sustained by Japanese-Americans.[69] Ultimately, however, Takezawa's view that the campaign for redress can be understood as a simultaneous manifestation of their reawakened and enhanced sense of ethnic identification as well as of the Japanese-Americans' embrace of American values makes sense.[70]

In Canada, the redress movement reflected a transformation within the Japanese-Canadian community, during which the group became politicized and acquired the power to challenge the Canadian government. Kobayashi describes this development in terms of the group members' "ability to take possession of their cultural heritage and assert that heritage politically as an expression of multiculturalism."[71] On this point, Art Miki explained how the redress campaign had generated a certain amount of pride about being of Japanese origin and a corresponding interest in ethnic affairs. He also claimed, however, that most Japanese-Canadians have assimilated and that the group now married outside its own ranks at a rate of 95 percent. Contrary to the reigning, officially endorsed ideology of multiculturalism suggested by Kobayashi's remark earlier, Miki said flatly, "if you maintain your ethnicity, you are not Canadian."[72] Despite her earlier published view that redress allowed for the reclaiming of Japanese-Canadian heritage, Audrey Kobayashi claimed in our interview that the community largely fell apart after redress.[73] Partially because of the very small numbers of people involved, the redress campaign was unable to counteract larger forces toward assimilation that tended to attenuate Japanese-Canadian ethnic consciousness.

In the end, despite its importance for those who had lived through the internment experience, Japanese-American and Japanese-Canadian leaders agreed that for the Sansei and subsequent generations, that experience no longer formed a central component of a distinctive ethnic identity. The children of those who suffered the indignity of the camps do not, according to these community elders, consider themselves the heirs of the internment experience. As Japanese-Canadian activist Frank Kamiya noted, "My children are aware of the past discrimination, but they are not activists, they won't go and march."[74] Similarly, John Tateishi said, "Young people see the internment as something that happened to their parents or grandparents and they are not preoccupied with it."[75] One senses that the old adage "time heals all wounds" is of some relevance here, but whether the mere passage of time would have had this effect in the absence of a redress agreement cannot be known.

Museums and Commemoration

Among other efforts to promote reconciliation in the aftermath of past wrongdoing, states and private entities have funded a plethora of commemorative projects such as memorials and public education programs to focus on these past misdeeds and to discourage their repetition. Indeed, the creation of the Civil Liberties Public Education Fund following the Civil Liberties Act of 1988 was an important element of the overall redress legislation for Japanese-Americans. In Canada, the funding for the Canadian Race Relations Foundation that accompanied the redress settlement had a similar function. Charles Maier has stressed that part of public reconciliation involves nationalizing the memory of previous misdeeds and the commemoration of those misdeeds among groups beyond the immediate circle of survivors.[76] The task of commemoration involves making atonement for past wrong part of a wider public commitment, an issue that concerns the larger society as well as the descendants of those previously wronged. For what happens to a particular group pertains to the whole society—or at least making it so is the aim of many activists seeking commemoration of past wrongs.

Against this background, the redress movement may be viewed as not just about confronting the past, but also about how to incorporate this past into the history of the Japanese-American and Japanese-Canadian communities, as well as into that of the larger society. After all, the internment experience "was and is the central event in Japanese-American history . . . , the event from which all other events are dated and compared."[77] It was perfectly natural, therefore, that this experience would find a dominant place in efforts to represent and commemorate the Japanese-American experience. But what exactly is the role of internment in representations of Japanese-American history? Have those representations contributed to fostering in the community's members a sense of reconciliation and of having come to terms with the past? Mark Selden has examined textbook representations of this history, finding somewhat surprisingly that the textbooks were in some respects ahead of the politicians on this issue: "[R]ather than transmitting the official canon, [they] may have played a role in preparing public opinion to right one of the great injustices of American history."[78]

Textbooks play an important role in the political and civic education of the young. Increasingly, however, this function is also being assumed by museums that intend to educate people of all ages about political wrongs and to send the message, "Never again." Often, these museums are the undertakings of the group whose history is being represented; they are thus what one might call "roots museums," and they reflect the larger trend toward the groups' sense of "ownership" of "their" history.[79] Against this background, some would regard museums as playing a significant role in the relevant groups' self-understanding. For example, Ivan Karpf has argued that museums constitute powerful agents in the construction of identity.[80] They play a major role in representing, chronicling, revising, and displaying the past that supplies some of the raw materials of identity. The internment experience of Japanese-Americans and Japanese-Canadians has been no exception in this regard. How has this experience been portrayed to visitors in museums and other public *lieux de mémoire* (sites of memory)?[81]

The Japanese American National Museum (JANM), located in Los Angeles, seeks to depict the experience of the Japanese-descent population in the United States. As an undertaking largely financed by Japanese-Americans themselves, the museum reflects at least one version of the group's understanding of its own history. The World War II experience comprises the lion's share of the exhibition. In contrast to the textbooks studied by Mark Selden, however, the museum narrates the long story of discrimination and racism toward Japanese-Americans that culminated in the internment experience.[82] A sign at the JANM says that the internment experience was a "national disgrace—a tragedy that must never be forgotten." The message it attempts to send is the now-familiar rallying cry, "Never again!" Nor was this the message only of the more prominent Japanese American National Museum in Los Angeles. Similar narratives may be found in other museums that depict aspects of the Japanese-American experience, such as the Wing Luke Asian Museum in Seattle and the nearby Bainbridge Island (Washington) Historical Society. The internment experience constitutes the main—in some cases almost the only—concern in these museum displays as well.

These portrayals of the Japanese-American experience reflect the prevailing view among older Japanese-Americans that the internment episode is the cornerstone of their ethnic identity. The JANM and the two Seattle-area museums thus contain permanent exhibits on the internment experience. Furthermore, special exhibits focus on various aspects of the experience of confinement. For example, "The View from Within," a major exhibition of artwork produced during the internment, opened at the JANM on the occasion of the fiftieth anniversary of Executive Order 9066 in 1992. Although the perception of the centrality of the internment experience obviously contains some truth for older Japanese-Americans, one must remember that the political and ideological perspectives indicated in the museums' representation of the internment experience reflect a particular viewpoint—namely, that of those who control the museums' "means of representation." Such control amounts to a form of "symbolic capital" that tends to endow its holders with an image of disinterestedness that drapes the representations in the mantle of sincere, unchallengeable truth. This perception of truthfulness is reinforced by the implicit assumption that those who mount the museum's exhibitions have only the best interests of the community at heart. The partial and necessarily tendentious character of the museum's representations is thus obscured by the warm glow of good intentions that generally surrounds undertakings of this kind.[83]

As Carol Duncan has noted, what a museum presents as the community's history, identity, and values may represent only the interests of certain powers within the community.[84] In part because of the large sums of money necessary to mount the displays in the JANM, for example, the representation of the Japanese-American experience tends to reflect the point of view of the older, more prosperous, and more mainstream elements in the community. The emphasis on the internment experience in ethnic museums depicts what for a particular segment of Japanese-Americans constitutes the core of their ethnic identity. Yet because this self-understanding may not be generalizable to the entire community, such an emphasis should be regarded with some skepticism. Indeed, we have already seen evidence that the younger generation feels less connection with the internment experience than do its predecessors. The sensibilities of the JANM may or may not be in tune with those of younger, increasingly assimilated Japanese-Americans.

The story in Canada is similar in this regard. Part of the $12 million community fund mandated by the redress settlement was earmarked to support historical and cultural projects that would aid in "remembering our past, our culture and heritage."[85] These funds constituted an important part of the funding necessary to build the Japanese Canadian National Museum, which is located in Burnaby, British Columbia, just east of Vancouver. In contrast to the Japanese-Americans, their Canadian counterparts were too few in number and possessed too little wealth to bankroll such a project themselves. In any case, an important part of the museum's mission was to transmit an account of the history of Japanese-Canadians to future generations of Japanese-Canadians and to the broader public. According to Audrey Kobayashi, "The idea of the museum was that the redress movement was to be kept alive."[86] The inaugural exhibit, "Re-shaping Memory, Owning History," was designed to convey this narrative. It sought to depict the Japanese-Canadian experience of internment and redress, but also tellingly asserted a claim to "owning" the story in question. In addition to the Japanese Canadian National Museum, the Nikkei Internment Memorial

Centre in New Denver, British Columbia (in the relatively remote interior of the province) aims to remind visitors of "what is now acknowledged as a dark and shameful period of Canada's history. It is an all-too-vivid reminder of the pain and anguish that so many were forced to endure, but which so many also survived and overcame."[87]

Modern museum exhibitions tend to freeze time and to fix the memory of the viewers by selecting what "deserves" to be remembered.[88] In this respect, it should be emphasized that the stress on the internment experience in Japanese-American and Japanese-Canadian ethnic museums foregrounds the experience and the worldview of a particular generation. This generation is not only characterized by its historical proximity to the events under examination. In addition, it is the product of a wider contemporary discourse emphasizing that pasts worth representing are those marked more by needless suffering than by heroic achievement. Museum exhibitions are privileged arenas for presenting stories of suffering and survival. In such contexts, the exhibit encounter becomes a moral and emotional story of identity and endurance.[89]

Despite the apparent harmony of interpretation conveyed by museum representations, the meaning of the internment experience is a matter of debate and disagreement among community leaders and members. The various exhibitions seek to convey the message that the internment experience remains the cornerstone of Japanese-American history and is the anchor for the group's ethnic identity. There is a similarity here with Novick's argument concerning the way in which the Holocaust came to be regarded as the core of Jewish identity, at least in what has been called its "lachrymose" variant.[90] Yet it is not clear that this view of the past will be appropriate for subsequent generations of Japanese-Americans and Japanese-Canadians, or even that it is so today. As we have already noted, some argue that the internment plays a less central role in the self-understanding of the younger generations. Indeed, Japanese-American community leader John Tateishi said, "Young people can look at the internment historically." By contrast particularly with Jews, who in his view were unlikely to ever get over their concern with the Holocaust, the younger generations of Japanese-Americans are less likely to see themselves as the bearers of their parents' and grandparents' painful memories.

This intergenerational lapsing of memory, so to speak, raises the Nissei and Sansei's concern that later generations will forget about the internment experience. Such forgetting, they maintain, enhances the risk that such mistreatment might be repeated in the future. As Frank Kitamoto put it, "As memory fades, the danger of this happening again returns."[91] We need further research to show whether future generations will view the internment as the heart of Japanese-American ethnic identity, or whether, in fact, the redress legislation and the passage of time will consign this view to the past. Mary Waters points out that, without political or economic reasons for maintaining ethnic solidarity, ethnic identification tends to become less important and other sources of identification supervene. If this occurs, individuals will increasingly identify with characteristics associated with class or status rather than with ethnic concerns.[92] Unless entrepreneurs of memory do their work successfully—in this as in other cases—the past is likely to recede in significance.

The creation of the Japanese-American and Japanese-Canadian national museums was intended to preserve the heritage and cultural identity of the two groups, as well as to convey to future generations an awareness of the "hardships and triumphs of earlier generations."[93] Yet the two institutions operate under dramatically different conditions. The JANM has a budget of US$8 million, some 100 staff members, many hired consultants, and hundreds of volunteers.[94] The museum is a state-of-the-art work of architecture that occupies a substantial site in the historic Japantown district of Los Angeles. The building itself and the surrounding grounds comprise a significant tourist attraction.

Whereas the Japanese-Canadian community modeled its project to create a national museum on that of the Japanese-Americans, the Japanese-Canadians lacked the economic and human resources of their American counterparts. The creators of the Canadian museum had expected its community members to donate funds to the museum, but this expectation was not realized. According to Frank Kamiya, one of the founders of the museum, most visitors to the Japanese-Canadian museum are of the older generation. Though assisted by federal government funds, the museum operates with a very limited budget and only one full-time staff person. Moreover, Kamiya added, keeping the museum operating and bringing people in is one of the museum's major challenges.[95]

The differences in the experiences of the two museums reflect the two communities' different experiences during World War II. The harsher conditions of the Japanese-Canadian internment (economic, political and social) and the dispersal that followed made it more difficult for them to achieve the level of wealth of their American counterparts. As Frank Kamiya stated, "The Japanese-American situation is quite different because a lot of them were able to go back [to the places they had been forced to evacuate] and get their land back. They got rich, while Japanese-Canadians lost everything. They were dispossessed."[96] In addition, the number of Japanese-Canadians is roughly an order of magnitude smaller than that of the Japanese-American population, reflecting the approximately 10–1 ratio of population in the two countries generally. Even had it been able to attain the kind of wealth acquired by Japanese-Americans, it would have been difficult—though not necessarily impossible—for the Japanese-Canadian community to finance and sustain a large museum devoted principally to its own experience.

Similarities Between Past and Present: 9/11

Despite the relative economic success and high intermarriage rates of Japanese-Americans, have the political factors that generate ethnic identification really subsided for them, as Mary Waters's comment suggests? A large literature has developed around Asian-Americans as a model minority—a group lacking the negative social and cultural traits associated with other non-white minorities in the United States, especially blacks. But does this mean that Asian-Americans need not be concerned about discrimination in the present and future? According to Evelyn Hu-DeHart, "while Asians are seen as the model minority exhibiting good American behavior, they are still aliens, outside the boundaries of white America."[97] Is this the case? Alternatively, have Japanese-Americans attained sufficient reconciliation to move on from the unpleasant past?

Members of the Japanese-American community have actively engaged in activities intended to educate the entire national community about the internments. Despite the various public acts of reparation—a presidential apology, monetary compensation to the victims, and attempts to commemorate the internment—our research suggests that those who lived through internment have not achieved closure and a sense of reconciliation. They still tend to regard the internment as a sort of unfinished business, a violation of human rights that could happen again—if not to them, then to some other group.

Not surprisingly, the events of 9/11 catapulted Japanese-American organizations such as the Japanese American Citizens' League and the National Coalition for Reparations and Redress into a very active role in civil rights issues. In particular, they spoke out against restrictions on civil liberties and for the rights of Arab-Americans, whom they see as actual or potential victims of constitutional violations of the kind that they once suffered. The arrest without charges of many persons (mostly men) of Arab descent (and of others mistaken for them) in the United States since late 2001 reminded several of our interviewees of what had happened to the Japanese-Americans in the early 1940s. Frank Kitamoto said, "In a way it is happening again now . . . I cringe when I see the government bypassing judicial procedure by using military tribunals . . . You wonder where it's going to end."[98] In response to a question concerning the extent to which the deterrent aims of redress ("never again") had been achieved, John Tateishi replied that "the current climate is an echo of everything that was said in 1942." Moreover, he continued, "Under the wrong climate of crisis and with a non-white population involved, it [mass arrests and internment] could happen again despite the Japanese-American redress settlement. Every Arab could be targeted and the administration won't care about the Constitution and government protocol."[99] Similarly, when the Los Angeles NCRR announced the themes of the annual Day of Remembrance in 2003, they were "race, prejudice, war hysteria, failure of political leadership— then and now." One organizer of the event wrote in the publicity materials, "As we commemorate February 19, 1942 and its aftermath, American Arabs, Muslims, and South Asians are being targeted based on the same factors."[100]

These statements raise questions about the extent to which the redress settlement really contributed to the reconciliation and integration of Japanese-Americans. In this regard, Judy Balint argues that even if victims' demands are met, reconciliation will not necessarily ensue. In her view, reconciliation must be grounded in the everyday realities of people's lives and fears.[101] The situation facing Arab-descent persons in the United States since 9/11 has led Japanese-Americans to recall more vividly what was once done to them because of their ethnicity. Fears of possible government abuses remind us that, notwithstanding redress of past wrongs, many non-whites doubt that they can count on full societal acceptance and equal treatment. John Tateishi illustrates this point when he says: "As Nissei who suffered the war hysteria, evacuation, and internment, I understand the humiliations and harassment that can be heaped upon innocent people if they only look like the enemy."[102] According to another observer, "Japanese Americans—so traumatized by their World War II internment that they spent the next half century relentlessly pursuing the American dream of assimilation—were among the first to step up and stand behind Muslims and Arabs in the days after September 11."[103]

The Japanese-Canadian community has experienced the aftermath of 9/11 very differently—in large part simply because they were not living in the country attacked by Al Qaeda terrorists. The National Association of Japanese Canadians (NAJC) joined a number of other organizations in condemning the war against Iraq. They also wrote a letter to the government advising it that "facts could get out of hand" and that "the recent practices of racial profiling and the enactment of the Canadian 'Anti-terrorist Act' constitute a wake-up call for all Canadians." In her letter to the media, the president of the NAJC stated, "We know this danger from our own experience."[104] But because there were no 9/11-related racial incidents in Manitoba, according to its own leaders the Winnipeg-based NAJC played a limited role in public discussions, in contrast to the more active political stance taken by the Japanese American Citizens League in San Francisco. For its part, the NAJC has assumed an active role in advising other wronged groups—for example, First Nations aboriginal groups, the Ukrainian-Canadian community, and those in the Chinese community pursuing the "head tax" issue—in their efforts to pursue their claims against the Canadian government.[105]

Still, the situation triggered by 9/11 made many Japanese-Canadians aware that visible minorities could be easily targeted groups in times of fear. John Biles and Humera Ibrahim, two researchers from the federal Department of Canadian Heritage, state that after 9/11, the largest specter that arose was the question of internment, but "no domestic crises emerged that indicated any fundamental failures of the 'Canadian diversity model'."[106] In regard to the possibility that the internment experience might be repeated with Iraqi Canadians in the context of the U.S.-led war on Iraq, Frank Kamiya responded that the internment experience "could happen again, but the redress made people aware that this did happen and that it shouldn't happen again."[107]

In sum, our interviewees appeared confident about the Canadian government's official stance against racism and the effectiveness of the culture of inclusion implicit in the official policy of multiculturalism. Kobayashi's conclusion regarding the effects of redress summarizes this attitude: "The . . . settlement between the federal Government and the Japanese Canadians strikes an important blow against racism. It sets a precedent for officially redressing the wrongs of the past . . . [it] provides a model for understanding the experience of racism and the social changes through which racism's effects can be ameliorated."[108] Comparatively speaking, Canada seems to have been more persuasive in atoning for its past misdeeds vis-à-vis Japanese-Canadians than the U.S. government has been with regard to Japanese-Americans, and this has paid dividends in terms of political legitimacy and social cohesion. This greater willingness to address the past head-on is at least in part a product of the fact that Canada need not fear that, by openly acknowledging past wrongdoing vis-à-vis this particular population group, it may be "opening the floodgates" with regard to another group that comprises a substantial segment of the overall population, such as has occurred in the United States with regard to black Americans. To be sure, other claimants are making reparations demands in Canadian society, but such groups are primarily Indians/First Nations people. A Royal Commission on Aboriginal Peoples has produced a major report that has guided subsequent discussion and negotiations.[109]

Conclusion

To what extent, then, do reparations and coming to terms with the past bring about a sense of reconciliation for previously wronged groups? An examination of the consequences of redress legislation to make amends for internment during World War II indicates that reconciliation is more a *process* than a clear-cut outcome for once-victimized groups. At one level, government acknowledgment and attribution of responsibility did bring a sense of vindication and restore a sense of honor and equal status. At another level, the interviews highlighted the varying degrees of reconciliation achieved by redress. Our findings confirmed Balint's view that, in order to achieve an enduring reconciliation, this has to be framed by institutional change.[110]

Yet events since 9/11 have made Japanese-Americans and Japanese-Canadians realize that injustices that *should* happen "never again" *can* happen again because structural conditions in the society have not changed, such as the potential targeting of certain ethnic groups as "threats without evidence." Canada's official policy on multiculturalism and its relatively stronger official stance against racism made Japanese-Canadians more confident than their American counterparts about their government's likely response to a crisis. In contrast, the Japanese-American leadership in the United States perceived the historical causes identified by the 1982 Commission on the Wartime Relocation and Internment of Civilians (CWRIC) for the internment of some 120,000 Japanese and Japanese-Americans during World War II—namely, racial prejudice, war hysteria, and failure of political leadership—as threatening the nation again. This led Japanese-Americans to reevaluate their own experience in terms of what is happening to another ethnic community and to mobilize around civil rights issues in the aftermath of 9/11. Their political participation has been more vigorous than that of their Canadian counterparts, who see their role less as that of leading civil rights struggles and more in terms of actively helping other wronged groups make their claims for redress.

Representations of the internment experience in American and Canadian museums—like those everywhere—aim to consecrate a particular view of the past. Within this perspective, the internment was the seminal event in the history of the Japanese-Americans and Japanese-Canadians. Yet this is the point of view of a group that, though once mistreated, subsequently grew relatively successful in each country. Having reestablished themselves after the internment they do not serve as such a significant model for the younger generations. As the older generation fades from the scene, younger Japanese-Americans and Japanese-Canadians—themselves increasingly assimilated and intermarried with the larger population—seem unlikely to continue to regard this portrayal of the ethnic experience as reflecting their own perspective.

On another level, as part of the redress settlement in both Canada and the United States, government established special foundations to "sponsor research and public education activities so that the causes and circumstances of this and similar events may be illuminated."[111] In the United States, the impact of the violation of Japanese-Americans' constitutional rights on the broader society remains relatively vague. As John Tateishi put it, "I don't know what the larger society thought of this [the internment and redress]."[112] It would be valuable to know to what extent the broader public has learned lessons from this past and may thus be prepared to take a stand should similar circumstances arise. Certainly, the history of the Japanese-American internment has had some effect on recent discussions of the treatment of Arab-Americans, reminding the public of a dishonorable past experience and warning against repetition. In Canada, however, the broader society appears more aware of the importance of supporting multiculturalism as a core Canadian value to help fight intolerance and racism, separate and apart from the internment experience.[113]

Although reparations have not necessarily led to a full sense of reconciliation among Japanese-Americans and Japanese-Canadians, the redress legislation does seem to have provided "a specific, narrow invitation for victims to walk between vengeance and forgiveness."[114] Comparatively speaking, the wrong done to those of Japanese-descent persons was mild; none was intentionally killed or tortured in carrying out the policy euphemistically referred to as "evacuation." Where more severe harms have been perpetrated, the achievement of reconciliation is likely to be correspondingly more difficult. The example of slavery and its aftermath in the United States constitutes a case in point.

CHAPTER 4

Forty Acres:
The Case of Reparations
for Black Americans

On Tuesday, March 26, 2002, a young black lawyer named Deadria Farmer-Paellmann filed suit in U.S. District Court for the Eastern District of New York against FleetBoston Financial Corporation, Aetna Insurance, and a railroad company named CSX Corporation, their respective predecessors, and up to 1,000 "Corporate [John] Does" that, like the named companies, may have profited from American slavery. The suit sought damages and compensation for 35 million descendants of African slaves, although the plaintiffs asserted that any award would go not to individuals but toward a fund to improve the health, education, and housing opportunities for blacks generally. According to Roger Wareham, one of several lawyers who prepared the legal action, "This is not about individuals receiving checks in their mailbox."[1] The suit—actually one of three suits seeking redress for slavery-related wrongs that were filed that day—reflected the recent upsurge of efforts to pursue "reparations" for blacks in the United States.

The announcement of the suits, which received considerable media attention, might have been expected to generate jubilation among those who have been promoting the idea of reparations as a means of rectifying the economic inequalities and social stigmatization endured by blacks in the United States. Yet the reaction to the suit by the best-known reparations activists was muted at best. Instead, those activists responded with notably faint praise. They seem to have regarded the Farmer-Paellmann suit as being out of step with their larger political strategy for enhancing the living conditions of black Americans by means of reparations claims-making. Beyond demands for mere economic compensation, that strategy includes naming the U.S. government as a defendant in reparations lawsuits in order to highlight the fact that reparations are a matter not just of money, but of a national political responsibility to repair the broader damage caused by three centuries of slavery and segregation as well.

Notwithstanding their divergent aims, Farmer-Paellmann's suit and others filed by reparations activists elsewhere reflect a remarkable efflorescence in the use of law to address past injustices perpetrated by states, churches, and private firms. The transformation of political conflict into legal disputation—an old story in American life, observed already by Tocqueville 175 years ago[2]—is consistent with a larger human interest in the pacification of social relations, and this may be a successful way of achieving certain political ends during an age of retrenchment concerning racial equality and social justice more generally. This way of approaching political problems has been particularly facilitated in the United States by the 1966 codification of the modern class-action suit. This mechanism was originally intended to help amalgamate small consumer claims, but in the meantime it has been used for vastly different purposes with much higher stakes.[3] Lawyers, always prominent in American public life, have played a crucial role in defining the terms on which political conflict is fought out as the notion of reparations has grown more widespread. The litigiousness often regarded as as a peculiarity of American society has increasingly gone global as a result. Because much of the legal maneuvering with regard to past injustices that occurred elsewhere now takes place in courtrooms in the United States, one senses that John Locke had it backward: it was not so much "in the beginning" that all the world was America, but rather "in the end."[4]

Yet there is a price to pay for doing politics through legal means. This mode of carrying on political disputes privileges lawyers over citizens and courtrooms over more widely accessible sites of debate and deliberation. The juridical pursuit of political aims is also vulnerable to being hijacked by people pursuing their own private agendas rather than the common good, especially when those political aims concern primarily economic matters. This kind of manipulation has had deleterious consequences for the wider political goals sought by those using the courts as a vehicle for broader purposes. Finally, it is not clear that legal casuistry is well-suited for bringing about substantive social change; for such change to occur, legal maneuvering may provide some help, but popular mobilization is an essential element as well.

The Struggle for Reparations for Black Americans

Slavery, rather than territorial conquest, has generally been regarded as the most fundamental abrogation of the deep rhetorical commitment to freedom in U.S. history. Along with simple demographic facts that have left Indians a marginal population in most parts of the country, the problems of African-Americans have therefore received more attention in American public life than those of indigenes, who have been the major focus of reparations politics in other settler (post-)colonial contexts (especially in Canada and Australia). Few would argue the importance of the civil rights revolution for blacks, but many wonder how substantial the gains have actually been, particularly in view of large and persistent disparities between blacks and other groups in rates of incarceration, poverty, unemployment, mortality, and the like. The social and economic progress of blacks in the United States continues to be the subject of anguished, if inconclusive, debate.[5] The economic stagnation of parts of the black population, despite the achievement of legal equality in the 1960s and the emergence of a substantial black middle class, has perhaps inevitably prompted a resurgence of arguments asserting the existence of hereditary differences between races and claims that blacks are lazy or otherwise disinclined to work as hard as others.[6]

In the meantime, affirmative action, which was so long regarded as the appropriate approach to dealing with inequalities rooted in past injustices affecting blacks in the United States, fell from political favor and was forced to confront a serious challenge in the U.S. Supreme Court. This outcome came about in part because affirmative action, originally aimed at blacks, was extended to the waves of new non-white immigrants entering the country after the reforms of the mid-1960s. More generally, it has fallen into disfavor because the majority now view it as a violation of the American commitment to individual opportunity as opposed to policies benefiting groups.[7] One major consequence of the challenge to affirmative action was a renewed call among many, especially in the black intelligentsia, for reparations to blacks to make amends for the inequalities purportedly caused by slavery and segregation. In his discussion of the case for reparations for African-Americans, for example, Robert Westley straightforwardly enunciated the relationship between the flagging popular support for affirmative action and the demand for reparations. Writing before the legal challenge was aired in the Supreme Court in 2003, Westley insisted,

"Affirmative action for Black Americans as a form of remediation for perpetuation of past injustice is almost dead," and it is thus necessary to "re-
vitalize the discussion of reparations."[8]

Although this motivation for reviving the discussion of reparations may
be more prominent in the thinking of activists, there may also be a more
complex set of circumstances leading to this upsurge in reparations talk.
Partially, of course, the movement was rekindled by the success of the
Japanese-American struggle for redress, which represents a frequent point
of reference for black reparations activists. Yet a more subtle reason may
be behind the burgeoning concern over reparations. As a result of changes
in immigration policies since the mid-1960s, the face of the United States
has changed dramatically. Asians have arrived in substantial numbers, and
the largest cohorts of new immigrants come from the United States' own
backyard, Latin America. These demographic changes, along with a broader
global embrace of multiculturalism, have begun to subtly revise the traditional American perception of racial differences. Whereas "the American
dilemma" at midcentury exclusively concerned the relationship between
whites and blacks, blacks now jostle with waves of non-white immigrants
who were not previously a significant part of the population mix. With the
postwar delegitimation of legally sanctioned racial discrimination of any
kind, those groups have also been seen as deserving of greater respect and
recognition. Against the background of multiculturalist agnosticism regarding the divergent historical trajectories of ethnoracial groups in the
United States, the campaign for reparations might be said to symbolize the
reassertion of the distinctiveness of the black experience vis-à-vis that of
other non-whites. However discriminated against or marginalized socially,
no other non-white group could claim to have been systematically uprooted
from their homelands and enslaved in North America. The black experience
was unique in this regard, and their reasons for demanding reparations
were equally unique.

Westley's remark also reminds us that the current round of reparations
claims-making, which found expression in the Farmer-Paellmann suit, is
hardly the first. Others have pursued reparations for blacks in the past,
though with relatively little success. Indeed, the notion of some sort of
compensation for the wrongs and the exploitation involved in American
plantation slavery goes back at least to the Civil War era.[9] In early 1865,
General William Sherman announced a plan to make available for settlement by freed blacks the Sea Islands and a portion of the lowlands south

of Charleston, South Carolina. According to Special Field Order No. 15, each family was to receive 40 acres of land, and Sherman subsequently authorized the Army to loan them mules. The promise of the two jointly gave rise to the notion of "40 acres and a mule." By June 1865, some 40,000 blacks occupied 400,000 acres, and the Freedmen's Bureau planned to extend this pattern to a total of 850,000 acres of the land under its control. After taking office, however, President Andrew Johnson rescinded the Bureau's plan, forgiving Confederate owners and restoring to them their land. As a result, the freedpeople of the plantations were left with few resources and a deep sense of betrayal as they embarked on the road to freedom.[10]

The bitter disappointment arising from the federal government's retreat from efforts to redistribute land to blacks after the war has given the phrase "40 acres and a mule" great resonance among subsequent campaigners for reparations. The symbolism for blacks of the number 40 has thus come to parallel the way in which the number 442—deriving from the number of the heroic, much-decorated regiment of Japanese-American soldiers during World War II—came to play an important symbolic role in the pursuit of redress for persons of Japanese descent interned in the United States during that war.[11] Just as H.R. 442, the bill mandating redress for interned Japanese-Americans, was named after the 442d Regiment, Congressman John Conyers's H.R. 40—calling for a study commission to examine the question of reparations for African-Americans—is drawn from the abortive possibility of distributing lands to freedpeople after the Civil War.

With the end of Reconstruction after 1877 and the gradual imposition of segregationist legislation culminating in *Plessy v. Ferguson*'s ruling (1892) that "separate but equal" facilities were constitutional, blacks were compelled simply to fight for their basic civil rights and against the extralegal violence of such organizations as the Ku Klux Klan. Thus, the idea of reparations fell largely into abeyance until the upsurge of pressure for racial equality during the civil rights movement beginning in the 1950s. The Civil Rights Act of 1964 and the Voting Rights Act of 1965 constituted the movement's signal legislative victories, endowing blacks with the legal rights that had been nominally accorded to them in the post–Civil War amendments (the Thirteenth, Fourteenth, and Fifteenth), but that were rarely enforced after Reconstruction ended. But these legislative changes, significant though they were, hardly brought an end to police brutality, rat-infested ghettos, and sharp economic inequalities between whites and blacks. Meanwhile, the interracial movement that had spearheaded the campaign for those laws and for a larger "beloved community" subsided in the aftermath of its significant legislative victories.

Soon, along with other mobilized racial minorities, some black radicals in the United States began to see themselves as an "internal colony," a population exploited for its cheap labor—or simply left to make its own way—and kept under control not so much by laws as by untrammeled police violence.[12] Subsequent to Stokely Carmichael's 1966 declaration of "Black Power," the civil rights movement was gradually supplanted by the activities of the groups that would pursue the "identity politics" of the coming period, for which the black movement was a model. Those groups that could make a plausible case for a trajectory similar to the black experience would usher in a "minority rights revolution."[13]

In this context, the idea of reparations for slavery and legal segregation experienced a brief resurgence in the 1960s and early 1970s. At the time, the notion may not have seemed so wild-eyed as it is sometimes thought to be, since no less a figure than President Lyndon Johnson had announced in 1965: "You do not take a person who, for years, has been hobbled by chains and liberate him, bring him up to the starting line of a race and then say, 'You are free to compete with all the others,' and still justly believe that you have been completely fair . . . It is not enough just to open the gates of opportunity. All our citizens must have the ability to walk through those gates."[14] Johnson was effectively endorsing a notion of affirmative action of the sort that had been adumbrated in the civil rights legislation of the mid-1960s.

Yet many felt that these notions did not go far enough and that more concrete changes had to take place before blacks would be able to compete in the race of American life. "Queen Mother" Audley Moore, a one-time Garveyite and former Communist, is often said to have been the first, or at least the first well-known person in the postwar period to raise the demand for reparations. The idea was soon incorporated into the political agendas of black radical groups, especially the Black Panthers, although the term was frequently interpreted to mean restitution or redistribution of land.[15]

The main episode that returned the idea of "reparations" to public awareness involved the so-called Black Manifesto of radical activist James Forman. The Manifesto was originally adopted by the National Black Economic Development Conference, which met in Detroit in late April 1969.

According to Forman's own account, he worked out the text of the document with a number of activists from the Detroit-based League of Revolutionary Black Workers and proclaimed it to the conference with their support. The Manifesto demanded "five hundred million dollars in reparations from the racist white 'Christian' churches and the Jewish synagogues" in compensation "for the centuries of exploitation and oppression which they had inflicted on black people around the world." In the minds of its drafters, the Manifesto was not merely a claim for monetary compensation, but "a call for revolutionary action . . . that spoke of the human misery of black people under capitalism and imperialism, and pointed the way to ending those conditions." The promulgation of the Manifesto at the Detroit conference at first attracted little attention other than that of FBI Director J. Edgar Hoover and Attorney General John Mitchell. It received more notice, however, when Forman delivered it—unscheduled and uninvited—to a dumbstruck congregation at the famously liberal Riverside Church in New York on Sunday, May 4, 1969. The Black Manifesto articulated a number of demands for economic improvements for blacks of the kind that would appear in subsequent efforts to obtain reparations, such as banks, universities, and job training programs designed to benefit blacks.[16]

The minister whose Riverside Church service had been interrupted, Ernest Campbell, eventually responded favorably to the basic outlook of the Manifesto, as did the Episcopal Church hierarchy. An article by Charles Willie, a black sociologist then at Syracuse University, wondered in print whether the document was "prophetic or preposterous," but was fundamentally sympathetic to the aims—if not the addressee—of the Manifesto. In a critique that would reemerge later in the context of the recent lawsuits for reparations for slavery against private companies, Willie argued that the Manifesto's focus on the church was misguided because compensation from religious institutions cannot "absolve the government of what is government's responsibility."[17]

Yet the wider response to the Manifesto was unsympathetic, at best. Despite the fact that Forman had developed the Manifesto in collaboration with activists in the League of Black Revolutionary Workers, not all of that organization's members endorsed the cause. According to Michael Dawson, both rank-and-file adherents and leaders of the League saw the programs envisaged in the Manifesto as "a diversion from what should be the main thrust" of the group's efforts.[18] The mainstream NAACP also rejected the demands laid out in the Manifesto. In the pages of the *New York Times*,

NAACP leader Roy Wilkins urged churchmen to "shun reparations as [a] delusion."[19]

Eventually, even those who had initially supported the aims outlined in the document backtracked as well. Worse still, monies paid by some churches to the Interreligious Foundation for Community Organizations, to which James Forman had urged payments to be made on behalf of the Black Economic Development Conference, were diverted, Forman wrote, "in very opportunistic ways . . . This betrayal by greedy black churchmen was a serious disappointment."[20] The tensions between more radical and nationalist forces, on the one hand, and the black churches, on the other, would echo down through subsequent black politics.[21] Ultimately, Forman's chronicle of the experience reads as a cautionary tale that anticipated the squabbles generated by reparations payments to the survivors of Nazi-era wrongs.[22]

Nonetheless, the notion of reparations had once again come to be associated with the injustices experienced by blacks in the United States. Within a couple of years after Forman's promulgation of the "Black Manifesto," Boris Bittker, the Sterling Professor of Law at Yale, published his analysis of *The Case for Black Reparations*.[23] Arguing that blacks had suffered disproportionately among American racial and minority groups, Bittker suggested a number of ways to calculate the amount of compensation owed them. Regardless of the method of calculation, however, the sums involved were very large indeed because the purpose was not merely to acknowledge and apologize for past wrongs but to redistribute wealth with the goal of enhancing black economic equality. Yet perhaps even more important than Bittker's suggestions about how to assess the amount due was his argument concerning the way in which the compensation should be paid. Bittker asserted that individual payouts would lead to fruitless expenditures on consumption, whereas what was needed was long-term investment. He therefore argued that payments should be made to blacks collectively in the interest of long-term institution-building.[24]

The book was soon reviewed by Derrick Bell, a civil rights activist and professor of law at Harvard whose visibility grew dramatically in the early 1990s when he tangled very publicly with that august institution over its failure to hire women of color on the Law School faculty.[25] Bell has long been an analyst of the "elusive quest for racial justice" who has despaired of "the permanence of racism" in the United States.[26] Given his demonstrated commitment to racial equality, Bell might have been expected to be enthusiastic about Bittker's proposals for a reparations scheme to enhance the conditions of American blacks.

Yet his review, entitled "Dissection of a Dream," concluded that the many constitutional and legal obstacles to such an undertaking were insurmountable. "Racial reparations," he wrote, "are more a vision than a legal possibility." In the end, according to Bell, the achievement of the aims set forth in Bittker's book depended not on legal disputation but on political developments. "Even if Professor Bittker had devised a fool-proof legal theory for black reparations litigation, few judges or legislators would be moved in the absence of some dramatic event, major crisis, or tragic circumstance that conveyed the necessity or at least the clear advantages of adopting a reparations scheme . . . Legal analysis cannot give life to a process that must evolve from the perceptions of those responsible for the perpetuation of racism in this country."[27] Bell's emphasis on politics over legal disputation in the pursuit of reparations has considerable plausibility. Despite Bell's critique, however, Bittker's book remains influential among some of those who support the idea of reparations, though they tend to see its analysis as having been superseded by subsequent developments.[28]

Indeed, the response to Bittker's book at the time was "mild"[29] in part, no doubt, because the militancy of blacks and other minorities began to flag by the early 1970s. At that point, the idea of reparations for blacks largely went underground again until the late 1980s, in the immediate aftermath of the Civil Liberties Act of 1988 that recompensed Japanese-Americans interned during World War II to the tune of $20,000 each (see Chapter 3). Soon thereafter, Detroit Congressman John Conyers resurrected the idea of reparations for blacks by proposing legislation to institute a commission to study whether blacks still suffer from slavery and segregation and, if so, to explore possible remedies. Under the symbolically laden rubric H.R. 40, Conyers introduced the bill into Congress in an environment that was flush with the reparations victory of a group that had been wronged, to be sure, but in a manner and to a degree that hardly seemed comparable to what black Americans had endured during their long sojourn in America. It was also in 1988 that John L. Lewis, the civil rights veteran and congressman from Georgia, began submitting a bill for the creation of a National Museum of African-American History and Culture on the Mall in Washington, D.C. that has since come to fruition.[30]

In contrast to the success of Japanese-American redress, however, Conyers's bill never got out of committee. Presumably the members of Congress realized that the mere installation of a commission of inquiry was likely to generate substantial pressures for some sort of reparations. Once the Commission on Wartime Relocation and Internment of Civilians (CWRIC) was in place to examine the factors that led to the Japanese-American internments, the political momentum built steadily until President Ronald Reagan was forced to endorse the notion of redress. It took approximately eight years from the invocation of a congressional commission of inquiry to the signing of compensatory legislation.[31] At the same time, the members of Congress may simply have been acting in accordance with the views of their constituents; a 1997 poll found that while two-thirds of blacks supported the idea of both an apology and compensation for slavery, two-thirds of white respondents resisted even an apology, and fully 88 percent opposed the notion of paying reparations.[32] In any event, the result is that Conyers's legislative proposal has gotten nowhere. Still, the issue of reparations for blacks has received greater public attention ever since Conyers put the issue back on the agenda,[33] and Conyers himself has said that he believes that reparations has now "entered the mainstream."[34] It is to these more recent developments that we now turn.

Reparations for Blacks in the United States: The Latest Chapter

Those backing the campaign for reparations for blacks in the United States have recently insisted more and more loudly that—after payments to Holocaust survivors, to persons of Japanese descent incarcerated as enemy aliens in North America during World War II, and to a variety of Indian groups—"it's our turn."[35] In 1994, during the early stages of the most recent wave of reparations claims-making, one observer correctly suggested that his readers "soon will be hearing that word [reparations] with greater frequency."[36] In the meantime, a number of city councils have adopted resolutions supporting the idea, and the city of Los Angeles has adopted an ordinance requiring every company doing business with the city to report whether it ever profited from slavery.[37] But whether the campaign for reparations ever becomes a successful movement probably depends on whether its backers succeed in creating a substantial popular base capable of pressuring lawmakers about the issue, just as Derrick Bell argued in the early 1970s. There are only inchoate signs that they can or will do so.

While reparations talk spread during the second half of the 1990s, attention to the issue surged with the appearance, in 2000, of Randall Robinson's highly publicized book *The Debt: What America Owes to Blacks*.[38] Coincident with its publication, Robinson convened a meeting of a number of leading black politicians, intellectuals, and activists in the Washington, D.C. offices of the TransAfrica Forum, the organization he founded to lobby the federal government on American foreign policy with respect to Africa and the African diaspora (especially in the Caribbean).[39] The subject of the meeting, at which Congressman John Conyers was a keynote speaker, was to discuss "The Case for Black Reparations." Although no mention was made of the earlier "Black Manifesto" during the discussions, the portion of the TransAfrica Forum Web site chronicling the meeting included a link to a text called "The Reparations Manifesto"; the heading of that document reads, "Restatement of the Black Manifesto."[40] Presumably some connection was being made to James Forman's demands of the late 1960s, but TransAfrica Forum's "Reparations Manifesto" made no mention of the culpability or responsibility of the churches. Instead, the document focused on the liabilities of the U.S. government.

The issue of reparations for blacks soon became so prominent that it found its way into mainstream media and prime time television, though mostly of the high-brow sort. Early in 2000, the popular NBC drama series *The West Wing* screened an episode in which the subject of reparations came up, resulting in a nasty exchange between Josh Lyman, the White House deputy chief of staff, and Jeff Breckinridge, a black lawyer whom the fictional Bartlett administration wanted to nominate for the post of assistant attorney general. There was one small problem, however; Breckinridge had written an enthusiastic blurb for the dust jacket of a book by Otis Hastings called *The Unpaid Debt*—a fairly transparent reference to Robinson's book. As the jousting over the problem unfolded in Josh's office, Breckinridge noted that "In the 60s, you could hear the looters shouting, 'That was my 40 acres, I'll be back for the mule'." The discussion continued with some brief sparring over whether, as Josh contended, "600,000 white men died over the issue of slavery" in the Civil War. After a "fascinating abstract discussion" of reparations for slavery that Josh clearly found exasperating, he said, "You know, Jeff, I'd love to give you the money, I really would. But I'm a little short of cash right now. It seems the SS officer forgot to give my grandfather his wallet back when he let him out of Birkenau [one of the camps in the Auschwitz complex]." Breckinridge argued that the redress given to Japanese Americans interned during World War II was a relevant precedent. Ultimately, Josh let the argument go, though whether he really conceded Breckinridge's points is unclear. In any event, Josh seemed to accept Breckinridge's position that he would be a vigorous defender of civil rights as assistant attorney general, and it appears that he would stand by Breckinridge's nomination. The dialogue is a tribute to the savvy of the series's writer and creator, Aaron Sorkin; the episode raised with great economy many of the central features of the controversy over reparations for blacks in the United States.[41] Following on this episode, by the end of 2000 *Harper's* ran a "Forum" on the issue of reparations, airing the views of a number of high-profile litigation attorneys on the question of the best strategy for pursuing reparations in the courts.[42]

Along with the attention and activism generated by Robinson's book among those supportive of the reparations idea, others who were less sympathetic were paying attention as well. On May 30, 2000, the conservative publicist David Horowitz wrote an attack on the idea of reparations in the online magazine *Salon*. The piece was headlined "The latest Civil Rights Disaster," with the subtitle, "Ten reasons why reparations for slavery are a bad idea for black people—and racist too."[43] The article appeared in an outlet not widely consulted by nonintellectuals and so generated little discernible echo.

But Horowitz, knowledgeable as he is about a wedge issue, was not finished with the matter. In early 2001, he attempted to place ads under the "Ten Reasons" heading in the campus newspapers of a number of leading colleges and universities across the United States. Most of the newspapers declined to run the ad. Those that did so saw copies spirited away from distribution boxes or had their editorial offices besieged by protesters—perhaps most notably at Berkeley, the proverbial birthplace of the Free Speech Movement. The student newspaper at Brown University published the ad, resulting in a fiasco. The furor provoked by the ad campaign stimulated a front-page article in the *New York Times* noting that "overlooked in much of the uproar over the [Brown University] newspaper's publication of the advertisement is the deeper national debate on reparations over slavery, which could have found fertile ground for discussion on this campus."[44] Horowitz wanted controversy, and the publicity that attends it, and he got both—in spades.

Much ink was subsequently spilled on the controversy that Horowitz provoked, with published responses from even so distinguished a commentator as John Hope Franklin, chairman of Bill Clinton's "Dialogue on Race," who dismissed Horowitz's ad as a "diatribe."[45] A former left-wing publicist himself (he was editor of the influential New Left publication *Ramparts* before his conversion to conservatism), Horowitz knew who he was dealing with when he placed the ad in campus newspapers, and his probable anticipation that it would reveal an inclination toward censorship among some on the left was not disappointed. He subsequently made considerable hay out of the matter, including a debating tour of college campuses with a representative of the National Coalition of Blacks for Reparations in America (N'COBRA), the major group working (in relative obscurity) on the reparations issue before Randall Robinson put it back on the map.[46] Horowitz also used the affair for his own fundraising purposes. He vigorously denounced the "hucksters" in the "racial shakedown racket" who are behind the "reparations scam," but he was apparently not averse to exploiting the issue for his own purposes.[47] A year or so after the controversy stirred up by Horowitz and his antagonists, the once-venerable organ of liberal opinion *The New Republic* also ran a lengthy, scathing attack on the idea of reparations—thinly disguised as a review of Robinson's book *The Debt*—by Berkeley linguistics professor John McWhorter, a rising star on the right for his relatively conservative views on racial issues.[48] By this time, the matter of reparations had become something of a *cause célèbre* in progressive circles and a *bête noire* in conservative ones.

Despite being primarily a domestic U.S. issue, the debates about reparations that took place prior to the World Conference Against Racism (WCAR) in Durban, South Africa in late summer 2001 put the matter on the worldwide political agenda. During the run-up to Durban, the prominent nongovernmental organization Human Rights Watch issued a document titled "An Approach to Reparations" that sought to bridge the gap between reparations for those who have themselves suffered wrongs and those who are seeking to rectify the long-term consequences of systems of domination and exploitation—that is, between commemorative and anti-systemic reparations.

In one of the most thoughtful and innovative interventions in the reparations discussion to date, Human Rights Watch proposed the creation of what would be "effectively truth commissions" to investigate "specific multiracial countries such as the United States, Brazil, and South Africa" that have been the foci of reparations debates because of their legacies of slavery and racial domination, as well as other bodies of inquiry "for specific countries that would examine the degree to which the slave trade and colonialism, as opposed to the subsequent practices of the post-independence government, have contributed to the destitution of the country's population."[49] Yet Human Rights Watch's nuanced approach to reparations, which sought to overcome the distinction between reparations for those who had directly suffered harms and those who suffer today from the *consequences* of earlier wrongs, especially the neediest among them, was soon lost in the flood. With the deterioration of discussion at Durban into shouting matches that included anti-Semitic remarks, the attacks of September 11, 2001, and the civil liberties and human rights challenges that soon followed, Human Rights Watch abandoned its plans to pursue the reparations inquiries that it had outlined. The Durban conference did issue a declaration that slavery was a crime against humanity, however, providing further fodder for reparations activists.

In the atmosphere created by *The Debt*, David Horowitz, and Durban, public opposition to the idea of reparations by a black person had begun to appear something like a betrayal of other blacks. Yet Jack E. White, who had been present at the TransAfrica Forum gathering in early 2000, wrote in his column in *Time* that "the fight for slave reparations is a morally just but totally hopeless cause."[50] A columnist for *Time* might be written off by supporters of reparations as too mainstream, but the same cannot be said of the only other prominent contemporary left-wing black critic of the idea of whom I am aware, the New School University political scientist Adolph Reed. Reed's progressive credentials are difficult to impugn; he has for some years written the "Class Notes" column for *The Progressive* magazine. Yet Reed pulled no punches in his published discussion of the reparations cause, dismissing the pursuit of reparations as a "political dead end."[51] On the assumption that it was "so obviously a nonstarter in American politics," Reed sought to make sense of why the idea of reparations had gathered such momentum in a political climate in which the fortunes even of affirmative action had declined substantially.

Reed argued that the idea of reparations had three relevant dimensions: material, symbolic, and psychological. He agreed that the economic wrongs inflicted on the American black population by slavery and legal segregation manifestly deserved to be remedied. He also understood the symbolic dimension of reparations, the yearning for public acknowledgment of the injustices of the past. But this, he asserted, "does not require the rhetoric of reparations," and it fit what he called "the Clintonoid tenor of sappy public apologies and maudlin psychobabble about collective pain and

healing." But Reed was most critical of the arguments of reparations activists with regard to the third, psychological dimension. In particular, he rejected their assumption that it is important "to restore or correct racial consciousness that the legacy of slavery is supposed to have distorted or
destroyed." He refers to this notion as the "damage thesis,"[52] which main-
tains that blacks have been psychologically disturbed by their experiences
of oppression. This approach to understanding the plight of blacks, he argues, "ensconces a particular guiding role for upper class blacks" who think
they have escaped the psychological damage they diagnose among others.

Like many other critics, Reed found insuperable the complications involved in reparations compensation—who would be the recipients? If payments were made to a corporate entity, how would that entity be held
accountable? Reed subsequently extended this critique by arguing that it's
one thing to compensate people who have directly suffered physical harms
and another to pay reparations to their descendants. Reed made the point
in connection with a much-noted exhibition on the appalling history of
lynching in the United States: "If there's a case to be made for reparations,
based on existing precedents, it seems like this would be it. There are victims with names and culprits with names, and there's a specifiable harm."[53]
In effect, Reed was distinguishing between "victims" and "the dispossessed"—which corresponds from the opposite perspective with a distinction between perpetrators on the one hand and beneficiaries on the other—
in a manner that some have used to distinguish among different kinds of
reparations claims and to argue that reparations are likely to be paid only
in case of identifiable victims.[54] The compensation paid to the victims of the
Rosewood massacre, a 1923 attack on blacks in Florida, and the sums recommended for those terrorized in the race riots in Tulsa, Oklahoma in 1921
fit this pattern well. Rather than being compensation for the generalized
wrongs done to blacks historically under slavery and Jim Crow, these cases
involved reparations for harms done to specific individuals and their families.[55] Yet even the lawsuit seeking to realize the recommendation for reparations to the surviving victims of the Tulsa race riot has so far been un-
successful, on statute of limitations grounds.[56]

Ultimately, however, Reed's objections to the idea of reparations were
political: "What strikes me as most incomprehensible about the reparations
movement is its complete disregard for the simplest, most mundanely prag-
matic question about any political mobilization: How can we imagine
building a political force that would enable us to prevail on this issue?"

Moreover, at a time when "common circumstances of economic and social insecurity have strengthened the potential for building broad solidarity across race, gender, and other identities," he argued, the "demand for racially defined reparations . . . cuts precisely against building such solidarity." In short, Reed opposed the idea of reparations as politically divisive—not with respect to some airy, nonexistent American community, but rather with regard to those elements of American society who are worst off because of their shared class position and who might be mobilized to seek political and social change on that basis.

Reed's has remained a lonely voice on the left. Yet the difficulties of squaring the pursuit of reparations for black Americans with traditional left-wing politics becomes apparent in an article by Ben Dalby in the *International Socialist Review* addressing the problem of "Slavery and the Question of Reparations." Dalby shares Reed's view of Randall Robinson as "elite-oriented," but reserves his main criticisms for Robinson's tendency to view the fundamental social divide that reparations is to ameliorate as *racial* rather than economic. Dalby argues that "the ruling class" has always used racism as a way of dividing workers along racial lines, to their disadvantage and to the benefit of that ruling class. Hence, analyses that stress the advantages to all whites that have accrued from slavery and racism miss the mark: "The legacy of slavery and institutionalized racism has meant lower unionization rates, and lower wages for Black *and* white workers . . . The potential combination of the struggle against racism with class consciousness was a constant danger." The correct answer to the reparations demand, therefore, is to "make the rich capitalists who benefited from slavery pay." Yet the ruling class shrinks from countenancing this demand, in this account, because its implications are too profound: "This is more than just resistance to paying out large sums of money . . . [If blacks receive reparations, w]ho will we have to pay next, the Bushes and Rockefellers of this country might ask? American Indians demanding land and the billions stolen from them? The entire working class who have been systematically robbed for profit?"[57]

The problem with this analysis is that it transforms "the working class" into a quasi-racial entity that persists relatively unchanged across generations. Nonetheless, the argument points toward a transformation of the idea of reparations from a race-based to a class-based demand. While perhaps having better prospects politically, one wonders whether the term *reparations* is useful in achieving what would amount simply to a~~policy of~~ wealth redistribution, whether intended to fix *past* injustices or current and future ones. The *International Socialist Review*'s attention to the reparations demand nonetheless suggested the extent to which the idea of reparations had taken hold in left-wing circles. The magazine's treatment also made clear, however, that this was an awkward demand from the point of view of traditional left-wing, class-based universalism.

Adolph Reed's sharp critique of the campaign for reparations for blacks raised the unavoidable question of the political mobilization behind, and hence the practical feasibility of, reparations for blacks. In recent years, two main groups have been active in the reparations cause. First is the high-profile Reparations Coordinating Committee (RCC), which was initially co-chaired by Harvard Law School professor Charles Ogletree and by Randall Robinson. The RCC was first formed in August 2000. The other group pushing the reparations idea—N'COBRA, the acronym of the aforementioned National Coalition of Blacks for Reparations in America—is less well known, though it has been in existence since 1987. The differences between the two groups are striking. The RCC includes some of the most visible and successful black intellectuals and professionals in the United States today. The involvement of such persons in the issue appears to reflect a disillusionment about the prospects for racial equality that is fueled by their own evident success in American life. Though this is by no means to impugn the integrity of their commitment to the issue, that commitment has something of the quality of a "survivor's guilt."[58] By contrast, those associated with N'COBRA are substantially less well-known and much more likely to have the African-sounding names typical of black nationalists in the United States. The two groups seem a somewhat unlikely match.

Neither the RCC nor N'COBRA issued a ringing endorsement of the March 2002 suit filed by Deadria Farmer-Paellmann, which from their perspective seems to have been something of a maverick enterprise. Indeed, in an apparent effort to regain the upper hand for their own approach to reparations claims-making, the RCC's Ogletree observed disapprovingly on the Op-Ed page of the *New York Times* later the same month that the suit "is limited to FleetBoston, Aetna, CSX, and other to-be-named companies." In contrast, "the broader reparations movement seeks to explore the historical role that other private institutions and government played during slavery and the era of legal racial discrimination that followed. The goal of these historical investigations is to bring American society to a new reckoning with how our past affects the current conditions of African-

Americans and to make America a better place by helping the truly dis-advantaged."[59] In other words, the Farmer-Paellmann suit was confined to seeking mere monetary compensation rather than aiming to stimulate a public debate about slavery, segregation, and their consequences, as the Reparations Coordinating Committee envisioned.

For its part, about three weeks after the filing, on April 13, 2002, the N'COBRA National Board issued a "Membership Advisory" indicating that while it "applauded" Ms. Farmer-Paellmann's efforts, it had declined her invitation to act as co-lead counsel because it was not informed of the pending lawsuit until twelve days before it was filed and the board did "not want to participate in a litigation strategy that has been developed and implemented . . . without the input of its legal team." More particularly, "it appears that the strategy developed may include not filing actions against the United States government," in contrast to N'COBRA's stress on "the central role that the government played in the enslavement of Africans and [that it] continues to play in maintaining the vestiges of slavery."[60] In short, the two principal organizations spearheading the recent drive for repara-tions for black Americans were inclined to keep their distance from the Farmer-Paellmann lawsuit mainly because it was limited to suing private enterprises rather than the federal government. Their criticisms of Farmer-Paellmann for targeting only private companies echoed Charles Willie's ear-lier critique of the Black Manifesto for directing its attack at the churches rather than what they regarded as the proper addressee, the government.

In addition to their stated objections, the RCC and N'COBRA may also have been reluctant to go along with Farmer-Paellmann's suit because of the involvement of controversial reparations attorney Edward Fagan. The newly prominent lawyer earned considerable notoriety as counsel in some of the legal actions that brought in more than a billion dollars in reparations for Holocaust survivors in the late 1990s—as well as perhaps millions in legal fees for himself. Fagan's controversial involvement in the Holocaust-related actions garnered him a scathing front-page feature in the *New York Times* examining his often-questionable tactics and practices.[61] Yet Fagan was only getting started when he helped compel the Swiss to pay victims of the Holocaust for their suffering. Having moved on to help put together the Farmer-Paellmann suit in late March 2002, he was also the lead lawyer in a $50 billion class-action suit against Citigroup, UBS, and Credit Suisse filed two months later on behalf of victims of South African apartheid.[62] From the point of view of reparations activists, his participation in the

Farmer-Paellmann suit might have been seen as likely to complicate the perception of reparations as a political rather than a merely legal issue.

In all events, Fagan beat N'COBRA and the RCC off the mark, and thus preempted—at least to some degree—whatever strategy they may have had in mind. The fundamental problem here may not have been so much Fagan's possible huckstering as the difficulty of pursuing a legally oriented strategy for obtaining reparations in the absence of a broader grassroots movement supporting that demand. Until this time, the RCC and N'COBRA appear to have had at least formally an arms-length relationship, although Adjoa Aiyetoro, N'COBRA's chief legal consultant, was present as a participant at the TransAfrica Forum meeting on reparations in January 2000 and she and Charles Ogletree have long known one another personally.[63] Soon after the Farmer-Paellmann lawsuit was launched, however, N'COBRA and the Reparations Coordinating Committee issued a joint statement agreeing to work together more closely. The statement bespeaks the RCC's recognition of the fact that it is an undertaking of the contemporary equivalent of W. E. B. Du Bois's "talented tenth," and an attempt to overcome the relative isolation of that group from the remainder of the black population. The planned cooperation between the two groups, according to the statement issued by N'COBRA, "links the RCC with the constituency of African Descendants that are both [N'COBRA's] clients and the beneficiaries of our work . . . The breadth of the N'COBRA network assures the important linkage of the RCC to the broad-based grassroots movement for reparations."[64] The two groups apparently believed that they had to work together more closely if they wished to achieve their common goals.

Despite the rapprochement between the two organizations and the statement's invocation of a "broad-based grassroots movement," the evidence for the existence of such a movement is weak. For example, March 21, 2002 was declared "Reparations Awareness Day" in the city of New York, but even a sympathetic observer from *The Village Voice* reported that an event in Brooklyn celebrating the occasion produced only a scene of "Ivy Leaguers and comfortable activists talking to each other" that was "replayed at reparations forums around the city."[65] Similarly, a "Citywide Millions for Reparations Mobilization Rally" scheduled to take place at the Harriet Tubman School in Harlem in May 2002 produced little discernible echo.[66] The Harlem event was intended to drum up support for the "Millions for Reparations National Rally" scheduled for Saturday, August 17, 2002 in Washington, D.C. Turnout for the rally was relatively meager—perhaps a few thousand—although RCC co-chair Charles Ogletree agreed with the *New York Times* account that it was a very "energetic" group.[67]

Oddly, the Millions for Reparations Rally was not organized by either the RCC or N'COBRA, but by a number of black nationalist groups including the National Black United Front, the New Black Panther Party,[68] and the United Negro Improvement Association, the group originally founded by the early twentieth-century Caribbean-born "back-to-Africa" leader Marcus Garvey. In addition to calling attention to the demand for reparations, the August rally was also supposed to honor Garvey on the 115th anniversary of his birth.[69] The Garveyite and Afrocentric infrastructure underlying the march bears witness to political scientist Michael Dawson's recent finding that, as a result of the relative weakness of other currents in contemporary black politics, "black nationalism is enjoying more grassroots success than it has had in three-quarters of a century"—that is, since Garvey was at the height of his influence.[70]

Yet Dawson's claim that "the language of reparations" is part of the "common understanding" of black politics is doubtful—or at least it doesn't tell us much about blacks' degree of commitment to achieving reparations.[71] Examining the extent of support for reparations among black youth, one analyst argued that the urban black young of the hip-hop generation are almost entirely unaware of the reparations lawsuits and their aims. A figure familiar to hip-hoppers, the impresario and founder of Def Jam records, Russell Simmons, pledged to promote knowledge of the reparations cause among his customers, and to support research and action on the matter. Simmons also bankrolled the Hip Hop Summit Action Network, whose president, former NAACP president Benjamin (Chavis) Muhammed, had committed himself to getting out the reparations message to blacks. In a bid to take the campaign to the streets, Simmons developed plans for a publicity campaign based on the theme of "Forty Acres and a Bentley"— because, he said, the luxury car "has become the highest American aspiration for this generation, unfortunately." Whatever its appeal to the hip-hop generation, this choice of theme may not be well-calculated to inspire enthusiasm about the idea of reparations among the non-black segments of the population, who will be crucial in determining the eventual political outcome of the quest for reparations. The bottom line, according to the *Voice* writer, is that if the reparations movement is going to get anywhere, "the lawyers and academics will have to roll up their sleeves, kick off their expensive shoes, and get their feet dirty walking the streets, looking for a way to bridge the divide" between "the old civil rights guard" and the "reigning hip-hop generation."[72]

If history is any guide, in order for the campaign to have any prospect of becoming a mass movement, reparations activists will need to gain the support of mainstream civil rights organizations and the black churches. Yet an examination of the Web site of the NAACP found no discussion of the issue, much less any stated position on the matter.[73] Notably, however, the NAACP Web site posts the results of several polls concerning the reparations issue. A poll created on July 23, 2001 asks, "Will reparations help America address a long delayed moral obligation?" Thirty-four percent of the respondents said that it would, but 56 percent said that it would not. Another poll, created in March 2002, indicates that 71 percent of the respondents oppose a governmental inquiry into possible reparations for slavery. Finally, in a poll created in early April 2004, soon after a judge dismissed a number of lawsuits against businesses that had allegedly profited from slavery, the NAACP asked whether respondents "agree or disagree with lawsuits for reparations against companies that insured slave ships?" Fewer than one-third agreed, while 61.5 percent disagreed with such actions. It is unclear how the parameters of these polls were drawn, but the respondents were presumably NAACP members; in all events, the NAACP would appear at least to want these negative findings to be known.[74]

Given the apparent dearth of grassroots mobilization behind the reparations idea, perhaps the most striking feature of the campaign so far has been the relative absence from its ranks of the black churches. The pulpits have historically been the most reliable channel between elite black opinion and mass grassroots activism. One may reasonably regard with skepticism the hope that leaders of the hip-hop movement will substitute for the churches and play a substantial role in generating support for reparations, especially if Bentleys are the stated aspiration.[75]

Presumably those who are promoting the campaign for reparations envision the legal route as a catalyst that will generate enthusiasm for the reparations idea among both blacks themselves and the public at large. In order to assess this strategy, one should remember that the civil rights movement did not emerge full-blown with sit-ins, boycotts, and marches on Washington; it took time for the movement to gather steam. It began in the unpromising, famously (though misleadingly) conformist 1950s, but ultimately led to a "second Reconstruction."[76] One of the sparks that eventually lit the fuse in the dark days of the 1950s was the decision in *Brown v. Board of Education*, which declared an end to the era of legalized segregation. In most accounts of the rise of the civil rights movement, the *Brown* decision is identified as a watershed episode. Gerald Rosenberg has disputed the widespread assumption that *Brown* was a key moment heralding the possibility of wider changes, however, arguing that political developments outside the courtroom were more decisive in achieving equal rights. Yet he relies on a positivistic methodology that assumes that one must find copious references to *Brown* in, say, the speeches of Martin Luther King in order to demonstrate its significance for the civil rights movement. In fact, *Brown* had an immediate and welcome impact on many participants in the struggle for civil rights, and they saw the ruling as a beacon of wider changes.[77] Rosenberg is correct, however, to insist that court rulings in themselves do little to change matters "on the ground"; that requires political mobilization and enforcement of the law.[78]

One of the more striking conclusions of Michael Dawson's study *Black Visions* concerns the extent to which black political discussion and debate take place in terms that lead it to be extensively overlooked by the mainstream media. An important result is that political analysts tend to underestimate the significance of nationalist perspectives among blacks. Dawson shows that nationalism has been resurgent in recent years largely because of the widespread disillusionment—among even the country's most successful blacks—regarding the prospects for progress toward racial equality in the United States. The idea of reparations for blacks has bubbled along in the black nationalist underground for some years and has surfaced with some force since the late 1990s both because of the larger context of successful reparations claims by other groups and because of the high profile of some of the campaign's leading advocates.[79] Despite attracting the rhetorical support of many blacks, it has continued to be largely a marginal preoccupation spearheaded by a relatively small though often highly visible group. There is no sign that the wider society has grown appreciably more sympathetic to the idea of reparations for blacks in the United States since the latest round of reparations activism began.

Conclusion

Against this background, what is achieved by pursuing the seemingly unlikely goal of gaining reparations for the injustices suffered by blacks in American history, real as they have been? Employing the legalistic language of reparations may offer some advantages, but it entails substantial disadvantages as well. Supporters of reparations for blacks often point to the precedent set by the reparations paid to Jews for their Holocaust-related suffering, as well as to persons of Japanese descent for their unjust internment during World War II. These cases do indeed raise questions about why blacks might not similarly demand compensation for the wrongs to which they have been subjected and for their uncompensated contributions to the wealth of the contemporary United States. Yet there is something to the argument that payments to Holocaust survivors and interned Japanese-Americans are a different matter than compensation to those who are ("merely") the descendants of slaves rather than themselves the victims of atrocities. It is for this reason that the lawsuits in the Tulsa Race Riot case seemed more promising than a more general attempt to rectify inequalities of wealth through the mechanism of reparations. As we have already noted, however, the lawsuit seeking reparations in that case was dismissed on statute of limitations grounds.[80] If the campaign for reparations for blacks is to be successful, in all events, the focus has to be shifted from *perpetrators* to *beneficiaries*. This presents very difficult obstacles that arise from the fact that the people for whom the campaign is being undertaken—the most disadvantaged blacks in American society—are not necessarily the victims of actionable legal offenses, as were Japanese-Americans.

To the extent that Americans have come to associate the term *reparations* with monetary payments to individuals, such a goal would seem likely to be a nonstarter politically, as a number of commentators on this issue— black and white—have suggested. Although many reparations activists seek such measures as college scholarship funds, small business loans, and educational programs designed to call greater attention to the history of racial oppression in America, for the uninitiated use of the term *reparations* tends to conjure up images of monetary payouts that would have to be rather large to make any significant impact on individual blacks. In addition, the idea of individual payments raises eyebrows among those potentially responsible for the resulting tax burden. Some of the estimates of what would be owed for back wages, lost opportunities, and the like are, not surprisingly, astronomical sums.[81] The prospect of individual payments to black Americans, in the manner of the funds recently developed by the German government to compensate those exploited as slave labor under the Nazis therefore seems dim.

But individual payments are probably not the real objective of most supporters of reparations for black Americans. In response to some of these objections, Charles Ogletree has argued that "the billions, or perhaps trillions, of dollars that come from a successful reparations lawsuit not be distributed in the form of a check to every African-American," but that "all of the money be placed in a trust fund, administered perhaps through the churches or other reputable organizations in the community, and made available to the 'bottom stuck,' those African-American families that have not been able to realize the American Dream fully . . . It is a paternalistic approach, of course, but one that is entirely necessary to overcoming the problems we face."[82] Yet if this is the objective, use of the term *reparations* in connection with the pursuit of these policy objectives may well be counterproductive, suggesting as it does the notion of individual payments. For this is simply a policy of redistribution of wealth to the black poor, which in any case is not an objective with strong prospects in contemporary American politics. The notion that the funds should be distributed by "reputable organizations in the community" is sure to provoke controversy, as Ogletree is well aware. More significantly, the notion that the money will become available through a single successful reparations lawsuit seems far-fetched. This is especially true in view of the fact that the Tulsa reparations suit—on which Ogletree stakes so much importance and which he claimed "avoids the modern critique of reparations lawsuits" (namely, that they must involve living victims)—was dismissed after he wrote his memoir.[83]

In the end, the use of legal stratagems such as lawsuits for reparations to achieve the goals of racial equality in the United States must be understood above all in tactical terms. Does the pursuit of reparations contribute to a better understanding of the ways in which slavery and segregation have created a society that frequently mistreats and denigrates blacks and denies them their full share in American life? Does it contribute to a more complete recognition of the role of blacks in creating the prosperity enjoyed by Americans? Does it contribute to improving the lives and opportunities of the most disadvantaged black Americans?

The legal path is appealing because the political context is so frustrating. "Court is the one place we can achieve what we can't achieve in the popular vote," Ogletree has said.[84] Yet this approach leaves the movement open to interlopers less interested in their political aims and for whom the courtroom is the only venue in which they seek victory. Similarly, the pursuit of money—as opposed to the civil rights movement's search for equal legal treatment—raises hackles because it appears to invoke a notion of economic equality to which the United States has never had any commitment, constitutional or otherwise. Even were the issue not so difficult, the march through the courts appears likely to be a long one. Commenting on the prospects of success of reparations legal actions, NAACP Legal Defense Fund litigator Ted Shaw noted that these efforts were taking place "in a context in which the Supreme Court is as conservative as any we have seen in our lifetime," and "they will be hostile to anything we could bring."[85]

The juridification of politics is not necessarily auspicious when the goal is broad economic redistribution and the legal and political climate is so unpromising. Political scientist and long-time analyst of American racial politics Jennifer Hochschild expressed the matter succinctly when she argued that "using the court system to debate a deeply political and moral issue distorts the case for reparations by framing it in 'legalese' . . . There are . . . deep costs to demanding monetary recompense for what was national policy for over three centuries—especially if there is no real chance of seeing the cash."[86] Carol Swain is almost certainly correct in her claim that "talk about reparations at the present time is ill-advised and can be positively harmful in terms of improving race relations and garnering support for policies to help the truly distressed. Current reparations talk inflames the white electorate, undermines the bridge-building process across racial lines, fuels white nationalist sentiments, and is insufficiently targeted in its aims to help those members of minority groups who are most in need."[87]

The campaign for reparations for blacks has shown few signs of growing into a movement because there seems little prospect that the U.S. government is going to dispense largesse to a group defined by its race. In order to mount a serious challenge to the widening disparities of wealth and power in the contemporary period, it will be necessary to build an interracial movement to challenge contemporary inequalities that appeals to broad segments of the population.[88]

This was precisely the approach adopted by those supporting the University of Michigan's efforts to defend the use of affirmative action in its admissions policies. Faced with a major court challenge, supporters of the policy rallied their forces, including representatives of corporate business, the military, academia, Jewish groups once opposed to "quotas," and others. These authorities warned that, without a diverse student body and, subsequently, a diverse corps of well-educated persons, the United States would eventually suffer damage to its legitimacy and well-being. Their arguments emphasized efficiency and effectiveness, the possibilities and promise of the future rather than the wrongs of the past.[89] In considerable measure, this view appears to have been crucial in gaining the (limited) support of the Court's swing vote in the Michigan law school case, that of Justice Sandra Day O'Connor. The result was that affirmative action seems to have been preserved, in a somewhat opaque form, for a generation.[90]

In the end, although racial inequality in the United States cannot be understood without some reference to the historical legacy of slavery, solutions will have to be couched in forward-looking terms that a politician can articulate, not in legal terms that stress the past violations of slavery and Jim Crow. These arguments must be able to address satisfactorily the gains—in many respects remarkable—that blacks have made in the last four decades. Reparations is too blunt a tool for the problem at hand. Projects such as a Museum of African-American History and Culture on the mall in Washington also seem to be a promising means of recognizing the role of blacks in American life and the almost biblical nature of their sojourn in the United States. At the same time, of course, it will do little to transform the conditions of the poorest blacks. In the terms outlined in Chapter 2, the museum will address the cultural aspects of the historic wrongs that have been done to blacks, but not the economic wrongs. Ameliorating the economic wrongs will require a broader-based political movement devoted to greater economic equality for all Americans. There are indications that elements of the socialist left have begun to adopt the banner of reparations and to make it part of a broader egalitarian agenda, but that development remains in its infancy. Its prospects for incorporation into a mass, cross-class movement remain unclear at best.[91]

Meanwhile, the forms of reparations claims-making that have been championed by some American blacks have also had a powerful impact on Southern Africa, where other kinds of historical injustices have nonetheless been assimilated to the Holocaust and to the experience of slavery. It is to those claims that we now turn.

CHAPTER 5

Post-Colonial Reparations: Reparations Politics in Post-Apartheid Namibia and South Africa

Until World War II, as we have noted previously, the term *reparations* was used mainly in connection with the damages owed to victors in war; these were state-to-state transactions that sought to make amends for the ravages of war. Yet in its literature, the South African Reparations Movement (SARM), which came into being around the turn of the millennium, defines reparations as "a term that refers to what is owed by the wrongdoer to the oppressed and dispossessed."[1] For SARM and other movements like it, *reparations* is not about punishing former wartime enemies in any traditional sense, but rather about coming to terms with and making amends for the past misdeeds of states and private enterprises vis-à-vis the groups and individuals (or their descendants) that were once victimized. In contrast to earlier progressive views of the relationship between history and emancipation, SARM and various other reparations-seeking groups suggest that coming to terms with the wrongs of the past has become the main route to a brighter future.

This chapter explores the spread and development of reparations politics in Southern Africa, specifically Namibia and South Africa. It seeks to demonstrate that reparations politics in the region exemplify the range of meanings of the term *reparations*—from commemorative reparations, which are closer to identity politics, to anti-systemic reparations, which are closer to commonality politics. As will be seen, American (or American-trained) lawyers, American courts, and American understandings of the relationship between law and politics play a central role in reparations politics in Southern Africa (and, by extension, elsewhere). Finally, the chapter will show that reparations politics in Southern Africa is part of a larger global trend toward the juridification of politics.

Reparations Politics in Namibia

In Namibia, the former German South-West Africa, representatives of the Herero people have for some time pursued a campaign for reparations from German entities in compensation for a series of pre–World War I atrocities that sharply reduced the group's numbers between 1904 and 1907. The atrocities in question followed a period of tensions arising from settler colonial expansion into Herero lands and rumors of a revolt by the Herero against German colonial overlordship. The result was a genocidal campaign by the Germans to eradicate Herero resistance to European rule in the north of the territory, along with a more or less simultaneous war against the Nama in the south. In August 1904, after their defeat in the battle of the Waterberg, in the northeast, the Herero fled by the thousands into what they knew as the Omaheke *sandveld* (the Kalahari Desert). The Germans cut them off from waterholes in the west, south, and northeast, forcing them into inhospitable parts of the Omaheke.[2] Those who did not reach Bechuanaland (present-day Botswana) either succumbed to the desert or were picked up by German patrols and put in concentration camps. In 1904, camps had been set up in the capital, Windhoek, in Okahandja to the north, and in the coastal town of Swakopmund, where conditions were often fatal.[3] As a result of the Germans' persecution, the Herero population declined markedly during the next two years or so. Although estimates of the pre-1904 Herero population vary, they range from an estimated 50,000 to 120,000, falling to around 15,000 as a result of the German assault—a devastating outcome by any standard.[4]

The Herero demands that the Germans make good on this past are complex, dating back to events that took place almost a century ago.[5] The claims against Germany and German companies are based, somewhat ambiguously, on charges of both genocide and dispossession. According to Herero Paramount Chief Kuaima Riruako, the Germans' actions violated the 1899 Hague Convention on the Laws and Customs of War by Land. Although the notion of genocide did not come into existence until World War II, that term—along with the notion of a Herero Holocaust—appears often in the group's rhetoric as a characterization of the Germans' scorched-earth policy against the Herero. Beyond the killings and persecution resulting frequently in death, the Hereros were, Chief Riruako said, widely reduced to the condition of "slaves" and to performing forced labor.[6] Indeed, according to the historian Jan-Bart Gewald, "Between 1905 and 1908 the majority of the Herero survivors were incarcerated in concentration camps and allocated as forced labourers to civilian, administrative and military enterprises alike. The majority of the camp inhabitants were women." The Germans sought to transform the Herero men, as well as those of the Nama people, "into a single amorphous black working class."[7]

In addition to the killings and coercive labor arrangements, the Herero were extensively dispossessed of cattle and land. Indeed, "Germany terminated by conquest all Herero land rights in German South-West Africa, leaving the [Herero] nation with no land at all" and laying the foundation of white control of farmland in the north-central and northeastern part of Namibia.[8] The advantages accruing from this unjust transfer persist to the present day, as Europeans—especially Germans and Afrikaners—and their descendants retain the dominant economic position in the country, despite the advent of majority rule in the political sphere.[9] In sum, no one disputes that indefensible wrongs were done to the Herero. But the question of compensation is a complex one because the wrongs were committed so long ago; because of the uncertain legal basis of the claims; and because it is not entirely clear that other groups—especially the Nama—might not make similar claims regarding ethnically motivated killing and dispossession if they were inclined or able to do so.

The demands raised by the Herero claimants have a particular resonance, however, because the massacre of the Hereros has been seen as a parallel to, or indeed as the dress rehearsal for, the Nazi Holocaust.[10] According to Chief Riruako, "What Hitler did to the Jewish people was something that originated in German colonization of Namibia. The Holocaust started with us here; Hitler was a continuation of what happened here." The putative parallel derives in part from the fact that the Hereros were massacred and driven into the wilderness on the basis of a still-extant extermination order issued by German Lieutenant General Lothar von Trotha, acting under the authority of Kaiser Wilhelm himself.[11] The fruit of von Trotha's order was an extended spree of killing and expulsion. Unlike in the case of the Jews, however, the Herero took up arms against invaders, though they were substantially outgunned and soon overwhelmed. The Herero suffered the typical fate of those colonized by Europeans in the course of what is known, rather euphemistically, as "European expansion."[12] In contrast, the Jews were very much a part of the society over which the Nazis assumed control and were butchered simply for what they *were* rather than for any threat they might have posed to German rule. Moreover, in the case of the Jews, no extermination order has ever been found, even if there is no doubt that the genocide against them was sanctioned at the highest levels.[13]

The framing of the Herero Holocaust as a prelude to the now-canonical one is further reinforced by later developments. Before World War I, Dr. Eugen Fischer, an ethnologist who later became director of the Kaiser Wilhelm Institute of Anthropology in Berlin, serving from 1927 to 1942, had conducted studies of Namibia's "Rehoboth Bastards"—a population from the area south of Windhoek that was descended of unions between Boer (Afrikaner) settlers and native blacks—on the basis of which he concluded that the offspring of racial intermixing were always intellectually and socially inferior to the "superior race." Hitler read these studies while incarcerated in Landsberg Prison, where he wrote *Mein Kampf*, and Fischer's work eventually became the basis for Nazi policies of forced sterilization.[14] Against this background, it is difficult to ignore Hannah Arendt's insight in the early post–1945 period that the racialist depredations of the era of European imperialism constituted the training ground for totalitarian violence, especially that of the Nazis.[15] This view supports the notion that the atrocities against the Herero were the dress rehearsal for the assault on the Jews.

Despite the demonstrable horrors to which the Herero were subjected,[16] the German government has declined to apologize or pay reparations. Perhaps most intransigently, when Chancellor Helmut Kohl visited in 1995, he refused to meet with representatives of the Herero at all. During a 1998 trip to Namibia, then-President of the Federal Republic Roman Herzog eschewed any apology, arguing according to one newspaper account that "international laws requiring reparations were not in place" during the period in question. Still, he "promised to take the Herero petition" back to the German capital for further consideration.[17]

Nothing seems to have happened; the German government remained unbending about the Hereros' claims. On a state visit to the country in October 2003, Foreign Minister Joschka Fischer, a leading representative of perhaps the most liberal party in Germany (the Greens), refused to make a formal apology for the massacre of the Hereros. Fischer chose his words in Windhoek meticulously, averring that he would not "undertake any statement that would be relevant to compensation." The official position of the German government is that the legacy of colonialism cannot be rectified with compensation.[18] This position has been reaffirmed in subsequent statements by German diplomats in the region. Early in 2004, Ambassador to Namibia Wolfgang Massing expressed his "regret" for the actions of the Germans during the pre–World War I era, "the closest a German government representative has come to an apology." At the same time, the ambassador insisted that "development aid was for all Namibian citizens and not one specific ethnic group." Still, he did suggest that the German government would contribute to the commemoration of the 1904 massacres— the term *genocide* has not been used—and to "some specific projects which will help to preserve your [Herero] traditions and culture."[19] Later, in July 2004, the German ambassador in Botswana expressed his government's regret for the killings of Hereros in the early twentieth century but insisted that German development aid was intended to benefit all Namibians rather than one specific group.[20]

In contrast to the protestations of the German government that their "aid" is for all Namibians, the representatives of the Herero insist that racism accounts for the German refusal to pay reparations. According to Professor Mburumba Kerina, a leading Herero figure and aide to Chief Riruako, the difference between their claims and those of the Jews is that "the Jews are white; we are black."[21] To be sure, this misreads the dynamics of race in the minds of the Nazis, who aimed to purify the German national body of all kinds of *lebensunwerten Lebens* ("life unworthy of life"), including Jews, Gypsies (Sinti and Roma), the mentally ill, the handicapped, and homosexuals. The Nazis also likened the Jews to Indians (i.e., Native Americans), among other undesirables. But that is irrelevant to the point here, which is that the Herero leadership claims that it is being penalized twice over for its racial difference from the German conquerors and that this difference is the basis of the Germans' recalcitrance on the reparations question.

But there is yet another important source of opposition to the Hereros' claims—the Namibian government under Sam Nujoma, the long-time head of the ruling Southwest Africa People's Organization (SWAPO), which led the armed struggle for liberation from South African rule, and his successor, Hifikepunye Pohamba. From the perspective of Herero leaders Chief Riruako and Professor Kerina, the Namibian government is controlled by the Ovambo. Indeed, the Ovambo constitute the majority of both the overall Namibian population and of SWAPO itself, and opposition parties are said to be organized chiefly along ethnic lines as well.[22] As a result of this configuration, according to Mburumba Kerina, "Nujoma has sought to marginalize the Hereros. Everything now goes to the North."[23]

In this view, the SWAPO government refuses to back the Hereros' claims because it is reluctant to antagonize the Germans, who are the country's chief source of foreign aid. Indeed, since independence in 1990, the German government has contributed some 500 million Euros (approximately $575 million) to the economic and social reconstruction of the country, which has only 3 million inhabitants. In addition, SWAPO has been seen as resistant to explorations of the past in part because it has its own atrocities to reckon with, which are themselves the focus of reparations claims of a more immediate if less "systemic" kind. Indeed, the SWAPO government faces substantial questions about its actions during the liberation struggle. As a result, the issue of reparations for those detained by SWAPO during the struggle "has monopolized human rights discussion in post-Independent [sic] Namibia," not least because of a "lack of cohesion among victim groups" and "a dearth of organizations that advocate for victims other than SWAPO ex-detainees."[24] The matter of reparations for the pre–World War I period has received more attention in the West, however, in part because of a renewed interest in the question of the extent to which the Herero Holocaust comprised a run-up to the Jewish Holocaust.

Clearly, as Foreign Minister Joschka Fischer expressed it, the German government feels a particular "responsibility for the colonial history."[25] Yet as the foregoing references to development aid suggest, the Germans prefer not to portray these payments as resulting from pressure for reparations. The foreign assistance might nonetheless be viewed as reparations if either government wanted to call it so; the issue is in part purely terminological. Foreign assistance to the Namibian government—even if represented as reparations—goes (at least nominally) to the whole country, whereas reparations specifically to the Herero would presumably benefit them (assuming they can be identified) more than the rest of the population. For whatever reasons, the German government prefers to portray its economic transfers to Namibia as development aid, not as reparations, and to insist that the payments go to the entire society, rather than to any one group.

Because the Nama might well mount similar claims regarding German mistreatment, the Hereros' claims apparently contain an element of identity politics, Namibian-style. Chief Riruako and Professor Kerina were ambiguous when asked who would benefit from reparations to the Herero (the

Herero only or the whole country?), but the chief did observe that "trib-alism is the death of Africa."[26] Sidney Harring has argued that "the Herero nation is asking for reparations from roughly the same position as the State of Israel." Although he acknowledges that "a 'tribe' is not a 'state' . . . nothing in the international law of reparations requires that aggrieved people be represented by a state."[27] Harring is correct, of course; many nonstate groups have succeeded in obtaining reparations from *their own* governments, and this is a major part of what makes the contemporary usage of the term *reparations* so novel. But the difficulties the Herero have faced vis-à-vis the German government indicate that it is a more compli-cated matter for a nonstate entity to bring reparations claims against a for-eign government that is providing extensive financial assistance with a clear statement of "responsibility" for historical wrongdoing in the whole country. When the Germans provided reparations to the nascent state of Israel in the early 1950s, the link between its assistance and the wrongdoing in question was clear, unambiguous, and very recent.[28] These links are not so obvious in the Herero case.

In pursuing their claims, the Herero have been bolstered by the success of comparable efforts elsewhere. Despite the differences from the Israeli case, in their arguments for reparations the Herero frequently cite the prec-edent set by postwar German reparations to Jewish entities. In 1998, Mbu-rumba Kerina pointed to another parallel case, though one that has not been especially successful in garnering reparations for its claimants. Upon hearing of the Japanese acknowledgment of crimes against some of those whom they sexually exploited during World War II, Professor Kerina—who like many Herero has a German grandparent—said, "I thought, hey, that's my grandmother—a comfort woman. And I thought, if the Japanese could pay for that, the Germans could [too]."[29] Yet the compensation for the comfort women and for the Japanese-descent persons incarcerated in North America during World War II have involved reparations to those persons who had actually suffered the wrongs in question. (In the U.S. case, as noted earlier, this formula was arrived at precisely as a way of forestalling claims from blacks for reparations for slavery.) It is not possible to make this claim with respect to the Hereros, whose historical distance from the injustices in question makes their case a more difficult and convoluted one.

The proponents of reparations for the Herero have sought to further their aims through the courts. They found a willing ally in Washington, D.C., attorney Philip Musolino, who regarded the Hereros' case as winnable because the claims were "relatively circumscribed, egregious, and provable" and because the existence of "an actual extermination order makes the case more prosecutable."[30] Following the precedent set by recent Holocaust-related cases, in 2001 Musolino sued Deutsche Bank and two firms that had been active in German South-West Africa at the time of the atrocities. The two companies were Woermann Line, now known as Deutsche Afrika Linien or SAFmarine, and Terex Corporation, also known as Orenstein & Koppel, the principal railroad construction concern in South-West Africa during the period in question. The suit sought $2 billion in relief for the plaintiffs—the Herero People's Reparations Corporation, the Herero Tribe, its Paramount Chief Kuaima Riruako, and dozens of individual Hereros.

According to the court filing, the defendants were selected based on the theory that, "in a brutal alliance with Imperial Germany," they had "relentlessly pursued the enslavement and genocidal destruction of the Herero Tribe . . . Foreshadowing with chilling precision the irredeemable horror of the European Holocaust only decades later, the defendants and Imperial Germany formed a German commercial enterprise which cold-bloodedly employed explicitly-sanctioned extermination, the destruction of tribal culture and social organization, concentration camps, forced labor, medical experimentation and the exploitation of women and children in order to advance their common financial interests."[31]

Given the difficulties the Herero had previously encountered in their efforts to extract compensation from the German government, it is perhaps not surprising that they initially chose to sue only corporate defendants. Reflecting on such actions more broadly, Joel Paul has asked, "Why has international law turned its gaze to multinational corporations at this time and in this way? . . . One simple answer to the question is that the companies may be the only tortfeasors [wrongdoers] still available to provide any compensation. The individual bad actors are often dead, missing, beyond jurisdictional reach of domestic courts, or unable to satisfy large damage claims. The immortality of the multinational corporate entity, its size, wealth and omnipresence in a variety of jurisdictions make it uniquely attractive as a defendant."[32] It turns out, however, that not all corporations are equally immortal. Subsequent to the initial filing, the plaintiffs dropped defendant Terex Corporation from the lawsuit in response to its claim that it had been under different management at the time of the wrongs in question. In Terex's stead, Musolino filed an additional $2 billion lawsuit against the German government.[33]

As in the case of the various efforts seeking reparations for slavery, some of which have been criticized for failing to highlight governmental responsibility for the injustice, suing private entities for monetary compensation may be regarded by some as a trivialization of the wrongdoing by states. In addition, corporate settlements may involve payments to "make this go away," without any acknowledgment of culpability or regret. Those Hereros who wish to have an apology from the German government are not likely to be satisfied only with money.

It is not entirely clear, however, whether an apology is an important element of the Hereros' demands, other than as a precursor to monetary payments. In commenting on the lawsuit filed against the German government in September 2001, Chief Riruako said, "The Germans paid for spilled Jewish blood. Compensate us, too. It's time to heal the wound"; there was no mention of an official apology or statement of regret.[34] In January 2004, Chief Riruako said similarly: "The wounds of the past must be healed. Our reparation claim must only be seen as an effort to regain our dignity and help us restore what was wrongfully taken away from us . . . I once again invite the German government to accept the genocide of my people and engage in a dialogue with the Herero to iron out issues of mutual interest."[35] Indeed, I cannot recall seeing a demand for an *apology*, as opposed to one for *compensation*, in any of the literature on the Herero claims that I have examined.

Yet not everyone involved in reparations politics is concerned about getting an apology. For example, as was noted earlier, John Tateishi, a chief architect of the Japanese-American redress campaign in the 1980s, originally was uninterested in an apology and wanted only financial compensation. "An apology," he said, "is just words."[36] As far as he was concerned, only money would demonstrate the government's seriousness in acknowledging its prior wrongdoing. Eventually, however, he was persuaded that this approach was misguided, and the interned Japanese-Americans ultimately got both an official apology and financial compensation.

But if German entities, including the government, are the target of the suits, why are the legal actions being filed in the United States? In view of official German recalcitrance regarding the claims for reparations, the Hereros might well feel that their prospects in German courts would not be good. In fact, according to one report, the Hereros filed their suit in the United States "because they believe they have a greater chance of success there."[37] But why should that be the case? In part, it is "the natural product of a legal culture that relies on private lawsuits both as a means to obtain compensation for injuries and also as a tool to address societal problems." In addition, various features of the American legal system make it an appealing venue for undertaking these kinds of actions—notably, there is no penalty for losing, punitive damages (on top of compensation for losses) are possible, and the like.[38] The crucial law here is the Alien Tort Claims Act, a late-eighteenth-century statute originally designed to facilitate claims for losses due to piracy that has been little used until fairly recently. Moreover, in the early 1980s case of *Filartiga v. Pena-Irala*, "U.S. courts recognised that aliens could sue for reparations for human rights abuses committed against them by individuals who were not citizens of the U.S."[39] Along with similar cases, the door has opened wider during the subsequent years to litigation of human rights and reparations claims in U.S. courts.

Even in the United States, however, the legal route has had its bumps. In June 2003, a District of Columbia court declared the Herero lawsuit beyond its jurisdiction. In response, the plaintiffs filed another suit, this time in a New York court.[40] The legal wrangling promises to drag on for some time. The difficulties facing the Herero legal actions raise the familiar question of "how far back should we go." Harring notes that the Herero were effectively barred from making claims while they lived under South African rule, and that post-apartheid South Africa permits claims for restitution of property as far back as the Native Land Act of 1913—a period roughly comparable to that in which the Hereros suffered the wrongs for which they seek compensation.[41] Moreover, the State of Brandenburg in Germany recently concluded a treaty with the Vatican under the terms of which Brandenburg would pay the Church more than a million Euros as "compensation for church property confiscated *during the time of the Reformation* as well as *at the beginning of the 19th century.*"[42] Such an agreement might seem to lift all statutes of limitations on how far back we can go.

This opening of vistas for reparations claims brings us to the complicated matter of reparations politics in contemporary South Africa, where claims range from those that are very recent to those dating from the very arrival of Europeans on South African soil.

Reparations Politics in Post-Apartheid South Africa

The post-apartheid context in South Africa has been the locus of a remarkable profusion of reparations politics. These campaigns have generally been of three types. One involves chiefly what I have called symbolic claims, and arises from the reparations mandate of the Truth and Reconciliation Commission (TRC) and the activism of the Khulumani Support Group. Next, there have been anti-systemic reparations claims arising from the anti-globalization activism of such groups as Jubilee South Africa, though these claims relate more or less exclusively to the apartheid-era past. Finally, a more radical version of anti-systemic reparations has involved challenging the dispossession of Africans from their lands during the entire history of European colonization since 1652. Proponents of reparations of this kind respond to the question "how far back should we go?" with the answer, "very far back indeed."

Yet even this list of reparations claims-makers does not exhaust the array of groups that have mobilized around reparations issues. Not to be ignored, Afrikaner groups have pressed the British queen to apologize for the use of concentration camps in the Boer (South African) War at the turn of the century.[43] If the poignancy of the Herero claims has been heightened by the notion that the events in pre–World War I Namibia were a dress rehearsal for the Jewish Holocaust, the demands for an apology from the British crown were ennobled by the assertion that the Boers had been the first to find themselves incarcerated in a concentration camp. The rancor of the Afrikaners under the post-apartheid regime is another story, however. In what follows, we will focus on those seeking reparations for apartheid specifically or for colonialism more generally, for these have constituted the most significant claims for reparations in post-apartheid South African society.

Before examining the different types of reparations claims being pursued in contemporary South Africa, it should be noted that the idea of reparations itself seems to have had some difficulty taking hold among South Africans and was to a considerable extent brought to the region from outside, especially by American (or at least American-trained) lawyers.[44] As of 1997, according to a valuable study of reparations politics in South Africa by Chris Colvin of the Centre for the Study of Violence and Reconciliation, the TRC regarded the number of victims identified by the commission as "embarrassingly low"; in response, the body began using the idea of reparations to get people to participate in the process of testifying before it.[45] In other words, reparations was at that time not so much a demand of the putative victims, but a carrot used by the TRC to encourage involvement in its activities.

That relative indifference to reparations claims on the part of victims would change dramatically over the coming years. A particularly significant role here in promoting the idea of reparations may be accorded to an activist lawyer named Art Serota, whose name came up in numerous interviews with reparations activists and others in the region. Serota has a long history of participation in causes related to racial justice in the United States and Southern Africa, and in 1996 he published a book arguing the need for reparations in the United States.[46] One hesitates to attribute the emergence of reparations politics largely to a single individual, but undeniably his tireless activism on the reparations issue has left a mark throughout Southern Africa and in the United States as well. Similarly, Jeremy Sarkin, a Harvard-trained South African lawyer and law professor at the University of the Western Cape who has also practiced in New York State, serves as counsel to the Herero.

One might also note the high level of cooperation and collaboration that has emerged between Southern African and U.S.-based activism in connection with the reparations-for-apartheid issue. This development has been a notable feature of the leadership at the Transafrica Forum in Washington, D.C. After trade unionist Bill Fletcher took over from founding president Randall Robinson (who retired to the Caribbean to write) early in the new millennium, the connections between reparations activists on the two continents appear to have grown more intense. For example, Fletcher is listed as one of the contact persons for information concerning the November 2002 lawsuit seeking reparations for apartheid-related profiteering (see below). One might argue that Du Bois's notion of the color line as a global rather than a national phenomenon is being rejuvenated in connection with campaigns to gain reparations for Africans and their descendants in the diaspora. Although the discourse of reparations may have played a significant role in bringing these groups together recently, this is not the first time that such a sensibility has developed among blacks in the United States and Africa. Many of those involved in the civil rights movement of the 1950s and 1960s also saw their activities as part of a worldwide effort to overcome racial injustice.[47]

Commemorative Reparations Claims-Making in South Africa

For many good reasons, the South African Truth and Reconciliation Commission has assumed an exalted status among those around the world

seeking means for coming to terms with the past. Even though it was neither the first nor necessarily the most successful of the truth commissions,
the TRC is now seen as a model for all cases of transitional justice.[48] This
venerable position is probably a function of two facts: first, that the body
was led by two churchmen, Archbishop Desmond Tutu and Alex Boraine,
who stamped the proceedings with a Christian sensibility of forgiveness and
reconciliation, and, second, that the commission sat in final judgment of a
system of racial domination that had become a bizarre anomaly by the time
it was finally brought down and hence deserving of worldwide attention
and opprobrium.

The TRC's now almost mythical status for giving perpetrators and victims
alike an opportunity to air their stories tends to distract us, however, from
the fact that it left behind a good deal of unfinished business.[49] The TRC
failed to have a bigger impact on post-apartheid South African life in part
because it did not—and perhaps, given the terms of its mandate, could
not—address the sharp economic inequities between black and white that
the apartheid state left behind. As Mahmood Mamdani has noted, the TRC
was concerned only with the relations between *perpetrators* and *victims,* not
those between *beneficiaries* and *disadvantaged.* It viewed the apartheid regime
purely as an *authoritarian state,* not as a *colonial state.*[50]

Yet the Committee on Reparations and Rehabilitation of the TRC was
charged with making recommendations regarding reparations for victims at
least of politically motivated crimes. Early in its existence, the Committee
administered an urgent reparations program to over 14,000 victims of
human rights violations. Then, in its Interim Final Report in 1998, the TRC
proposed a plan for reparations that had been developed by the Committee
on Reparations and Rehabilitation. The government did little to implement
these recommendations, however, stimulating a growing sense of dissatisfaction among potential recipients. Whereas the reparations issue was initially a less prominent feature of the overall process of coming to terms
with the past, as noted earlier, in the meantime "the issue of individual
financial reparations has taken centre stage . . . [Financial r]eparations have
come to signify not simply one contentious part of a broader, long-term
reparations process and program—rather it has come to function as the key
indicator of government's political, legal and moral commitment to justice
for victims."[51]

As a consequence of the growing saliency of reparations and the perception that it has been stalling on the issue, the South African government,

headed by the African National Congress (ANC), has been "engaged in an increasingly acrimonious conflict with representatives of victims who claim the government has dragged its feet, failing to design and implement a final reparations policy."[52] As of early 2003, a number of TRC-registered victims had received "Urgent Interim Reparations" in relatively small amounts in the range of R2000–5000 ($300–750) each.[53] But this settlement did not begin to address the expectations of large numbers of victims. The growing dissatisfaction with the government's implementation of the reparations scheme recommended by the TRC led to heightened mobilization by victim groups who sharply criticized government policy and practice. In response, government officials adopted the position that "people didn't get involved in the struggle for the money."[54] This may well be true, but as Reverend Michael Lapsley, director of the Institute for the Healing of Memories, pointed out, it appears like stonewalling when coming from people who have benefited handsomely from the new order while others remain in need.[55]

In the view of one prominent observer, this acrimonious situation could have been avoided had the ANC government handled the matter with greater political skill. In an interview, Mary Burton, a member of the South African Truth and Reconciliation Commission, argued that "had the government said 'this is reparations' every time it opened a clinic, [it would have been] better off" because people would feel as though (more) reparations had been paid and that the government was responding to popular needs more effectively. Burton's comment recalls the point, already considered in the discussion of the Herero claim, that reparations is in part a terminological matter, and hence one of perception—reparations may be whatever transfer one chooses to call reparations. Nonetheless, Burton observed, "once the recommendations [of the TRC] were made, expectations were raised," and the cat was out of the bag, so to speak. Contrary to Mary Burton's position, however, one might argue that the ANC simply misjudged the significance of the reparations issue. This would not be entirely surprising, inasmuch as the demand was made relatively late in the game. In all events, in response to the perception of government intransigence on the reparations issue, various individuals and groups began to mobilize to pursue reparations claims, including through legal channels.[56]

Indeed, some engaged high-profile lawyers with Holocaust-related experience in order to do so. Soon enough, the seemingly omnipresent Ed Fagan—well known for his efforts in gaining $1.25 billion for Holocaust victims from Swiss banks and hence anathema to many in Switzerland—emerged as the lead lawyer in a $50 billion class-action suit against Citigroup, UBS, and Credit Suisse filed in Geneva in June 2002 on behalf of four victims of apartheid. Perhaps the best-known of the plaintiffs was Lulu Petersen, whose then thirteen-year-old brother Hector became a worldwide symbol of the barbarity of apartheid when he was photographed being carried off in the arms of a friend after being shot to death in the Soweto uprising of 1976.[57] The suit charged that the defendant companies had profited from loans made to the government during the apartheid era, propping it up despite the fact that the regime had been condemned by the United Nations and was under a U.N. embargo from 1985 to 1993. The lawyers filing the suit told the press that they hoped hundreds of thousands of South Africans would add their names to the action. The TRC arguably opened the door to actions of this sort when it wrote in its Interim Final Report that a "vast body of evidence points to a central role for business interests in the elaboration, adoption, implementation and modification of apartheid policies throughout its dismal history."[58] Whether the claims will hold up in court is another question, however.

For reasons already discussed in connection with the Herero case, the suit was filed in American courts. According to Fagan's co-counsel, Dumisa Ntsebeza, "We believe that there is a statute in the U.S. that can be used by any person to proceed against people that have been complicit in crimes against humanity."[59] Although Ntsebeza appears to have had in mind the Alien Tort Claims Act, he is referring more generally to the post-*Filartiga* environment of openness in the United States to human rights litigation for actions committed anywhere in the world.

Fagan has been prominently involved in both creating and exploiting that context. As noted earlier, the apartheid-related suit came two months after Fagan's participation in Deadria Farmer-Paellman's case seeking reparations for slavery in the United States. As in that action, however, the suit seeking damages for apartheid-related profiteering appears to fit an unfortunate pattern of suits in which Fagan is a participant. The debt relief activist organization Jubilee 2000 South Africa had been planning for some time to sue German and Swiss financial institutions for their support of and profits from apartheid.[60] In late November 2001, the *Forward* reported that Fagan and a prominent Washington, D.C., attorney also involved in Holocaust-related litigation, Michael Hausfeld, had been consulting with the group about its plans for legal action.[61] But in a story about the June 2002 lawsuits, Hausfeld indicated that, whatever cooperation may have existed previously, Fagan scooped him in the June 2002 suit. The piece noted that Hausfeld had been "working with a group of about 20 lawyers and academics to file a different suit on behalf of apartheid victims," which "will be filed . . . after it is thoroughly researched." Hausfeld is also said to have criticized Fagan's suit as "premature" and to have said that it "denigrated the entire issue by trying to hold a small number of companies responsible for the 'entirety of evil'."[62]

Hausfeld was by no means Fagan's only critic in reparations activist circles. Terry Collingsworth, the lead attorney in a suit against oil giant Unocal for its alleged use of slave labor in Burma/Myanmar, took a similar view. According to an account by *Southscan,* a publication specializing in South African affairs, Collingsworth told them that "Fagan's suing of virtually all companies that were doing business in South Africa during apartheid was a 'clear overreaching of the legal process.' It provided corporate opponents 'a poster child for their position that companies are being exposed to burdensome litigation under the ATCA [Alien Tort Claims Act]. A theory that simply investing in South Africa during apartheid is sufficient to have caused an injury to a group of victims is not even remotely likely to prevail,' said Collingsworth."[63] Hlengiwe Mkhize, chair of the Committee on Reparations and Rehabilitation of the Truth and Reconciliation Commission, said of the lawsuit that "legal battles make . . . a mockery" of the TRC's efforts to promote reconciliation and that it would "open doors to unlimited claims."[64] More claims were indeed just around the corner.

From Symbolic to Anti-Systemic Reparations Claims

In addition to the legal mobilization on the part of Fagan and his clients, the ANC government's foot-dragging on reparations issues stimulated a greater focus on reparations claims by other groups as well. The chief group in this regard is the Khulumani ("Speak Out!") Support Group, an organization established in 1995 to support victims in connection with the TRC process. Over time, however, Khulumani became increasingly involved in the reparations issue, pressing the government to adhere to the recommendations of the TRC's Interim Final Report. By April 2000, the group had organized a march on Parliament and a petition to the president urging the government to pay the outstanding claims. It has since organized other such actions to advance the claims of its constituency.[65]

Frustrated by the ANC government's lack of responsiveness, Khulumani also opted to use legal channels in its pursuit of reparations. According to one report, "One of the South African plaintiffs said she was going down this road because of what she called the government's disregard of the promises of reparations it had made to apartheid victims."[66] In pursuing reparations via lawsuits, the Khulumani Support Group joined forces with Jubilee South Africa, an organization that had first emerged in the late 1990s as part of the broader Jubilee 2000 movement for debt relief. The Jubilee movement, with its main headquarters in London, was based in part on the biblical notion of a moratorium on debt every fifty years. In addition, Jubilee activists argued that much Third World debt was "odious debt," contracted by the governments in question under terms so imbalanced—or by regimes so immoral—as to render illegitimate the debt currently facing the countries in question. Although the movement had its successes (not least as a result of the high-profile involvement in debt relief issues of Bono, the lead singer of Irish mega-rock band U2), it had a limitation built into its very name. Both for this reason and as a result of internal developments stemming at least in part from Art Serota's advocacy, the South African branch of the group eventually dropped the "2000" from its name and increasingly began to shift its focus toward a concern with reparations.[67] By November 2002, the group had joined forces with the Khulumani Support Group in the Apartheid Debt and Reparations Campaign.

It was this alliance that launched the lawsuit to which Washington lawyer Michael Hausfeld had referred in his earlier criticisms of Ed Fagan's tactics. On November 12, 2002, Hausfeld and other attorneys filed suit against twenty "foreign corporations and banks that aided and abetted the system of Apartheid." The suit was brought in the United States "because it is the only country in the world that allows for this type of litigation to be brought in its jurisdiction." Initiated on behalf of individual members of the Khulumani Support Group, the legal action took as its point of departure the aforementioned assertion in the TRC Interim Final Report that businesses had played a role, even if a subsidiary one, in sustaining and supporting the apartheid regime. According to a statement issued by Jubilee South Africa in conjunction with the court filing, "[These corporations] made massive profits while the suffering of the victims of apartheid intensified. The banks and businesses have consistently ignored our attempts to engage in discussion about their role in supporting broad social programmes for the reconstruction and development of affected communities and in compensating specific individuals for the damage that the corporations made possible." The lawyers filing the suit contended that while the TRC offered businesses as well as individuals an opportunity to come forward and request amnesty in exchange for their testimony about their complicity in the state's wrongdoing, none did so. "As a result, we believe that foreign corporations and banks have forfeited their rights to claim any entitlement under the spirit of the Promotion of National Unity & Reconciliation Act [the statute that created the TRC] and have opened themselves to litigation."[68]

In advance of filing the lawsuit, South African reparations activists had sought to make their case to a broader international audience and to stress the redistributive thrust of their actions. At a meeting of development NGOs from the European Union and Southern Africa in Copenhagen on November 3–5, 2002, the attendees held an extensive debate about the issue of apartheid debt and reparations, "to the dismay of at least some EU governments." The participants ultimately "passed a resolution supporting the class actions in principle . . . The resolution demands EU governments recognise that EU banks and corporations supported apartheid and cooperated with its regime. 'The peoples of Southern Africa . . . therefore have a right to debt cancellation and compensation payments', [the resolution] states." According to this report on the meeting, "the demand for debt relief and victim compensation is receiving ever larger resonance" around the world.[69]

Although the Khulumani/Jubilee South Africa suit follows the Fagan suit in suing businesses that profited from the apartheid system, the group was critical of Fagan's approach in his June 2002 lawsuit and activists from Khulumani distanced themselves publicly from his legal action. As in his slavery-related suit in the United States from early 2002, Fagan tended to focus on monetary rather than political claims and so antagonized those who view reparations politics as part of a broader politics of redistribution. According to George Dor, then general secretary of Jubilee South Africa, "For us, this [reparations claims-making] is just one way of maintaining momentum. For us, it's a social movement leading the legal cases, not the other way around. Individual reparations are legally most important, but politically they're least important. Monetary reparations are not irrelevant, but they're only a catalyst for broader social transformation. We in [Jubilee South Africa] have to be continually on our guard against people enriching themselves through reparations." From Dor's perspective, then, talk of individual reparations is purely a tactical matter, a way of mobilizing people for redistributive aims in the aftermath of the collapse of apartheid. After that epochal event, he argued, it was more difficult to keep people engaged in politics because the target of their dissatisfaction was no longer as apparent as it had been under National Party rule.[70] Dor's remarks, perhaps more clearly than any others, reflect the anti-systemic view of reparations politics. That is, reparations are not seen as an end in themselves, or as unconnected to broader efforts toward social transformation, or as benefiting only one particular group. Rather, they are perceived as a way of pursuing a politics of economic redistribution and equality in a period that is peculiarly preoccupied with coming to terms with the past.

Like the Namibian government, the South African government has kept its distance from these legal actions, and for the same reasons. It has expressed concern that the reparations suits will complicate the country's efforts to attract investment capital from abroad.[71] Yet whether these suits will lead potential investors to shun South Africa—by far the most important economic power in Africa and thus a crucial market for international capital—is a matter of dispute. Nobel Prize–winning economist Joseph Stiglitz has insisted that reparations would not negatively affect the investment climate in South Africa, as government officials have claimed.[72] In any case, under pressure to do something about the reparations issue, President Thabo Mbeki made a "one-off" offer of R30,000 (approximately $4,700) to apartheid victims coincident with the submission of the TRC's Final Report in April 2003. In addition, the government accepted "the TRC's recommendations for the 'rehabilitation of communities' and systematic programmes to 'project the symbolism and the ideal of freedom.' These include erecting symbols and monuments that exalt the freedom struggle, including new geographic and place names." At the same time, Mbeki rejected the idea of a "wealth-tax" on businesses that was intended to raise funds to pay reparations and criticized the lawsuits that had been filed in U.S. courts. Meanwhile, at least some of the victims were not happy; one said, "We only want the country to acknowledge us. What they are giving us is too little."[73]

Yet Mbeki's hopes that these lawsuits would go away have been dashed. In an effort to advance a more winnable case than that filed in June 2002, Ed Fagan filed a $100 million lawsuit in New York in November 2003 accusing a number of companies, including Union Carbide and Dow Chemical, of defrauding their South African workers by negligence in the management of their pension, health, life insurance, unemployment, and retirement funds. While the outcomes remain uncertain, the discourse and legal activism generated by the notion of reparations have continued to grow. Some analysts have suggested that, although the lawsuits may not lead to individual reparations payments, they

> may . . . persuade the companies to make payments into various social funds inside South Africa, or to be pliable on the issue of black economic empowerment . . . There seemed to be hints in this direction in [the] ANC website newsletter, penned by [President Thabo] Mbeki. He noted again that there should be "resource transfers" to the "second economy" from the developed part of the economy and society. And analysts believe the large companies based in SA may also be urged in this direction by the political mobilisation developing around the cases. The government does not either want to appear unsympathetic to its mass constituency—or to allow an issue to fester which may lead to greater political mobilisation.[74]

The government nonetheless felt strongly enough about its position to publicly dismiss Archbishop Desmond Tutu's support for the Khulumani/Jubilee South Africa lawsuit.[75] Again, the legal maneuvering promises to go on for some time to come, with outcomes that remain to be seen.

Radical Anti-Systemic Reparations Claims: SARM

According to George Dor of Jubilee South Africa, that organization began to move away from its focus on debt relief and toward a greater concern with reparations as a result of Art Serota's arrival from the United States and participation in the organization's discussions and activities. As a result of disagreements over Jubilee's future direction, Serota left the organization in mid-2000 and began pursuing alternative concerns. A workshop in Johannesburg around this time resolved to create a national reparations movement, and steps were taken toward building such a movement. These efforts led to the creation of the South African Reparations Movement (SARM), whose initial meeting took place in Durban in December 2000.[76]

The group's first major public event, the First National Reparations Congress, was held in Johannesburg in January 2002. The event brought together "indigenous reparations leaders" from a number of different ethnic groups in Southern Africa "who have [brought] or are in process of bringing reparations claims against wrongdoer entities." These groups included representatives from Namibian (Herero), Zimbabwean, Khoi, San (often known as Bushmen), Griqua, and Korana groups. Other participants in the Congress included "labour, religious, environmental justice, youth, rural development and other grassroots organisations." The theme of the Congress was "Free the Mind, Free the Land, Free the People."[77]

Land claims are thus at the heart of the group's activities. According to its literature, SARM "is adamant that the land stolen by invading forces must be returned to the people from whom it was stolen." Such land was, the organization claimed, for the most part communally owned. It also demanded reparations for forced labor and for "stolen wealth through lost inheritance, stolen assets, stolen minerals and natural resources. Moreover, the damage and destruction to language and culture and other forms of exploitation and human rights abuses, including slavery, require full redress, and compensation." Any resources acquired via reparations would be used to pay for economic development and "community and nation building." More broadly, SARM promoted

- Reclamation of our African identity, in which are enshrined the values of equitable sharing
- The power of indigenous knowledge systems
- Repossession of the land of the indigenous people, administered by traditional leadership
- Reconstructing the agricultural integrity of African tradition
- Enhancing and respecting our traditional institutions
- Redressing all the imbalances from slavery through colonialism, racism and capitalism
- Addressing institutional racism and white supremacy in ways which eradicate both from our society.[78]

The stress on African identity, culture, and values reflects SARM's roots in the Black Consciousness Movement, which is perhaps most widely associated with the figure of slain student leader Steven Biko.[79] More significantly, the organization is the only one in Africa of which I am aware that specifically infuses the notion of indigenism into its approach to reparations. It thus introduced into South African reparations politics a relatively novel discourse that has grown increasingly powerful since the 1960s in other white settler societies, though primarily those outside of Africa.[80] The South African Reparations Movement is thus unique in South African reparations politics, making it resemble the North American or Australian scene more than was previously the case.

Although its approach is distinctive, SARM is not the only group in South Africa that is active on land issues. As in the case of reparations per se, mobilization around land claims has been sparked in part by the slow implementation of government obligations. Since the end of the apartheid system in 1994, according to one report, as of late 2001 only 12,676 of 54,324 outstanding land claims had been settled.[81] Also pursuing land claims are an NGO called the National Land Commission; the Pan-African Congress (PAC), an anti-apartheid organization of long standing that has traditionally supported land redistribution; and the somewhat better-known and more powerful Landless People's Movement. The specter of major social conflict over land haunts the South African landscape not least owing to the proximity of Robert Mugabe's Zimbabwe.[82] These other groups, however, are interested only in land and not in SARM's "indigenous" agenda.[83] Indeed, this aspect of SARM's program gives it a rather unique twist.

In addition, SARM differs from other reparations-seeking groups in its basic tactics and outlook. For example, although SARM had cordial relationships with and offered moral support to the Khulumani Support Group in its legal efforts, SARM is not itself pursuing reparations lawsuits. Instead, it works at a grassroots level, organizing constituencies around the issues on which it focuses. SARM thus opened a total of four branch offices in the Northern Cape and Free State provinces during 2002, focusing on research and the development of claims. Some of these claims involve efforts to gain reparations for damage done by the operations of foreign businesses involved in the extraction of South Africa's natural resources, such as mines that damaged communities and workers' health, or pollution in waterways.[84]

Fundamentally, however, the difference between the various groups in South Africa pursuing reparations for past injustices concerns the "cutoff date" toward which they are oriented. Ed Fagan and his clients only go back to 1976 (the year of the Soweto uprising that led to Hector Petersen's death), and the Khulumani Support Group is an offshoot of the TRC process, which took under its purview crimes dating back to the beginning of the armed struggle against apartheid in the early 1960s. In contrast, SARM is "looking for reparations for damages beginning in 1652."[85] The ANC government may regard the lawsuits initiated by Fagan, Khulumani Support

Group, and Jubilee South Africa as threatening to the investment climate and the larger well-being of South African society, but SARM's demands are considerably more radical. Whereas these other groups seek compensation for injuries incurred only under the apartheid order, SARM raises claims calling into question the land and economic arrangements that have arisen during the entire history of South Africa since the first arrival of the Dutch at the Cape of Good Hope. The group thus addresses Mahmood Mamdani's critique that the TRC treated South Africa only as an *authoritarian* state, but not as a *colonial* state.

The issue of indigenous lands has become increasingly significant in Southern Africa in recent years. In early 2001, for example, leaders of Khoi, San, and Griqua groups gathered in a major conference demanding "redress for past wrongs, the return of stolen land and official recognition as South Africa's first indigenous nation."[86] Later that year, about 60,000 ethnic Khoikhoi of the Goringhaicona tribe, led by paramount chief Calvin Cornelius, sought to regain large sections of Cape Town's valuable Victoria and Alfred Waterfront district, a revamped harbor that now plays host to 10 million visitors annually and provides 14,000 permanent jobs. The group's effort would require the reversal of a provision in the post-apartheid South African constitution limiting land claims to those dating no further back than the Native Lands Act of 1913. The Khoi activists envision a flow of revenue and preferential treatment in hiring for jobs on their traditional lands.

Not everyone is convinced that this is the best way to rectify the injustice done to the people of the area. According to Glenda Glover, director of the Cape Town–based Surplus Peoples' Project, a group pressing land claims, the restoration of lands to earlier owners may help only a few, especially tribal chiefs or male heads of household. "We feel the focus should be on the redistribution process in terms of needs and affirmative action," Glover said. "It should be about recognizing this huge unequal distribution and doing something about it. It is the majority that has been dispossessed, so it is the majority that needs to be helped."[87] These Khoikhoi claims offer an excellent example of a much more general dilemma connected with the land claims of indigenous peoples: namely, whether helping groups that have unarguably been dispossessed through restoration of lands will not generate a new round of injustices to others, many of whom may be disadvantaged themselves. Cases in dense urban areas such as this one tend to be settled through some arrangement for financial compensation, whereas rural land claims are more likely to be resolved by transfers of land, which of course is typically less valuable and hence less controversial.

Resolving claims in this way has been further strengthened by a decision of the South African Supreme Court, which found that "the indigenous Richtersvelder people [a branch of the San/Bushmen straddling the border between South Africa and Botswana] had both communal land ownership and mineral rights over their territory," and that "laws which tried to dispossess them were 'racial discrimination'."[88] The Botswana government's expulsion of the "Bushmen" from their traditional lands in the Central Kalahari Game Reserve has provoked concern among both nongovernmental organizations involved in indigenous issues and the United Nations. The government is said to have implemented the "destruction of the Bushmen's water supply, [a] ban on the Bushmen hunting for subsistence, and refusal to allow Bushmen to enter their land without a permit."[89] Only time will tell whether the South African court decision will also apply to Botswana, or whether we will witness in the case of the Kalahari Bushmen a disaster of the sort that befell black Southern Africans at the hands of European invaders in the course of colonization. Indeed, Botswana's treatment of the Bushmen of the Central Kalahari Game Reserve sounds curiously like the Germans' dealings with the Herero before World War I—though no extermination order is known to exist.

In all events, pressures from groups seeking restitution of lands in general have been a powerful force in South African politics. For example, the Landless People's Movement has threatened to start taking over white farms if its demands are not met.[90] Although the government hoped to finalize all outstanding land claims by 2005, the deadline laid down by President Thabo Mbeki,[91] such finalization seems unlikely. The problem of reparations in the form of restitution of indigenous lands is likely to grow rather than diminish as the politics of indigenism becomes more widespread.

Conclusion

The different versions of reparations politics in contemporary Southern Africa demonstrate the many and varied meanings of the term *reparations*. More particularly, the various campaigns indicate the extent to which reparations can range from a commemorative and symbolic approach that is close to identity politics to an anti-systemic understanding of reparations that has stronger affinities with traditional left-wing commonality politics. The reparations claims against the Germans raised by the Hereros for the pre–World War I killings and dispossession can perhaps be situated nearest to the identity pole of the continuum. Their claims seem intended primarily to make *them* better off, not the whole society of which they are now a part. The commemorative reparations promised by the South African Truth and Reconciliation Commission were intended primarily to demonstrate the government's acknowledgment of previous wrongdoing and to stand as a warning against future repetition of such acts. In the terms of the schema laid out in Chapter 2, money has a more symbolic than economic meaning in these claims. Despite the fact that the lawsuits initiated by Ed Fagan on behalf of his clients against target companies that profiteered from apartheid, they are again mainly attempts to benefit them as individuals, not South African society as a whole. Fagan and his clients have had tense relations with those committed to an anti-systemic vision of reparations politics, who view such efforts as part of a broader struggle for economic justice and for whom the meaning of money is primarily economic rather than symbolic.

Meanwhile, the claims being pursued by the Khulumani Support Group and Jubilee South Africa's Apartheid Debt and Reparations Campaign are a hybrid bridging commemorative and anti-systemic reparations. In these cases, money has a predominantly economic significance. Initially motivated by a failure of the commemorative variant of reparations, the legal actions of these two groups have become much more closely intertwined with an anti-systemic understanding of reparations, especially in the eyes of the leadership of Jubilee South Africa. Rather than seeking to improve the lives only of a select group of victims, the lawsuits are part of a larger anti-corporate, anti-globalization politics from which all South Africans— indeed, all ("working") people—are the intended beneficiaries. In this case, more clearly than with someone like Ed Fagan, legal action is, to borrow a phrase from Clausewitz, "a continuation of politics by other means."

Finally, the claims being raised by the KhoiSan and other indigenous peoples, as well as by the South African Reparations Movement, return us to the identity pole but in a more ambiguous way than in the Herero case. By pursuing the return of lands on which other South Africans live, SARM seeks to challenge a whole colonial-cum-capitalist order. In doing so, however, they focus on and may enhance the well-being of relatively small groups of indigenes. But in some instances at least, they will unavoidably pit those groups against larger segments of the population, some of which will themselves have been victims rather than beneficiaries of apartheid.

Whatever the specifics of each case, it is remarkable that the notion of reparations—until relatively recently a term that referred exclusively to international obligations flowing from war-inflicted damages—has stimulated a great deal of activism, debate, and political action around the world. In Southern Africa, this development no doubt drew upon a broader discourse that had taken wing especially in the aftermath of the Japanese-American and Japanese-Canadian redress settlements of the late 1980s. But it was also advanced significantly by specific individuals who brought with them to the region an American-style legalistic approach to politics. Reparations politics in Southern Africa thus fits into a larger tendency in recent history that Habermas and others have described as the "juridification of politics." Rather than legal action being a continuation of politics by other means, law increasingly becomes the medium through which political struggles are carried out. This is another sense in which the world is being "Americanized," for better or worse.

Yet reparations politics has a certain peculiarity when viewed from the vantage point of the history of progressive politics. Almost by definition, earlier progressive politics saw the past as a lower, more backward period that was to be left behind as retrograde—or that, as a result of its dialectical contradictions, was the womb of a brighter future. Now, however, the past has been revalued in a sense; for many groups and activists (and academics), the route to the future is now thought to be *through the disasters of the past*. Only by coming to terms with the past, it is said, can we get to that brighter day. The spread of reparations politics thus challenges the old labor movement slogan, "don't mourn, organize"—the South African version of which was "don't mourn, mobilize." It may be correct, as Reverend Michael Lapsley—a Protestant minister and anti-apartheid activist whose hands were blown off by a letter bomb in the waning days of the old regime—put it, that this was "good politics, but bad psychology."[92] Still, the foregrounding of past injustice as a site for political struggle is an important novelty in progressive political discourse that has pitfalls as well as advantages. With the rise of Holocaust consciousness as the "point of departure" of our era, it is likely to structure our views of politics for some time to come. As Jubilee South Africa's George Dor said, however, "unless it's future-oriented, reparations is not a good idea."[93]

Conclusion

I have argued in the foregoing pages that the recent surge of campaigns for reparations for various historical injustices is a product of the coincidence of several factors. First, the Holocaust has come to play a central role in the historical consciousness at least of opinion-making elites, and that epoch-making event and the responses to it have furnished a template for a number of groups seeking attention to and, perhaps, compensation for wrongs done to them in the past. By designating as reparations the compensation paid to Jews and the state of Israel after World War II, the term began to undergo a major reinterpretation that would have significant political consequences. Once a name for the compensation paid by the losers of a war to the winners, the term increasingly came to refer to compensation paid by states to nonstate groups and individuals for the wrongs they suffered, whether in wartime or in other circumstances. The spread of reparations thus parallels the rise of human rights thinking, the emergence of substate groups and individuals as subjects of international law, and the juridification of politics in general. One need not subscribe to the view that all reality is only discourse to be impressed by the extent to which this terminological shift has shaped subsequent political realities; the idea of reparations has now been disseminated throughout the world and constitutes a crucial resource in the arsenal of contemporary politics. Yet more had to happen for these developments to take place.

In particular, the spreading concern with past injustices has been part and parcel of a tendency (at least among intellectual and political elites) to view our era as one that is "after" others—an era that is post-socialist, post-nationalist, post-modernist, post-utopian. In the process, the images of a brighter future that had been the hallmarks of socialism and the nation-state gave way to the pessimistic ironies of post-modernism. A still-unfinished project of modernity and its companion, historical optimism based on Enlightenment rationalism, came to be regarded among these elites as cruel illusions. As a result, the historical past increasingly assumed a more prominent place than the future in the eyes of many progressive thinkers and activists, who now saw the past rather than the future as the realm that could be "fixed." This posture was consistent with the fact that 1989 was a kind of Rubicon for the left, which sustained a historic defeat as advocates of free markets and liberal individualism gained the ascendancy over those who sought to rein them in. As a consequence, the politics of utopia lay in shambles.[1]

Against this background, a growing cadre of "entrepreneurs of memory" stresses to an unusual degree the continuing and nefarious vitality of the past in the present. The persistence of that unhappy past debilitates those subject to it, the entrepreneurs of memory insist, and those affected must therefore come to terms with the past in order to exorcise it and move on. It is not difficult to see the similarity between these arguments and those advanced by Freud and his therapeutic epigones. But the ranks of the entrepreneurs of memory, deeply influenced by these currents of modern culture, are much wider, especially including lawyers, theologians, historians, and political activists. As a result of their appropriating the ideas of reparations and coming to terms with the past, the project of "making whole what has been smashed" has become a major preoccupation of many groups, individuals, and institutions.

This project resonates with a larger tendency in the culture toward an embrace of victimization rather than heroism, of nurturing grievance rather than overcoming adversity. Robert Hughes was prescient to diagnose ours as a "culture of complaint," as was Jean-Michel Chaumont when he analyzed the new "competition of victims" that followed the growth of Holocaust awareness beginning in the 1960s.[2] More recently, David Garland, an analyst of crime and punishment patterns, has noted the apotheosis of the victim as a figure in contemporary culture. "It is no longer sufficient to subsume the individual victim's experience in the notion of the public good: the public good must be individuated, broken down into individual component parts. Specific victims are to have a voice . . . There is, in short, a new cultural theme, a new collective meaning of victimhood."[3] Garland's characterization calls our attention to privatization of criminal justice, which has many other dimensions as well. The transformation described by Garland with regard to the criminal law context has its analog in the realm of state-sponsored atrocities.

Just as the administration of justice has increasingly been privatized, so has history.[4] That is, as the past in recent years has been "democratized"— taken out of the hands of experts—it has also increasingly been multiplied and utilized as an instrument of social conflict. There are now many "histories," not a single "history"; this is a result not merely of post-modernism's resistance to unitary narratives, but also of the spread of groups mobilized around efforts to call attention to or to promote the reconsideration of particular pasts. The stakes in these cases are social recognition of various kinds. To be sure, as Orwell pointed out long ago, political stakes are always involved in our understanding of the past. Yet there is a distinction between interpretations of the past that have *political* implications and those that are *politicized*—"weapons forged for a current ideological contest"[5]—and that distinction needs to be maintained.

The fragmentation of the body politic is the other side of the privatization of justice and history, and in certain respects the condition of their possibility. Well-meaning though it may be, the idea of multiculturalism has helped strengthen this propensity in the more liberal-democratic societies by encouraging a sense of separateness from the larger polity and an embrace of "imagined communities" below the level of the citizenry as a whole. This in turn has been reflected in the rise of identity politics, which makes political claims on the basis of people's membership in groups defined by sociological characteristics rather than by virtue of their common membership in a politically defined community of fate.[6] With the aid of the upgraded attentiveness to victims and their experiences, identities can now be forged, or at least strengthened, through an embrace of the erstwhile victimization of one's group. Perhaps the leading example of this phenomenon has been the Holocaust, which—despite its dependence on what some Jews reject as the "lachrymose version of Jewish history"—has been used by some within organized Jewry as a way to sustain a waning sense of identification with the group.[7] The Nanking massacre has played a similar function for the diaspora Chinese, as has the Armenian genocide of the early twentieth century for many overseas Armenians.[8]

Whereas much of the most sophisticated and serious writing on politics in the 1950s and 1960s wrung its hands about mass politics and conformism, our era faces entirely different problems.[9] Chief among these problems, perhaps, is the very idea of a coherent "public" that has any politics at all, much less utopian ones. In the United States, for example, the decline of mass publics is reflected in the relative deterioration of "market share" for the three top networks during the last three decades or so and the cession of audiences to the proliferation of cable channels. Such trends are underway elsewhere as well. As the rise of Italy's Silvio Berlusconi and even of Germany's Gerhard Schroeder suggests, politics and salesmanship look more and more alike. An era in which the citizen is challenged by the "customer" is not fertile ground for political engagement of any kind.[10] More broadly, the concept of citizenship itself has been challenged in numerous ways. Among intellectuals especially, doubts have been raised about the degree to which a common citizenship actually meets the needs of all members of a sociopolitical order; "one size fits all" has come to be seen as insupportably insensitive to difference.[11] In the meantime, American politics increasingly serves the interests of the only constituents whose views are attended to—namely, the well-heeled.[12]

Notwithstanding the conservative political background to the rise of victim-consciousness, the political commitments of those engaged in reparations politics vary across a spectrum ranging from those primarily concerned with the relatively narrow problems of specific groups to those who view their reparations activism in terms of a broader commonality politics. For those concerned with the narrow view, once the past to which they and their group have been subjected has been dealt with, they are more or less satisfied; these persons can be said to be pursuing a kind of identity politics. In the case of those for whom reparations politics is part of a broader political struggle, campaigns for reparations tend to be seen simply as a tactic in a much wider, more critical attempt to overcome inequalities for all people.

For those with a narrow view of reparations politics, the meaning of money in any reparations arrangement is chiefly *symbolic;* it is meant to commemorate the past suffering and to demonstrate to the one-time victims that the perpetrator is truly remorseful. Because "talk is cheap," the money that accompanies an apology "puts one's money where one's mouth is." An apology without money might be perceived as empty, and money without an apology might well be regarded as offensive. In cases of antisystemic reparations politics, however, the meaning of money is *economic,* so to speak; that is, any money that is distributed is intended above all to ameliorate economic inequalities flowing from the earlier injustices. The money is important for what it *does* more than for what it *says*. The meaning of money in reparations politics may be further modified by the extent to which those seeking redress believe that "their" culture has been damaged in the process. Privately owned items of real property—whether artworks or land and houses—tend to present fewer difficulties of this kind. The more difficult cases involve instances in which artifacts and territories are said to be imbued with a sacred or other profound cultural significance. In such cases, mere money cannot suffice, and it is the objects or lands themselves that the injured demand to have restored. In all events, responses to these pasts and to ameliorative arrangements will vary from person to person; the entrepreneurs of memory may or may not occupy a stance representative of wider elements of the relevant group.

One might sum up the preceding points by emphasizing that reparations politics is indeed a matter of *politics*. This statement should by no means be interpreted as suggesting that there are no moral claims involved; but to say that the claims are moral tends to sanctify them in a way that removes them from the mundane world of politics of which they are very much a part. I have tried to show that the rise of reparations politics is a response to a specific historical conjuncture in which entrepreneurs of memory concerned with a range of different pasts have adapted for their own purposes a particular discourse that has been productive for other groups in pursuing their commemorative and compensatory aims. Although some would argue that this is a "secular" development—that is, that reparations politics is a matter of a fundamental shift that has taken place in Western-oriented societies—this understanding captures perhaps only half of the story. To be sure, we have become more "civilized" in some ways: to take just one example, questions regarding the treatment of animals preoccupy us in a way that they did not do so, say, 100 years ago, and even eating animals is a subject that has captured the attention of moral theory in a way that is relatively novel.[13] This shift is reflected in the codification in U.N. documents, and hence in international law, of the right to reparations for gross violations of human rights.

Yet there are also signs that the saliency of "reparations" is declining in the public agenda. One major factor facilitating the rise of reparations politics in "the world's courtroom," the United States, is its relatively "permissive" legal environment. Early in 2003, however, a federal court of appeals in California dismissed a suit by a number of people seeking compensation for forced labor they performed for German and Japanese companies during

World War II, on the grounds that the statute of limitations barred them from suing. One legal commentator argued that this did "not bode well for what he called 'trans-historical claims' that involve the slavery of African-Americans in the United States."[14] In June 2003, a federal appeals court in Washington dismissed a suit against Japan that had been brought on behalf of fifteen women exploited as comfort women during World War II.[15] As we have already discussed, the lawsuit seeking reparations for the race riots in Tulsa, Oklahoma in the early 1920s was dismissed on similar, statute of limitation grounds, although that ruling was appealed.

More broadly, we have noted the significance of the Alien Tort Claims Act (ACTA) as an avenue through which those seeking to make claims for past wrongdoing by states and putatively allied companies could do so, as, for example, in the apartheid-related lawsuits. In June 2004, the Supreme Court was asked to determine whether the law, which was not used to sue corporations until the mid-1990s, "provides a basis for a federal court damage suit for violations of the 'law of nations,' and how to decide what sorts of legal injuries meet that definition." The Bush administration and business interests, wary of the chilling effect that such litigation may have on international investment by American companies, had urged the Court to rein in the ACTA.[16] Despite opposition by the Bush administration and the corporate community, the Court upheld the law's continued applicability, arguing that "it would take some explaining to say now that federal courts must avert their gaze entirely from any international norm intended to protect individuals." Still, the Court said that the law should be applied "with 'judicial caution'," particularly where foreign policy concerns are at stake. In this regard, the Court specifically cited cases pending against corporations that did business in apartheid-era South Africa. The South African government has opposed these suits, as we have noted, and the State Department has gone along with the ANC government's position. "In such cases," the Court said, "there is a strong argument that federal courts should give serious weight to the executive branch's view of the case's impact on foreign policy."[17]

Meanwhile, the energy associated with the demand for reparations for black Americans that was generated in the early years of the new century seems to have dissipated. One suspects that this has something to do with the political climate in the United States since 9/11; a major political undertaking of this sort may well have been deemed inadvisable under the circumstances. Without a substantial popular basis, which the campaign lacks, the effort to achieve reparations for black Americans seems relatively unpromising. Meanwhile, the legal maneuvering engineered by Ed Fagan and others has led some to shift away from lawsuits as a means of doing politics and toward grassroots organizing around the issues that concern them. Finally, those involved in the *causes célèbres* that opened the door to the upsurge of reparations politics after 1989—the Holocaust and the Japanese-American and Japanese-Canadian internments, and the processes intended to redress them—are passing from the scene. In short, the conjunctural forces that paved the way to the 1990s spike in reparations claims-making are disappearing, and other than those involving persons who themselves suffered under brutal regimes, the cases that remain tend to be rather complex and unpromising.

"Reparations" are thus likely to remain a part of the routine processes of transitional justice, as long as the victims who suffered injustices themselves—or perhaps their immediate relatives—are alive and able to receive compensation. The case of reparations for the Japanese-Americans and Japanese-Canadians suggests that such compensation is valuable for restoring a sense of dignity for those once wronged and of legitimacy for the state that undertakes such compensation. The United Nations' adoption of the "Basic Principles and Guidelines on the Right to a Remedy and Reparation for Victims of Gross Violations of International Human Rights Law and Serious Violations of International Humanitarian Law"[18] will help ensure that those wronged will receive their due, or at least something approximating it. With such guidelines in place, "the past" will offer less in terms of needs that have been unattended; only more distant pasts will remain to be dealt with, but these cases will be the most problematic to resolve.

We should also remember that the preoccupation with making whole what has been smashed has its negative sides. One problem is the tendency to view current difficulties as the product of what some past oppressor "did to us." This view may be true enough, of course, and needs proper accounting in the books that tell the chronicle of human history. But it can also offer excuses for perpetuating contemporary injustices. Consider Robert Mugabe's desperate attempt to stay in power in Zimbabwe by blaming his country's self-inflicted economic wounds on British imperialism. Many see through the ruse, but in a world in which the formerly colonized generally remain far behind their colonial overlords, the claim has sufficient credibility to give pause. More broadly, the tendency to mobilize past wrongdoing as an explanation for present iniquity may help to distract from recognizing the harmful policies implemented by the current holders of power in the post-colonial world. Similarly, although racism is an old and persistent feature of American society and must be included in any convincing account of racial inequality there, it cannot be the case that all such inequality is traceable to slavery and Jim Crow. Otherwise there would be no way to make sense of those blacks who have "made it" in America. We should recognize their achievement and understand the extent to which such accomplishment is possible for others, and how to make it more available to those to whom it is currently foreclosed. The reality of black progress since the 1960s makes the majority of Americans skeptical about ideas such as reparations, which seem too undiscriminating in their impact to be appropriate to the situation.

Ultimately, moreover, we must be careful not to reinforce the group differences that underlay past mistreatment. Given its effort to rectify wrongs carried out against groups, reparations claims-making can help to sustain boundaries between groups that were the basis on which the original injustices were perpetrated. It may be necessary to repair wounds across these boundaries, but the chief goal must be to tear down these walls between people. Given its concern to tend to the unjustly wronged and harmed, reparations politics tends to invoke a conception of people as weak and as permanently damaged by adversity. Indeed, some people are enduringly diminished by injustice and ill-treatment, but the goal should always be to inculcate an image of people as strong and resilient. Given its preoccupation with past injustices, reparations politics may tilt our attention excessively toward a history about which, in fact, little can be done.

The entrepreneurs of memory often remind us of William Faulkner's point that "the past isn't over—it's not even past." The dividing line between past, present, and future is fleeting and arbitrary, and certainly many of the social problems we seek to address today have their roots in past wrongs. Yet in a profound, even epistemological sense, we cannot "make whole what has been smashed." Without neglecting the ways in which the past ramify into and in a certain sense even constitute the injustices of the present, we must always bear in mind that it is only the future that we can really do anything about. "Coming to terms with the past" may be a contribution to making a better future, but it may also distract from that goal. Max Horkheimer was right when he wrote, "Past injustice is over and done with; the slain are truly slain."[19]

Notes

Introduction

1. *The New Yorker,* December 17, 2001. The cartoon is signed (Robert) "Mankoff."
2. "Four Generations of Americans Demand Sitcom Reparations," *The Onion,* www.theonion.com.
3. Wole Soyinka, *The Burden of Memory, the Muse of Forgiveness* (New York: Oxford University Press, 1999), p. 90.
4. Elazar Barkan, *The Guilt of Nations: Restitution and Negotiating Historical Injustices* (New York: Norton, 2000), p. 310.
5. "South Africa: Payouts for Apartheid," *New York Times,* October 20, 1998, p. A8. For more details, see Chapter 5.
6. See "Los Angeles to Draft Law Revealing Business Links to Slavery," *New York Times,* May 18, 2003, p. 29; Ross E. Milloy, "Panel Calls for Reparations in Tulsa Race Riot," *New York Times,* March 1, 2001, p. A12; and Brent Staples, "Coming to Grips with the Unthinkable," *New York Times,* March 16, 2003, p. A12.
7. I should perhaps state here that, for somewhat technical reasons, I will generally prefer the term "black Americans" or "blacks" to "African-Americans." The former term connotes a population descended in substantial degree from slave ancestors; they are a wholly American group, just as the Coloureds of South Africa are a distinctive product of South African history. (For an illuminating comparison of the two groups, see George Fredrickson, *White Supremacy: A Comparative Study in American & South African History* [New York: Oxford University Press, 1981], pp. 255–257.) Although the number of African immigrants remains relatively small, it is growing, and the experience of these immigrants differs rather sharply from that of black Americans. One group originated out of an involuntary migration, while the other did not; this is the crux of their different experiences. African-origin immigrants to the United States from the Caribbean represent a kind of in-between group; they too are generally the descendants of slave populations in the Caribbean, but their entry into the United States was likely to have been voluntary. This has meant that blacks from the Caribbean have had a rather different experience

167

in American society as well. Thus, there are often divisions and conflicts between these two populations; for a discussion of tensions in the area of access to elite institutions of higher education, see Sara Rimer and Karen W. Arenson, "Top Colleges Take More Blacks, But Which Ones?" *New York Times,* June 24, 2004, p. A19.

8. Campaign for Labor Rights, "April 16: Endorse the Demands," *Labor Alerts,* posted March 12, 2000; I am grateful to Todd Gitlin for calling this item to my attention.

9. Human Rights Watch, "An Approach to Reparations," July 19, 2001, *www.hrw.org.*

10. "U.S. Will Pay Reparations to Former Latin American Internees," *New York Times,* June 15, 1998, p. A19.

11. See Soyinka, *The Burden of Memory,* pp. 45–47.

12. On the role of North Africans in the slave trade, see Ronald Segal, *Islam's Black Slaves: The Other Black Diaspora* (New York: Farrar, Straus and Giroux, 2001).

13. Norimitsu Onishi, "Senegalese Loner Works to Build Africa, His Way," *New York Times,* April 10, 2002, p. A3.

14. See Mike Robinson, "Judge Dismisses Slave Reparations Suit," Associated Press, January 24, 2004, available at *www.usatoday.com;* and Associated Press, "Oklahoma Judge Dismisses Race Riot Suit," March 23, 2004, available at *www.prometheus6.org.*

15. See BBC News, "Apartheid Victims File Suit," June 19, 2002, available at *news.bbc.co.uk.*

16. For a good indication of the growing distance between ourselves and the experience of the Holocaust, see Daniel Mendelsohn, "What Happened to Uncle Shmiel?" *New York Times Magazine,* July 14, 2002, pp. 24–29ff.

17. Some of the main titles in the growing literature include Barkan, *Guilt of Nations;* Janna Thompson, *Taking Responsibility for the Past: Reparation and Historical Justice* (Malden, MA: Polity, 2002); Priscilla Hayner, *Unspeakable Truths: Confronting State Terror and Atrocity* (New York: Routledge, 2001); Roy Brooks, ed., *When Sorry Isn't Enough* (New York: New York University Press, 1999); Ruti Teitel, *Transitional Justice* (New York: Oxford University Press, 2000); Hermann Lübbe, *"Ich entschuldige mich": Das neue politische Bußritual* (Berlin: Siedler, 2001); Martha Minow, *Between Vengeance and Forgiveness* (Boston: Beacon Press, 1998); and my own edited volume, *Politics and the Past: On Repairing Historical Injustices* (Lanham, MD: Rowman & Littlefield, 2003). For an analysis of many of these issues that was ahead of its time, see Nicholas Tavuchis, *Mea Culpa: A Sociology of Apology and Reconcilation* (Stanford, CA: Stanford University Press, 1991).

18. See Hayner, *Unspeakable Truths.*

19. See John D. Skrentny, *The Minority Rights Revolution* (Cambridge, MA: Belknap/Harvard University Press, 2002).

20. See Michael Ignatieff, *Human Rights as Politics and Idolatry* (Princeton, NJ: Princeton University Press, 2001), pp. 21–22.

21. See Weber, "Politics as a Vocation," in Hans Gerth and C. Wright Mills, eds., *From Max Weber: Essays in Sociology* (New York: Oxford University Press, 1946), pp. 118–128.

1. The Surfacing of Subterranean History

1. For example, see John Ibbitson, "Campaign to Remember U.S. Slavery Takes Root," *Globe and Mail* (Toronto), July 15, 2002, p. A3.

2. Hyung Gu Lynn states that, "[A]s defined in Article 302 of the Treaty of Versailles, 'compensation' is claimed by individuals against states, while 'reparations' and 'indemnities' are settled between states." See Hyung Gu Lynn, "Systemic Lock: The Institutionalization of History in Post-1965 South Korea–Japan Relations," *Journal of American East Asian Relations* 9, no. 1–2 (Spring–Summer 2000): 72.

3. The boundaries of this term and its coherence are contentious matters; I use it here as a shorthand for the predominantly Christian world comprising (mainly Western) Europe and the Americas, or what some would call "Latin Christendom."

4. See Peter Novick, *The Holocaust in American Life* (Boston: Houghton Mifflin, 1999); Daniel Levy and Natan Sznaider, *The Holocaust and Memory in the Global Age,* trans. Assenka Oksiloff (Philadelphia: Temple University Press, 2005); and Jeffrey Alexander, "On the Social Construction of Moral Universals: The 'Holocaust' from War Crime to Trauma Drama," *European Journal of Social Theory* 5, no. 1 (February 2002): 5–86.

5. One of the more incendiary attempts to claim that the Holocaust had robbed attention from other crimes of the past—in this case, from those of Communism—was Stéphane Courtois, "Introduction: The Crimes of Communism," in Stéphane Courtois et al., *The Black Book of Communism: Crimes, Terror, Repression,* trans. Jonathan Murphy and Mark Kramer (Cambridge, MA: Harvard University Press, 1999), p. 23. I discuss this book and its impact toward the end of the present chapter.

6. The events in the Darfur region of Sudan may point to a shift away from the centrality of the Holocaust in thinking about past wrongdoing. In this case, the analogy has more frequently been to Rwanda than to the Holocaust. This shift may have resulted from a number of factors: the decline of the Holocaust as a touchstone as a result of the waning of claims related to it; the coincidence of the tenth anniversary of the Rwandan genocide in 2004; or the geographical (and perhaps "racial") propinquity of Sudan to Rwanda.

7. Thucydides, *History of the Peloponnesian War,* trans. Rex Warner (New York: Penguin, 1972), p. 402.

8. For an insightful analysis, see Jeffrey K. Olick and Brenda Coughlin, "The Politics of Regret: Analytical Frames," in John Torpey, ed., *Politics and the Past: On Repairing Historical Injustices* (Lanham, MD: Rowman & Littlefield, 2003).

9. Edmund Burke, *Reflections on the Revolution in France,* ed. Conor Cruise O'Brien (New York: Penguin Books, 1969 [1790]), pp. 246–247.

10. Karl Marx, "The Eighteenth Brumaire of Louis Bonaparte," in Robert Tucker, ed., *The Marx-Engels Reader*, 2nd ed. (New York: Norton, 1978 [1852]), p. 595.

11. See Karl Marx and Friedrich Engels, "The Communist Manifesto," in Tucker, ed., *The Marx-Engels Reader*, esp. Part I, "Bourgeois and Proletarians."

12. Friedrich Nietzsche, "On the Use and Disadvantages of History for Life," in Nietzsche, *Untimely Meditations*, trans. R. J. Hollingdale, ed. Daniel Breazeale (Cambridge: Cambridge University Press, 1997), pp. 102–103.

13. Walter Benjamin, "Theses on the Philosophy of History," in *Illuminations*, ed. Hannah Arendt (New York: Schocken Books, 1968), pp. 257–258. Benjamin wrote the "Theses" shortly before his death in 1940.

14. Sigmund Freud, *Civilization and Its Discontents*, trans. James Strachey (New York: W. W. Norton, 1961 [1930]).

15. Karl Jaspers, *Die Schuldfrage: Von der politischen Haftung Deutschlands* (Munich: Piper, 1987 [1946]); a new edition of the original 1947 English translation has recently appeared as *The Question of German Guilt*, trans. E. B. Ashton (New York: Fordham University Press, 2000). Although the term is generally translated as "responsibility," in the original German Jaspers typically uses not *Verantwortung* ("responsibility") but *Haftung*, which—perhaps significantly—is normally translated as "liability" as, for example, in the German equivalent of the phrase for "limited liability company" (i.e., *GmbH—Gesellschaft mit beschränkter Haftung*).

16. See the relevant essays in *Eine Art Schadensabwicklung: Kleine politische Schriften VI* (Frankfurt: Suhrkamp, 1987), which collects Habermas's contributions to the so-called *Historikerstreit* ("historians' debate"). For Habermas's appreciation of Jaspers's *Schuldfrage*, see the essay on Jaspers in Habermas, *Philosophical-Political Profiles*, trans. Frederick G. Lawrence (Cambridge, MA: MIT Press, 1983). For a discussion of Jaspers's text and Habermas's appropriation of its main themes, see Anson Rabinbach, "The German as Pariah: Karl Jaspers's *The Question of German Guilt*," in Rabinbach, *In the Shadow of Catastrophe: German Intellectuals Between Apocalypse and Enlightenment* (Berkeley: University of California Press, 1997).

17. For the divergent responses to the Nazi past in the two Germanys that emerged from the defeat of the Third Reich, see Jeffrey Herf, *Divided Memory: The Nazi Past in the Two Germanys* (Cambridge, MA: Harvard University Press, 1997). For an analysis of the efforts to come to terms with the past in postwar Germany and Japan that finds Japan wanting in comparison with Germany, see Ian Buruma, *The Wages of Guilt: Memories of War in Germany and Japan* (New York: Meridian, 1994).

18. Hannah Arendt, "Preface to the First Edition," *The Origins of Totalitarianism* (New York: Harcourt, Brace, 1973 [1951]), p. ix.

19. To borrow from the title of Eric Wolf, *Europe and the People Without History* (Berkeley: University of California Press, 1997 [1982]).

20. Lukas Meyer, "Inheriting Public Goods and Public Evils," unpublished ms., University of Bremen, June 1999, p. 15.

21. See Tyler Cowen, "How Far Back Should We Go?" unpublished ms., George Mason University, July 1999.
22. Jeremy Waldron, "Redressing Historic Injustice," ch. 2 of *Cosmopolitan Right*, ms. 2001, p. 20. See also Waldron, "Superseding Historic Injustice," *Ethics* 103 (October 1992): 4–28.
23. Quoted in Meyer, "Inheriting Public Goods and Public Evils," 29. My translation.
24. Andrew Schaap, "Guilty Subjects and Political Responsibility: Arendt, Jaspers and the Resonance of the 'German Question' in Politics of Reconciliation," *Political Studies* 49 (2001): 762.
25. Danny Postel, "The Awful Truth [about Lynching]," *Chronicle of Higher Education*, July 12, 2002. I am grateful to Todd Gitlin for calling this article to my attention.
26. See Ian Buruma, "War Guilt, and the Difference Between Germany and Japan," *New York Times*, December 29, 1998, p. A19. For a more extended discussion, see Buruma's "The Joys and Perils of Victimhood," *New York Review of Books* (April 8, 1999).
27. See their Web site, *www.nyu.edu*.
28. Anne-Marie Slaughter and David Bosco, "Plaintiff's Diplomacy," *Foreign Affairs* (September–October 2000): 102–116.
29. Nathan Glazer, *We Are All Multiculturalists Now* (Cambridge, MA: Harvard University Press, 1997).
30. For a vigorous critique, see Brian Barry, *Culture and Equality: An Egalitarian Critique of Multiculturalism* (Cambridge, MA: Harvard University Press, 2001).
31. Robert Hughes, *Culture of Complaint: The Fraying of America* (New York: Oxford University Press, 1993).
32. David Garland, *The Culture of Control: Crime and Social Order in Contemporary Society* (Chicago: University of Chicago Press, 2001), pp. 11–12. My italics.
33. Margaret Thatcher quoted in "AIDS, Education and the Year 2000!" *Woman's Own* magazine (GB), October 31, 1987, pp. 8–10.
34. First Inaugural Address, January 20, 1981.
35. See John Micklethwait and Adrian Wooldridge, "It Depends What the Meaning of 'Liberal' Is," *New York Times*, June 27, 2004, "Week in Review," p. 3.
36. Cass Sunstein, "The Right-Wing Assault," *American Prospect*, March 1, 2003, available at *www.prospect.org*.
37. For a provocative and compelling discussion of the politics of denial and acknowledgment of human rights violations, see Stanley Cohen, *States of Denial: Knowing about Atrocities and Suffering* (Malden, MA: Blackwell, 2001).
38. I would differ from Olick and Coughlin, "The Politics of Regret," on this point as well. The developmentalist position on which they draw, initially outlined by Norbert Elias, suggests a very *longue durée* style of approach to understanding the rise of reparations politics. This seems useful but is too unspecific historically. To clarify the relationship between their approach and my own, it may be useful to note Phil Gorski's distinction between types of theories. What Gorski calls first-order theories involve "a specific account of

a particular event or class of events in the social world (e.g., 'Perry Anderson's theory of absolutism')," whereas second-order theories offer "a general approach to the study of social life." My approach, which should be regarded as complementary to that of Olick and Coughlin, is more akin to a first-order theory, whereas theirs is more like a second-order theory. On this point, see Gorski, "Reply," *Comparative & Historical Sociology: Newsletter of the ASA Comparative and Historical Sociology Section* 15, no. 4 (Spring 2004): 8.

39. See Daniel Bell, *The Coming of Post-Industrial Society* (New York: Basic Books, 1976) and Alvin Gouldner, *The Future of Intellectuals and the Rise of the New Class* (New York: Continuum, 1979).

40. It is perhaps worth recalling here Thomas Cushman's point that, despite "the rapid growth of the 'genocide prevention industry'," the 1990s witnessed two major genocides in Bosnia and Rwanda—to which we might now add Darfur in Sudan. See Cushman, "Is Genocide Preventable? Some Theoretical Considerations," *Journal of Genocide Research* 5, no. 4 (December 2003): 526.

41. For a critical analysis of the role of this sort of discourse in coming to terms with past wrongdoing in South Africa, see Richard A. Wilson, *The Politics of Truth and Reconciliation in South Africa: Legitimizing the Post-Apartheid State* (Cambridge: Cambridge University Press, 2001).

42. Therapists and some therapeutically inclined sociologists; see Jeffrey Alexander et al., eds., *Cultural Trauma and Collective Identity* (Berkeley: University of California Press, 2004).

43. On the role of lawyers and historians in the pursuit of reparations for Holocaust-related wrongs, see Ariel Colonomos, "The Holocaust Era Assets and the Globalization of Shame," paper presented at the July 2001 meeting of the International Studies Association, Hong Kong.

44. Erving Goffman, *Stigma: Notes on the Management of Spoiled Identity* (New York: Simon & Schuster, 1963), p. 27.

45. Quoted in Edward T. Linenthal, *Preserving Memory: The Struggle to Create America's Holocaust Museum* (New York: Columbia University Press, 2001 [1995]), p. 21.

46. Goffman, *Stigma*, p. 38.

47. Joseph Berger, "The 'Second Generation' Reflects on the Holocaust," *New York Times*, January 17, 2000, p. A11.

48. See Dalton Conley, "Calculating Slavery Reparations: Theory, Numbers, and Implications," in John Torpey, ed., *Politics and the Past: On Repairing Historical Injustices* (Lanham, MD: Rowman & Littlefield, 2003), pp. 117–125.

49. Kerwin Lee Klein, "On the Emergence of Memory in Historical Discourse," *Representations* 69 (Winter 2000): 145.

50. For a profile of the International Center for Transitional Justice (ICTJ), see Lynda Richardson, "Helping Countries, and People, to Heal," *New York Times*, November 23, 2001, p. A25. See also Priscilla Hayner, *Unspeakable Truths: Confronting State Terror and Atrocity* (New York: Routledge, 2001). Hayner is a leading figure in the ICTJ.

51. Deborah Posel and Graeme Simpson, eds., *Commissioning the Past: Understanding South Africa's Truth and Reconciliation Commission* (Johannesburg: Witwatersrand University Press, 2002), pp. 1–2.

52. For a sharp critique of the waning commitment to the idea of equal citizenship, see Brian Barry, *Culture & Equality* (Cambridge, MA: Harvard University Press, 2001).

53. George Steiner, *Grammars of Creation* (New Haven, CT: Yale University Press, 2001), p. 3.

54. Jürgen Habermas, "Foreword," *The Postnational Constellation: Political Essays*, trans. Max Pensky (Cambridge, MA: MIT Press, 2001), p. xviii; my translation from the original, "Vorwort," *Die postnationale Konstellation: Politische Essays* (Frankfurt: Suhrkamp, 1998), p. 7.

55. See Todd Gitlin, *The Twilight of Common Dreams: Why America Is Wracked by Culture Wars* (New York: Metropolitan Books, 1995); see also the discussion of postmodernism and politics in Edward Rothstein, "Moral Relativity Is a Hot Topic? True. Absolutely," *New York Times*, July 13, 2002, pp. A13–15.

56. Steiner, *Grammars of Creation*, p. 329.

57. See Nietzsche, "On the Uses and Disadvantages of History for Life"; see also Charles Maier, "A Surfeit of Memory? Reflections on History, Melancholy, and Denial," *History and Memory* 5, no. 2 (Fall–Winter 1993): 136–151.

58. Ken Jowitt, "A World Without Leninism," in Jowitt, *New World Disorder: The Leninist Extinction* (Berkeley: University of California Press, 1992), p. 306.

59. Alexis de Tocqueville, *Democracy in America*, trans. and ed. Harvey Mansfield and Delba Winthrop (Chicago: University of Chicago Press, 2000 [1835]), pp. 395–396.

60. Karl Marx, *Capital*, vol. 1 in Tucker, ed., *The Marx-Engels Reader*, p. 435.

61. For a valuable discussion of the vicissitudes of race in the capitalist world-system, see Howard Winant, *The World Is a Ghetto: Race and Democracy Since World War II* (New York: Basic Books, 2001). Following Michael Adas's arguments in *Machines as the Measure of Men: Science, Technology, and Ideologies of Western Dominance* (Ithaca, NY: Cornell University Press, 1989), George Fredrickson doubts that race was a central *motivation* behind European global conquest and colonization, though it soon came to play a decisive role in structuring social hierarchies. See his *Racism: A Short History* (Princeton, NJ: Princeton University Press, 2002), pp. 108–109.

62. The reference is to Frantz Fanon's *A Dying Colonialism*, trans. Haakon Chevalier (New York: Grove Press, 1967 [1959]).

63. W. E. Burghardt Du Bois, *The World and Africa: An Inquiry into the Part Which Africa Has Played in World History* (New York: Viking, 1946), p. 258.

64. See George Fredrickson, *Black Liberation: A Comparative History of Black Ideologies in the United States and South Africa* (New York: Oxford University Press, 1995), esp. ch. 5, and Michael Dawson, *Black Visions: The Roots of Contemporary African-American Political Ideologies* (Chicago: University of Chicago Press, 2001), ch. 5.

65. See Mary L. Dudziak, *Cold War Civil Rights: Race and the Image of American Democracy* (Princeton, NJ: Princeton University Press, 2000) and Fredrickson, *Racism: A Short History*, pp. 129–132.

66. On the relative stagnation of progress in race relations globally since the early 1990s, see Winant, *The World Is a Ghetto*.

67. See Gustav Niebuhr, "Forgive Them Their Debts, World Council Says," *New York Times*, December 15, 1998, p. A10; Joseph Kahn, "Wealthy Nations Propose Doubling Poor's Debt Relief," *New York Times*, September 17, 2000, pp. 1, 10; Joseph Kahn, "International Lenders' New Image: A Human Face," *New York Times*, September 26, 2000, p. A5.

68. For a spectrum of views on the progress of the black population in the United States—or the lack thereof—since the civil rights movement, see Orlando Patterson, *The Ordeal of Integration: Progress and Resentment in America's "Racial" Crisis* (New York: Basic Civitas, 1997), which sees the glass as half-full; William Julius Wilson, *The Bridge over the Racial Divide: Rising Inequality and Coalition Politics* (Berkeley: University of California Press, 1999), which sees the glass as half-empty but open to improvement through a multiracial coalition politics that deemphasizes race in favor of a stress on class; and, at the most pessimistic, Dawson, *Black Visions*, which sees the glass as half-empty and with few prospects of improvement in sight.

69. Karl Polanyi, *The Great Transformation: The Political and Economic Origins of Our Time* (Boston: Beacon Press, 1944).

70. See Eric Hobsbawm, *The Age of Extremes: A History of the World, 1914–1991* (New York: Vintage, 1996 [1994]), p. 96 and *passim*. The term *creative destruction* is Joseph Schumpeter's; see his *Capitalism, Socialism, and Democracy* (New York: Harper & Brothers, 1942).

71. Robert Michels, *Political Parties: A Sociological Study of the Oligarchical Tendencies of Modern Democracy* (New York: Dover, 1959 [1915]; Philip Selznick, *The Organizational Weapon: A Study of Bolshevik Strategy and Tactics* (Glencoe, IL: Free Press, 1960).

72. See especially François Furet, *The Passing of an Illusion: The Idea of Communism in the Twentieth Century*, trans. Deborah Furet (Chicago: University of Chicago Press, 1999 [1995]) and Courtois et al., *The Black Book of Communism*. For a discussion of the *Black Book of Communism*, see my "What Future for the Future? Reflections on the *Black Book of Communism*," *Human Rights Review* 2, no. 2 (January–March 2001): 135–143.

73. For Tocqueville's critique, see *The Old Regime and the Revolution*, trans. Stuart Gilbert (Garden City, NY: Doubleday Anchor, 1955), pt. III, ch. 1.

74. See Hannah Arendt, *On Revolution* (New York: Viking, 1965 [1963]), p. 249.

75. The term *catching-up revolutions* is Jürgen Habermas's; see his *Die nachholende Revolution: Kleine Politische Schriften VII* (Frankfurt: Suhrkamp, 1990); on the "roundtables" throughout Eastern Europe, see Jon Elster, ed., *The Roundtable Talks and the Collapse of Communism* (Chicago: University of Chicago Press, 1996).

76. Steiner, *Grammars of Creation*, p. 7.

77. Michael Ignatieff has recently responded to the human rights movement's tendency to denigrate the state by pointing out that, without a functioning state, there is no law and hence no human rights. See his *Human Rights as Politics and Idolatry*, ed. Amy Gutmann (Princeton, NJ: Princeton University Press, 2001), p. 35.

78. Max Weber, 'The Nation,' in Hans Gerth and C. Wright Mills, eds., *From Max Weber: Essays in Sociology* (New York: Oxford University Press, 1946), p. 176.

79. See Ronald Niezen, *The Origins of Indigenism: Human Rights and the Politics of Identity* (Berkeley: University of California Press, 2003).

80. See Arendt, *The Origins of Totalitarianism* (New York: Harcourt, Brace, 1973 [1951]), ch. 9.

81. See her controversial 1959 essay "Reflections on Little Rock," in Peter Baehr, ed., *The Portable Hannah Arendt* (New York: Penguin, 2000), pp. 231–246.

82. See T. H. Marshall, "Citizenship and Social Class," in his *Class, Citizenship, and Social Development*, ed. Seymour Martin Lipset (Garden City, NY: Doubleday, 1964 [1949]), pp. 71–134. On the importance of social solidarity as the basis for a "thick" conception of citizenship, see David Abraham, "Citizenship Solidarity and Rights Individualism: On the Decline of National Citizenship in the U.S., Germany, and Israel," manuscript, Shelby Cullom Davis Center for Historical Studies, Princeton University, 2002.

83. See especially Will Kymlicka, *Multicultural Citizenship: A Liberal Theory of Minority Rights* (Oxford: Oxford University Press, 1995).

84. For updates on the controversy, see the home page of the Center for Research and Documentation on Japan's War Responsibility at *www.jca.apc.org*. See also the relevant essays in Laura Hein and Mark Selden, eds., *Censoring History: Citizenship and Memory in Japan, Germany, and the United States* (Armonk, NY: M. E. Sharpe, 2000) and in Andrew Horvat and Gebhard Hielscher, eds., *Sharing the Burden of the Past: Legacies of War in Europe, America, and Asia* (Tokyo: The Asia Foundation/Friedrich-Ebert-Stiftung, 2003).

85. See Sasha Polakow-Suransky, "Reviving South African History," *The Chronicle of Higher Education*, June 14, 2002.

86. Chang notes that her involvement in the cause of commemorating and seeking reparations for the Rape of Nanking was galvanized by her attendance at a 1994 conference of the Global Alliance for Preserving the History of World War II in Asia in Cupertino, California; see Iris Chang, *The Rape of Nanking: The Forgotten Holocaust of World War II* (New York: Basic Books, 1997). The Web site of the Alliance for Preserving the Truth of Sino-Japanese War, a member of the Global Alliance, can be found at *www.sjwar.org*.

87. See "Turkey: Warning to France," *New York Times*, January 13, 2001, p. A4; "Switzerland: Lawmakers Accept Armenian Genocide," *New York Times*, December 17, 2003, p. A8.

88. Randall Robinson, *The Debt: What America Owes to Blacks* (New York: Dutton,

2000). The activities of the Transafrica Forum, which Robinson founded some-twenty-five years ago, appears to nurture strong ties to the "African diaspora." I address this subject in greater detail in Chapter 4.

89. Albert O. Hirschman, *Exit, Voice, and Loyalty: Responses to Decline in Firms, Organizations, and States* (Cambridge, MA: Harvard University Press, 1970).

90. Hobsbawm, *The Age of Extremes;* Furet, *The Passing of an Illusion;* and Ernst Nolte, *Der europäische Bürgerkrieg 1917–1945: Nationalsozialismus und Bolschewismus* (Berlin: Propyläen Verlag, 1987).

91. Jürgen Habermas, "Learning from Catastrophe? A Look Back at the Short Twentieth Century," in Habermas, *The Postnational Constellation,* p. 46; my translation from the original, "Aus Katastrophen lernen? Ein zeitdiagnostischer Rückblick auf das kurze 20. Jahrhundert," in *Die postnationale Konstellation,* p. 75.

92. Charles Maier, "Consigning the Twentieth Century to History: Alternative Narratives for the Modern Era," *American Historical Review* 105, no. 3 (June 2000): 827. Hannah Arendt articulated this perspective in her *Origins of Totalitarianism,* but it was also common among those suffering under European domination in the colonial world. For an example of awareness among non-Europeans of the similarities between Nazism and European treatment of native Africans, see "A Declaration to the Nations of the World Issued by the Non-European United Committee, Cape Town, South Africa, 1945," reproduced in Du Bois, *The World and Africa,* pp. 39–41. George Fredrickson compares the "overtly racist regimes" of the United States, South Africa, and Nazi Germany in his aforementioned *Racism: A Short History.*

93. Mazower, *Dark Continent: Europe's Twentieth Century* (New York: Knopf, 1998), p. xiii. Adam Hochschild employs a similar motif in his recent history of the predations of King Leopold in the Congo: "[M]en who would have been appalled to see someone using a *chicotte* [a whip made of hippopotamus hide] on the streets of Brussels or Paris or Stockholm accepted the act, in this different setting, as normal. We can hear the echo of this thinking, in another context, half a century later: 'To tell the truth,' said Franz Stangl of the mass killings that took place when he was commandant of the Nazi death camps of Sobibor and Treblinka, 'one did become used to it'." See Adam Hochschild, *King Leopold's Ghost: A Story of Greed, Terror, and Heroism in Colonial Africa* (New York: Houghton Mifflin, 1998), p. 122.

94. Joseph Conrad, *Heart of Darkness* and *The Secret Sharer,* with an introduction by Albert J. Guerard (New York: Signet/New American Library, 1950 [1910]), pp. 69–70.

95. Hochschild, *King Leopold's Ghost,* p. 225.

96. The Stolen Generations Inquiry, officially known as the National Inquiry into the Separation of Aboriginal and Torres Strait Islander Children from Their Families, sought to examine the laws and policies under which these removals—and attendant physical and sexual abuse—took place. In one of the Inquiry's most striking conclusions, it found that the Australian government had committed genocide in its use of these practices. The rationale under-

lying this finding was that the practices in question fulfilled the clause in the U.N. Genocide Convention (1948) according to which "forcibly transferring children of the group to another group" constitutes an act of genocide. See "Bringing Them Home: Report of the National Inquiry into the Separation of Aboriginal and Torres Strait Islander Children from Their Families," available at the Web site of the Australian Human Rights and Equal Opportunity Commission, *www.austlii.edu.au*. See also Antonella Romeo, "Die geraubte Generation," *Die Zeit*, May 31, 2000, available at *www.zeit.de*; and Thomas Schmid, "Australiens Holocaust," *Die Zeit*, May 31, 2000, available at *www.zeit* *.de*.

97. See Stephen Kinzer, "Turkish Region Recalls Massacre of Armenians," *New York Times*, May 10, 2000, p. A3.

98. Novick, *The Holocaust in American Life*, pp. 100–101. A conversation with Ben Kiernan at the 2000 meeting of the Social Science History Association in Pittsburgh was a reminder of the importance of the genocide charges in the trials of these war criminals. It remains to be seen, however, whether the fear of prosecution will not lead some maniacal rulers to hold fast to the reins of power in order to stave off the threat of prosecution.

99. This has been the subject of much recent attention following the publication of Samantha Power's *"A Problem from Hell": America and the Age of Genocide* (New York: Basic Books, 2002).

100. Furet, *The Passing of an Illusion*, p. 502.

101. For one analysis of the nature of the "transition from socialism to capitalism," see Gil Eyal, Ivan Szelenyi, and Eleanor Townsley, *Making Capitalism Without Capitalists: The New Ruling Elites in Eastern Europe* (New York: Verso, 1998).

102. The meeting normally takes place in Davos, which has come to be used as a shorthand to refer to it; in 2002, however, it was held in New York in order to show confidence in that city in the aftermath of the attacks of September 11, 2001.

103. See Simon Romero, "Brazil Forum More Local Than Worldly," *New York Times*, February 7, 2002, available at *www.nytimes.com*.

104. Dan Diner, *Das Jahrhundert verstehen: Eine universalhistorische Deutung* (Frankfurt am Main: Fischer Taschenbuch, 2000), p. 66.

105. Ilya Ehrenburg and Vassily Grossman, eds., *The Black Book: The Ruthless Murder of Jews by German-Fascist Invaders Throughout the Temporarily-Occupied Regions of the Soviet Union and in the Death Camps of Poland During the War of 1941–1945*, trans. John Glad and James S. Levine (New York: Holocaust Publications, 1981). I am grateful to Rick Wolin for reminding me of this predecessor to *The Black Book of Communism*.

106. Courtois, "Introduction: The Crimes of Communism," in Courtois et al., *The Black Book of Communism*, p. 23.

107. The curious notion that, in comparison with the Holocaust, the misdeeds of Communism have not received their fair due has received an extensive airing in France in recent years. Yet the claim that Communism has been

underscrutinized compared to the Holocaust reflects the belated French reckoning with Communism rather than any lack of attention to that system while it still held sway in Eastern Europe. See Alain Besançon, *La malheur du siècle: Sur le communisme, le nazisme, et la unicité de Shoah* (Paris: Fayard, 1998). For a critique of Besançon's view of the "amnesia" about Communism and the "hypermnesia" about the Holocaust, see Henry Rousso, "La Légitimité d'une comparaison empirique," in Rousso, ed., *Stalinisme et nazisme: Histoire et mémoire comparées* (Paris: Editions Complexe, 1999), esp. p. 18. For a further discussion of the significance of *The Black Book of Communism*, see my "What Future for the Future? Reflections on *The Black Book of Communism*," as well as the other essays collected in the symposium on *The Black Book* in that issue of *Human Rights Review*.

108. Diner, *Das Jahrhundert verstehen*, p. 233.

109. See Margolin, "Cambodia," in Courtois et al., *The Black Book of Communism*, p. 634. For an extended discussion of the "racialization" of social groups and its relation to state-sponsored killing, see Eric Weitz, "Race, Nation, Class: Das 'Schwarzbuch des Kommunismus' und das Problem des Vergleichs zwischen nationalsozialistischen und sowjetischen Verbrechen," *Werkstatt Geschichte* 22 (1999): 75–91 and *A Century of Genocide: Utopias of Race and Nation* (Princeton, NJ: Princeton University Press, 2003).

110. Novick, *The Holocaust in American Life*. Novick's discussion is more measured than that in Norman Finkelstein, *The Holocaust Industry: Reflections on the Exploitation of Jewish Suffering* (New York: Verso, 2000).

111. Charles Maier has argued that, outside the Euro-Atlantic world, where the experiences and problems have been of a different nature, the Holocaust is regarded as a "parochial" preoccupation. See his essay "Consigning the Twentieth Century to History," p. 826. Accurate though it undoubtedly is at the level of popular historical consciousness, I suggest certain limitations to this view in my essay "'Making Whole What Has Been Smashed': Reflections on Reparations," *Journal of Modern History* 73, no. 2 (June 2001): 333–358.

112. See Soyinka, *The Burden of Memory, the Muse of Forgiveness* (New York: Oxford University Press, 1999), p. 83.

113. The report, issued on July 7, 2000 and titled *Rwanda: The Preventable Genocide*, is available at *www.visiontv.ca*. The quoted passage appears in ch. 24, "Recommendations," p. 266.

114. On this point, see Samantha Power, "To Suffer by Comparison?" paper presented at the 1999 Annual Meeting of the Social Science History Association, Fort Worth, TX, November 1999.

115. See Horst Möller, *Der rote Holocaust und die Deutschen: Die Debatte um das "Schwarzbuch des Kommunismus"* (Munich: Piper, 1999).

116. For representative examples, see Russell Thornton, *American Indian Holocaust and Survival: A Population History Since 1492* (Norman: University of Oklahoma Press, 1987) and David Stannard, *American Holocaust: Columbus and the Conquest of the New World* (New York: Oxford University Press, 1992). The notion that slavery and the subsequent mistreatment of blacks in the United States

is "America's Holocaust" is widespread among those promoting reparations
for African-Americans; for more on this, see the chapter on this subject
below.

117. Mazrui, "Who Should Pay for Slavery?" *World Press Review* 40, no. 8 (August
1993): 22.

2. An Anatomy of Reparations Politics

1. Charles S. Maier, "Overcoming the Past? Narrative and Negotiation, Remem-
bering and Reparation: Issues at the Interface of History and the Law," in
John Torpey, ed., *Politics and the Past: On Repairing Historical Injustices*
(Lanham, MD: Rowman & Littlefield, 2003), pp. 295–304.

2. Robert Paxton. *Europe in the Twentieth Century* (New York: Harcourt, Brace,
Jovanovich, 1975). This example is particularly relevant to the present discussion insofar as Paxton would soon write, with Michael Marrus, the defini-
tive study of French collaboration with the Nazis, *Vichy France and the Jews*
(New York: Basic Books, 1981).

3. See Wolfgang Mommsen, *Max Weber and German Politics, 1890–1920*, trans.
Michael S. Steinberg (Chicago: University of Chicago Press, 1984 [1959]),
pp. 312–320, esp. p. 313.

4. Paxton, *Europe in the Twentieth Century*, p. 221.

5. Karl Jaspers, *The Question of German Guilt*, trans. E. B. Ashton (New York:
Fordham University Press, 2000), pp. 112–113. I have slightly revised the
translation, on the basis of *Die Schuldfrage: Von der politischen Haftung Deutschlands* (Munich/Zurich: Piper, 1987 [1946]), p. 81.

6. Ibid. I have slightly modified the translation.

7. See T. H. Marshall, "Citizenship and Social Class," in Marshall, *Class, Citizenship, and Social Development* (Garden City, NY: Doubleday, 1964), pp. 71–134.

8. "Draft Basic Principles and Guidelines on the Right to a Remedy and Reparation for Victims of Violations of International Human Rights and Humanitarian Law," available at *www.unhchr.ch* (revised August 15, 2003); see also
Priscilla Hayner, *Unspeakable Truths: Confronting State Terror and Atrocity* (New
York: Routledge, 2001), p. 171.

9. For a skeptical view of the idea of sovereignty, see Stephen D. Krasner, *Sover-
eignty: Organized Hypocrisy* (Princeton, NJ: Princeton University Press, 1999).
Michael Ignatieff has noted that the post–World War II advance of the
human rights paradigm was an important aspect of the twentieth century,
belying those who would see the century as an unmitigated disaster. See
Michael Ignatieff, *The Rights Revolution* (Toronto: Anansi, 2000) and Ignatieff,
Human Rights as Politics and Idolatry, ed. Amy Gutmann (Princeton, NJ:
Princeton University Press, 2001).

10. An editorial in the *New York Times* regarding an official apology to native
American Indians makes this point as well. Describing Indian reactions to the
proposed apology, the *Times* editorial writers note, "Tribal leaders have been
offering mixed reactions of wariness ('words on paper') and approval some-

what short of delight ('a good first step')" because "no federal reparations or claim settlements are at stake." *New York Times,* June 28, 2004, p. A18. For more on the case of redress to Japanese-Americans and Japanese-Canadians, see Chapter 3 below.

11. See, for example, Elazar Barkan, *The Guilt of Nations: Restitution and Negotiating Historical Injustices* (New York: W. W. Norton, 2000).

12. Marj Brown et al., *Land Restitution in South Africa: A Long Way Home* (Cape Town: Idasa, 1998); Paul Brodeur, *Restitution: The Land Claims of the Mashpee, Passamaquoddy, and Penobscot Indians of New England* (Boston: Northeastern University Press, 1985).

13. *Personal Justice Denied: Report of the Commission on Wartime Relocation and Internment of Civilians* (Seattle: University of Washington Press, 1997 [1983]), p. 12.

14. See Martha Minow, *Between Vengeance and Forgiveness: Facing History after Genocide and Mass Violence* (Boston: Beacon Press, 1998), pp. 61ff.

15. Here I am borrowing the title of Phillip Rieff's *The Triumph of the Therapeutic* (New York: Harper & Row, 1966). For a skeptical view of the advantages of this triumph in American life, see Eva S. Moskowitz, *In Therapy We Trust: America's Obsession with Self-Fulfillment* (Baltimore, MD: Johns Hopkins University Press, 2001).

16. On the transformation of the concept of trauma from a physical to a mental notion, see Ian Hacking, *Rewriting the Soul: Multiple Personality and the Sciences of Memory* (Princeton, NJ: Princeton University Press, 1995), esp. pp. 185–186. On the spread more recently of the diagnosis of "post-traumatic stress disorder," see Allan Young, *The Harmony of Illusions: Inventing Post-Traumatic Stress Disorder* (Princeton, NJ: Princeton University Press, 1995).

17. For a useful typology, see Heribert Adam and Kogila Moodley, *Seeking Mandela: Negotiating Compromises in Divided Societies* (Philadelphia: Temple University Press, 2005); an earlier version can be found in their essay "Divided Memories: Confronting the Crimes of Previous Regimes," *Telos* 118 (Winter 2000): 87–108.

18. For a revealing use of the notion of the "field" as the unit of analysis in social research, see Pierre Bourdieu, "The Structure of the Scientific Field and the Social Conditions of the Progress of Reason," *Social Science Information* 14, no. 5 (1975): 19–47; reprinted in Charles C. Lemert, ed., *French Sociology: Rupture and Renewal Since 1968* (New York: Columbia University Press, 1981), pp. 257–292.

19. Nicholas Tavuchis raises doubts, however, about whether any meaningful apology can be made by those not directly involved in the acts for which an apology is now offered. See Tavuchis, *Mea Culpa: A Sociology of Apology and Reconciliation* (Stanford, CA: Stanford University Press, 1991), p. 49.

20. See Guillermo O'Donnell, Philippe C. Schmitter, and Laurence Whitehead, eds., *Transitions from Authoritarian Rule: Prospects for Democracy* (Baltimore, MD: Johns Hopkins University Press, 1986); Neil J. Kritz, *Transitional Justice: How Emerging Democracies Reckon with Former Regimes* (Washington, DC: United

States Institute of Peace Press, 1995); A. James McAdams, *Transitional Justice and the Rule of Law in New Democracies* (Notre Dame, IN: University of Notre Dame Press, 1997); Jon Elster, "Coming to Terms with the Past: A Framework for the Study of Justice in the Transition to Democracy," *European Journal of Sociology* 39 (1998): 7–48; and Ruti Teitel, *Transitional Justice* (New York: Oxford University Press, 2000). Once the paradigm of transitional justice had established itself, it was applied retroactively to postwar Europe; on the complexities of transitional justice in Europe immediately following World War II, see István Deák, Jan T. Gross, and Tony Judt, eds., *The Politics of Retribution in Europe: World War II and Its Aftermath* (Princeton, NJ: Princeton University Press, 2000).

21. See Samuel Huntington, *The Third Wave: Democratization in the Late 20th Century* (Norman: University of Oklahoma Press, 1991).

22. Of the increasingly vast literature on truth commissions and commissions of historical inquiry, see A. James McAdams, *Judging the Past in Unified Germany* (New York: Cambridge University Press, 2001); Antjie Krog, *Country of My Skull: Guilt, Sorrow, and the Limits of Forgiveness in the New South Africa* (New York: Three Rivers Press, 1999 [1998]); and the recent comprehensive study by Hayner, *Unspeakable Truths*.

23. See Theo van Boven et al., eds., *Seminar on the Right to Restitution, Compensation, and Rehabilitation for Victims of Gross Violations of Human Rights and Fundamental Freedoms* (Utrecht, The Netherlands: Studie- en Informatiecentrum Mensenrechten, Netherlands Institute of Human Rights, 1992). The once so-called van Boven principles have since been superseded by the Bassiouni principles as the determinative U.N. guidelines in this area; see "The right to restitution, compensation and rehabilitation for victims of gross violations of human rights and fundamental freedoms: Final report of the Special Rapporteur, Mr. M. Cherif Bassiouni, submitted in accordance with Commission resolution 1999/33," E/CN.4/2000/62, January 18, 2000, available at *www .unhchr.ch*. The most recent version of the "Basic Principles and Guidelines on the Right to a Remedy and Reparation for Victims of Violations of International Human Rights and Humanitarian Law" can be found at *www.hshr.org*.

24. On this point, see Huntington, *The Third Wave*. The recent U.N. Human Development Report 2002, *Deepening Democracy in a Fragmented World*, suggests that this "third wave"—the foundation on which the whole theory of democratic transitions was built—may be cresting. The full text of the report can be found at- *www.undp.org*; for a brief summary, see Barbara Crossette, "U.N. Report Says New Democracies Falter," *New York Times*, July 24, 2002, p. A8.

25. Tina Rosenberg, *The Haunted Land: Facing Europe's Ghosts after Communism* (New York: Random House, 1995). For Havel's analysis of the social underpinnings of Communist regimes, see his essay "The Power of the Powerless," in Vaclav Havel, *Living in Truth*, ed. Jan Vladislav (London: Faber and Faber, 1987 [1978]). For a useful typology of processes of coming to terms with past regimes, see Heribert Adam and Kanya Adam, "The Politics of Memory in Divided Societies," in Wilmot James and Linda van de Vijver, eds., *After*

the TRC: Reflections on Truth and Reconciliation in South Africa (Athens: Ohio University Press, 2001), pp. 32–47.

26. See Huntington, *The Third Wave.*

27. See Sharon Lean, "Is Truth Enough? Reparations and Reconciliation in Latin America," in Torpey, ed., *Politics and the Past.*

28. See Hayner, *Unspeakable Truths,* ch. 11.

29. Jon Elster, *Closing the Books: Transitional Justice in Historical Perspective* (Cambridge: Cambridge University Press, 2004).

30. Barrington Moore Jr., *The Social Origins of Dictatorship and Democracy: Lord and Peasant in the Making of the Modern World* (Boston: Beacon Press, 1966).

31. Aristide Zolberg et al., *Escape from Violence: Conflict and the Refugee Crisis in the Developing World* (New York: Oxford University Press, 1989), p. 255.

32. The best work on coming to terms with the past in the former Communist countries is Rosenberg, *The Haunted Land.* See also her editorial, "In Chile, the Balance Tips Toward the Victims," *New York Times,* August 22, 2000, p. A26. On restitution and privatization in Eastern Europe, see Barkan, *The Guilt of Nations,* ch. 6.

33. On the concept of internal colonialism, see Robert Blauner, *Racial Oppression in America* (New York: Harper & Row, 1972); an updated version is available in Blauner, *Still the Big News: Racial Oppression in America* (Philadelphia: Temple University Press, 2001).

34. The dams highlighted in the demands included one in Guatemala that was said to have been opposed by the Maya Achi indigenous group, and the Pak Mun Dam in Thailand. See the announcement of the "Issues Forum on World Bank, Dams, and Reparations" distributed by Aviva Imhof of the International Rivers Network, April 10, 2000, *aviva@irn.org.* I am grateful to Todd Gitlin for bringing this case to my attention.

35. I discuss this in greater detail below.

36. Mahmood Mamdani, "Degrees of Reconciliation and Forms of Justice: Making Sense of the African Experience," paper presented at the conference "Justice or Reconciliation?" at the Center for International Studies, University of Chicago, April 25–26, 1997, p. 6; quoted in Hayner *Unspeakable Truths,* p. 164.

37. Mahmood Mamdani, "A Diminished Truth," in James and van de Vijver, eds., *After the TRC,* p. 59.

38. John Torpey, "'Making Whole What Has Been Smashed': Reflections on Reparations," *Journal of Modern History* 73, no. 2 (June 2001): 333–358.

39. See, for example, Hayner's description of the reparations program in Chile, in *Unspeakable Truths,* pp. 172–173.

40. I am grateful to Philippe van Parijs for suggesting this distinction when I spoke about this project while a fellow at the Hoover Chair in Economic and Social Ethics, Université Catholique de Louvain, Louvain-la-Neuve, Belgium, October 23, 2003.

41. For the distinction between identity politics and commonality politics, see Todd Gitlin, *The Twilight of Common Dreams: Why America Is Wracked by Culture Wars* (New York: Metropolitan Books, 1995).

42. See especially Will Kymlicka, *Multicultural Citizenship: A Liberal Theory of Minority Rights* (New York: Oxford University Press, 1995); Kymlicka, ed., *The Rights of Minority Cultures* (New York: Oxford University Press, 1995); for a vigorous (though in some respects intemperate) rejoinder to Kymlicka and his allies, see Brian Barry, *Culture & Equality* (Cambridge, MA: Harvard University Press, 2001).

43. On the nature of the harms experienced by the comfort women, see Yamashita Yeong-ae, "The Re-Discovery of the 'Comfort Women' Issue in Korea," paper presented at the symposium on "Comfort Women of World War II: Their Suffering Must Not Be Forgotten," University of British Columbia, January 18, 2002, pp. 4–5.

44. Minow, *Between Vengeance and Forgiveness*, pp. 100–111 and 184n77. See also Warren Hoge, "A Curator of Lost Artwork and Found Memories," *New York Times*, May 25, 2002, p. A4.

45. On this issue, see Barkan, *The Guilt of Nations*, ch. 4.

46. Judith H. Dobrzynski, "Russia Pledges to Give Back Some of Its Art Looted in War," *New York Times*, December 3, 1998, p. A9.

47. Maier, "Overcoming the Past?" in Torpey, ed., *Politics and the Past*, p. 297.

48. Ruth B. Phillips and Elizabeth Johnson, "Negotiating New Relationships: Canadian Museums, First Nations and Cultural Property," in Torpey, ed., *Politics and the Past*, pp. 149–150.

49. Barkan, *The Guilt of Nations*, p. 171.

50. See Phillips and Johnson, "Negotiating New Relationships," in Torpey, ed., *Politics and the Past*, pp. 155–159.

51. See Michael Brown, *Who Owns Native Culture?* (Cambridge, MA: Harvard University Press, 2003) and Tiffany Jenkins, "Burying the Evidence," *Spiked Online*, November 24, 2003, available at *www.spiked-online.com*.

52. For a valuable discussion, see Ronald Niezen: *The Origins of Indigenism: Human Rights and the Politics of Identity* (Berkeley: University of California Press, 2003).

53. On this point, see Barry, *Culture & Equality*.

54. See Patrick Wolfe, "Land, Labor, and Difference: Elementary Structures of Race," *American Historical Review* 106, no. 3 (June 2001): 866–905.

55. Kymlicka, *Multicultural Citizenship*.

56. Tocqueville understood these dynamics concerning the response of American Indians to their conquest and colonization; see *Democracy in America*, trans. George Lawrence, ed. J. P. Mayer (Garden City, NY: Anchor Doubleday, 1969 [1835]), vol. 1, pt. II, ch. 10.

57. Chris Cunneen, "Reparations, Human Rights, and the Challenge of Confronting a Recalcitrant Government," *Third World Legal Studies*, Special Issue on "Into the 21st Century: Reconstruction and Reparations in International Law" (2000–2003): 183–201.

58. The document can be found at *www.ainc-inac.gc.ca*.

59. The RCAP report is discussed at length in Alan Cairns, "Coming to Terms with the Past," in Torpey, ed., *Politics and the Past*, pp. 77–80.

60. "Gathering Strength," *www.ainc-inac.gc.ca*.

61. For an example of the genre, see Arthur J. Ray, *I Have Lived Here Since the World Began: An Illustrated History of Canada's Native Peoples* (Toronto: Lester Publishing, 1996). For two skeptical views of Indian claims regarding the spiritual significance of specific lands, see Tom Flanagan, *First Nations? Second Thoughts* (Montreal: McGill–Queen's University Press, 2000) and Fergus Bordewich, *Killing the White Man's Indian: The Reinvention of Native Americans at the End of the Twentieth Century* (New York: Doubleday, 1996).

62. As noted previously, the phrase "creative destruction" is Joseph Schumpeter's, but it is also an apt characterization of Marx's understanding of capitalism as reflected in *The Communist Manifesto*.

63. Rhéal Séguin, "Cree, Quebec Sign Historic Deal," *The Globe and Mail* (Toronto), February 8, 2002.

64. See Chapter 5.

65. R. S. Ratner, W. K. Carroll, and Andrew Woolford, "Wealth of Nations: Aboriginal Treaty-Making in the Era of Globalization," in Torpey, ed., *Politics and the Past*, pp. 217–247.

66. For an excellent study of the treaty-making process in British Columbia today, see Andrew Woolford, "Between Justice and Certainty: Treaty Making in Modern-Day British Columbia," Ph.D. diss., Department of Anthropology and Sociology, University of British Columbia, 2002.

67. For a discussion of the importance of the end of colonialism for subsequent politics, see Geoffrey Barraclough, *An Introduction to Contemporary History* (New York: Penguin, 1967 [1964]), ch. 6, "The Revolt Against the West."

68. The charge of corruption is one among the litany of objections mounted in Flanagan, *First Nations? Second Thoughts*.

69. A number of Canadian political theorists have been arguing against the notion of equal citizenship for some time. Indeed, theories of minority group rights have been Canada's chief export on the international market of ideas in recent years. In addition to the works of Will Kymlicka cited above, see the writings of Charles Taylor and of James Tully, especially his *Strange Multiplicity: Constitutionalism in an Age of Diversity* (Cambridge: Cambridge University Press, 1995). For an approach that takes issue with the paradigm of group rights and the "nation-to-nation" vision it supports, see Alan C. Cairns, *Citizens Plus: Aboriginal Peoples and the Canadian State* (Vancouver: University of British Columbia Press, 2000).

70. See Philip A. Klinkner with Rogers M. Smith, *The Unsteady March: The Rise and Decline of Racial Equality in America* (Chicago: University of Chicago Press, 1999).

71. Tocqueville's pessimistic analysis of the consequences of the overlap between slavery and color remain relevant here. See *Democracy in America*, vol. 1, pt. II, ch. 10. For a valuable assessment of Tocqueville's pessimism, see George Fredrickson, "Race and Empire in Liberal Thought: The Legacy of Tocqueville," in Fredrickson, *The Comparative Imagination: On the History of Racism,*

Nationalism, and Social Movements (Berkeley: University of California Press, 1997), pp. 98–116.

72. See Randall Robinson, *The Debt: What America Owes to Blacks* (New York: Dutton, 2000).

73. This appears to be the approach taken by the lawyers who have been planning to launch a lawsuit against the U.S. government for reparations; see "Forum: Making the Case for Racial Reparations," *Harper's* (November 2000): 37–51.

74. Karl Marx, *Capital,* vol. 1, ch. 23, "The Genesis of the Industrial Capitalist," in Robert Tucker, ed., *The Marx-Engels Reader,* 2nd ed. (New York: Norton, 1978), p. 435.

75. Ali A. Mazrui, "Who Should Pay for Slavery?" *World Press Review* 40, no. 8 (August 1993): 22.

76. From the Web site of the Africa Reparations Movement, at *www.arm.arc.co.uk.* The Web site says, "Due to the sad death of Rt. Honourable Bernie Grant MP, this site is currently not being maintained." See also Barkan, *The Guilt of Nations,* p. 302.

77. Mazrui, "Who Should Pay for Slavery?" p. 23.

78. Wole Soyinka, "Reparations, Truth, and Reconciliation," in Soyinka, *The Burden of Memory, the Muse of Forgiveness* (New York: Oxford University Press, 1999), pp. 44–46.

79. Rhoda Howard-Hassmann, "Moral Integrity and Reparations to Africa," in Torpey, ed., *Politics and the Past,* pp. 193–215.

80. Walter Rodney, *How Europe Underdeveloped Africa* (Washington, DC: Howard University Press, 1972).

81. For an assessment of "the Third World's Third World," see Paul Kennedy, *Preparing for the Twenty-First Century* (New York: Vintage, 1993), pp. 211ff; see also the U.N. Human Development Report 2002, *Deepening Democracy in a Fragmented World,* available at *www.undp.org.*

82. Howard-Hassmann, "Moral Integrity and Reparations to Africa," p. 209.

83. Nacha Cattan, "Restitution Attorneys Plan Lawsuits Backing 3rd World Debt Relief," *The Forward,* November 30, 2001.

84. *Rwanda: The Preventable Genocide,* available at: *www.visiontv.ca,* Executive Summary ¶68.

85. For two representative positions in the debate, see Alan J. Kuperman, *The Limits of Humanitarian Intervention: Genocide in Rwanda* (Washington, DC: Brookings Institution Press, 2001) and Samantha Power, "Bystanders to Genocide," *The Atlantic Monthly* (September 2001), available at *www.theatlantic .com.* Kuperman's sober analysis reads like an apology for the failure of the outside powers to intervene, while Power's indictment of U.S. foreign policy bears remarkable similarities to that advanced by those who see the United States (and Britain) as responsible for the deaths of many Jews at the hands of the Nazis. The chief prosecutor here is David Wyman in his *The Abandonment of the Jews: America and the Holocaust, 1941–1945* (New York: The New

Press, 1998 [1984]). For critiques of this position, see Peter Novick, *The Holocaust in American Life*, ch. 3, and William D. Rubinstein, *The Myth of Rescue: Why the Democracies Could Not Have Saved More Jews from the Nazis* (New York: Routledge, 1997). See also Michael Innes, "Ordinary Bystanders?" *SAIS Review* 22, no. 2 (Summer–Fall 2002): 361–366.

86. John Dower, *Embracing Defeat: Japan in the Wake of World War II* (New York: Norton/The New Press, 1999), p. 459.

87. Daniel Levy and Natan Sznaider, "Memory Unbound: The Holocaust and the Formation of Cosmopolitan Memory," *European Journal of Social Theory* 5, no. 1 (2002): 87–106.

88. See Stef Vandeginste, "Victims of Genocide, Crimes Against Humanity, and War Crimes in Rwanda: The Legal and Institutional Framework of Their Right to Reparation," in Torpey, ed., *Politics and the Past*, pp. 249–274.

89. See Power, "Bystanders to Genocide."

90. For a representative example, see Théo Klein, "Putting a Price on Holocaust Guilt," *New York Times*, December 15, 1998, p. A31. See also Maier, "Overcoming the Past?" in Torpey, ed., *Politics and the Past*.

91. See the discussion in Laura Hein, "Claiming Humanity and Legal Standing: Contemporary Demands for Redress from Japan for Its World War II Policies," in Torpey, ed., *Politics and the Past*, pp. 127–147. For an extended treatment of the story, see George Hicks, *The Comfort Women* (New York: Norton, 1995) and Yoshimi Yoshiaki, *Comfort Women: Sexual Slavery in the Japanese Military During World War II*, trans. Suzanne O'Brien (New York: Columbia University Press, 2000 [1995]).

92. On these demands, see the Violence Against Women in War Network Japan at *www1.jca.apc.org*.

93. See Roy Brooks, "Reflections on Reparations," in Torpey, ed., *Politics and the Past*, p. 107.

94. Tavuchis, *Mea Culpa*, p. 49.

95. See Jeffrey K. Olick and Brenda Coughlin, "The Politics of Regret: Analytical Frames," in Torpey, ed., *Politics and the Past*, p. 56.

96. E. P. Thompson, *The Making of the English Working Class* (New York: Penguin, 1968 [1963]), p. 12.

97. Gayatri Chakravorty Spivak, "Can the Subaltern Speak?" in Cary Nelson and Lawrence Grossberg, eds., *Marxism and the Interpretation of Culture* (Urbana: University of Illinois Press, 1988), pp. 271–315.

98. See Dipesh Chakrabarty, *Provincializing Europe: Postcolonial Thought and Historical Difference* (Princeton, NJ: Princeton University Press, 2000).

99. See the writings of Manuel Castells, especially *The Rise of the Network Society*, vol. 1 of *The Information Age: Economy, Society and Culture* (Oxford: Blackwell, 1996).

100. Susan Buck-Morss, *Dreamworld and Catastrophe: The Passing of Mass Utopia in East and West* (Cambridge, MA: MIT Press, 2000).

101. See George Mosse, *Fallen Soldiers: Reshaping the Memory of the World Wars* (New York: Oxford University Press, 1990), pp. 24–25.

102. Paul Goldberger, "Requiem: Memorializing Terrorism's Victims in Oklahoma," *The New Yorker*, January 14, 2002, p. 91.

103. See Barry Meier, "Chroniclers of Collaboration: Historians Are in Demand to Study Corporate Ties to Nazis," *New York Times*, February 18, 1999, p. C1, and the contributions by Gerald Feldman and Harold James in Norbert Frei, Dirk van Laak, and Michael Stolleis, eds., *Geschichte vor Gericht: Historiker, Richter und die Suche nach Gerechtigkeit* (Munich: Verlag C. H. Beck, 2000).

104. Gerald D. Feldman, "Unternehmensgeschichte im Dritten Reich und die Verantwortung der Historiker: Raubgold und Versicherungen, Arisierung und Zwangsarbeit," in Norbert Frei et al., eds., *Geschichte vor Gericht*, p. 119. An English version of Feldman's article appeared in January 1999 as an Occasional Paper of the Center for German and European Studies of the University of California, Berkeley under the title, "The Business History of the 'Third Reich' and the Responsibilities of the Historian: Gold, Insurance, 'Aryanization,' and Forced Labor."

105. See the judicious article by Daqing Yang, "The Challenges of the Nanjing Massacre: Reflections on Historical Inquiry," in *The Nanjing Massacre in History and Historiography*, ed. Joshua Fogel (Berkeley: University of California Press, 2000), p. 151.

106. The quotation is from Zygmunt Bauman, *Modernity and the Holocaust* (Ithaca, NY: Cornell University Press, 1989), p. x, discussing the response to Hannah Arendt's claims in *Eichmann in Jerusalem* that the leaders of Jewish communities in Eastern Europe shared a heavy load of responsibility for the Holocaust. For a discriminating brief assessment of Arendt's arguments, see Michael Marrus, *The Holocaust in History* (New York: Meridian, 1987), pp. 110–113.

107. The seminal work unearthing the independent French role is Michael R. Marrus and Robert O. Paxton, *Vichy France and the Jews* (New York: Basic Books, 1981).

108. Henry Rousso, "Justice, History and Memory in France: Reflections on the Papon Trial," in Torpey, ed., *Politics and the Past*, p. 284. See also Rousso's seminal study, *The Vichy Syndrome: History and Memory in France Since 1944*, trans. Arthur Goldhammer (Cambridge, MA: Harvard University Press, 1991 [1987]).

109. See Cairns, "Coming to Terms with the Past," in Torpey, ed., *Politics and the Past*.

110. Donald Shriver, *An Ethic for Enemies: Forgiveness in Politics* (New York: Oxford University Press, 1995), p. 91; see also Minow, *Between Vengeance and Forgiveness, passim,* and, on analogous efforts by Japanese and Koreans, see Laura Hein and Mark Selden, eds., *Censoring History: Citizenship and Memory in Japan, Germany, and the United States* (Armonk, NY: M. E. Sharpe, 2000).

111. For a recent discussion, see Yasemin Soysal, "Teaching Europe," OpenDemocracy.net, available at *www.opendemocracy.net*.

112. See Susan Dwyer, "Reconciliation for Realists," *Ethics and International Affairs* 13 (1999): 81–98.

113. See Peter N. Stearns, Peter Seixas, and Sam Wineburg, eds., *Knowing, Teaching and Learning History: National and International Perspectives* (New York: New York University Press, 2000) and Hein and Selden, eds., *Censoring History;* note the recent rise in importance of Maurice Halbwachs's seminal studies of the social foundations of collective memory, collected in Lewis Coser, ed., *Maurice Halbwachs: On Collective Memory* (Chicago: University of Chicago Press, 1992); see also the writings of the German philosopher of history Jörn Rüsen, such as *Zerbrechende Zeit: Über den Sinn der Geschichte* (Köln: Böhlau, 2001). Peter Seixas has recently spearheaded the creation of the Centre for the Study of Historical Consciousness at the University of British Columbia; the Eva and Marc Besen Institute for the Study of Historical Consciousness at Tel Aviv University publishes the leading journal in the field, *History & Memory.*

114. See Novick, *The Holocaust in American Life* and Jeffrey K. Olick, ed., *States of Memory: Continuities, Conflicts, and Transformations in National Retrospection* (Durham, NC: Duke University Press, 2003).

115. I borrow these terms from Charles S. Maier, *The Unmasterable Past: History, Holocaust, and German National Identity* (Cambridge, MA: Harvard University Press, 1997 [1988]), p. 32.

116. Michael Ignatieff made this argument in his keynote speech at a symposium on "Redressing Historic Injustices: The Holocaust and Other Experiences," organized by Michael Marrus at the Munk Centre for International Studies, University of Toronto, January 23–24, 2002.

3. Commemoration, Redress, and Reconciliation

1. Lily Gardner Feldman, "The Principle and Practice of 'Reconciliation' in German Foreign Policy: Relations with France, Israel, Poland and the Czech Republic," *International Affairs* 75, no. 2 (April 1999): 333–356.

2. Priscilla Hayner, *Unspeakable Truths: Confronting State Terror and Atrocity* (New York: Routledge, 2001), p. 135.

3. See Heribert Adam, "The Presence of the Past: South Africa's Truth Commission as a Model?" in A. Tayob and W. Weisse, eds., *Religion and Politics in South Africa* (Muenster: Waxmann, 2000), pp. 140–158.

4. The terms *temporary detention center* and *internment camp* represent an important shift in the ways in which the history of this period has been understood, and debates over the proper terms to use in discussing this past have been central stakes in the controversy. The terms used here conform to the recommendations of the "Civil Liberties Public Education Fund Resolution Concerning Terminology"; see *www.momomedia.com.*

5. See Roger Daniels, *Concentration Camps: Japanese in the United States and Canada During World War II* (Malabar, FL: Robert E. Krieger Publishing Company, 1981), p. 188, and Maryka Omatsu, *Bittersweet Passage: Redress and the Japanese Canadian Experience* (Toronto: Between the Lines, 1992), p. 94.

6. Daniels, *Concentration Camps,* p. 3.

7. See Paul Spickard, *Japanese Americans: The Formation and Transformations of an Ethnic Group* (London: Prentice Hall International, 1996), p. 135.

8. Canadian Race Relations Foundation, "From Racism to Redress: The Japanese Canadian Experience" (1999) at *www.crr.ca*.

9. Ann Gomer Sunahara, *The Politics of Racism: The Uprooting of Japanese Canadians During the Second World War* (Toronto: James Lorimer & Company, 1981), p. 145.

10. Roy Miki and Cassandra Kobayashi, *Justice in Our Time: The Japanese-Canadian Redress Settlement* (Vancouver: Talonbooks, 1991), p. 55.

11. On these developments, see Robert Blauner, *Still the Big News: Racial Oppression in America* (Philadelphia: Temple University Press, 2001), ch. 4.

12. Interview with Art Miki, Winnipeg, Manitoba, July 7, 2003.

13. See Martha Minow, *Between Vengeance and Forgiveness: Facing History after Genocide and Mass Violence* (Boston: Beacon Press, 1998), p. 104.

14. Charles S. Maier, "Overcoming the Past? Narrative and Negotiation, Remembering and Reparation: Issues at the Interface of History and the Law," in John Torpey, ed., *Politics and the Past: On Repairing Historical Injustices* (Lanham, MD: Rowman & Littlefield, 2003), pp. 297–298.

15. Nicholas Tavuchis, *Mea Culpa: A Sociology of Apology and Reconciliation* (Stanford, CA: Stanford University Press, 1991), p. 17.

16. See Charles Maier, "Zu einer politischen Typologie der Aussöhnung," *Transit*, no. 18 (Winter 1999–2000), pp. 102–117.

17. See Judy Balint, "Law's Constitutive Possibilities: Reconstruction and Reconciliation in the Wake of Genocide and State Crime," in E. Christodoulidis and S. Veitch, eds., *Lethe's Law: Justice, Law and Ethics in Reconciliation* (Oxford: Hart Publishing, 2001), p. 144.

18. For an extended discussion of the meaning of "reconciliation," see Susan Dwyer, "Reconciliation for Realists," *Ethics and International Affairs* 13 (1999): 81–98.

19. See Roy Brooks, "Reflections on Reparations," in Torpey, ed., *Politics and the Past*, p. 16.

20. Interview with John Tateishi, San Francisco, CA, March 3, 2003.

21. I am grateful to Christian Joppke for pointing out this anomaly.

22. See Peter Novick, *The Holocaust in American Life* (Boston: Houghton Mifflin, 1999).

23. Alejandro Portes and Rubén Rumbaut, *Legacies: The Story of the Immigrant Second Generation* (Berkeley: University of California Press, 2001), p. 59.

24. See Stephen Fugita and David O'Brien, *Japanese American Ethnicity: The Persistence of Community* (Seattle: University of Washington Press, 1991), p. 152.

25. See ibid.; Donna Nagata, *Legacy of Injustice: Exploring the Cross-Generational Impact of the Japanese American Internment* (New York: Plenum Press, 1993); Mitchell Maki et al., *Achieving the Impossible Dream: How the Japanese Americans Obtained Redress* (Urbana: University of Illinois Press, 1999); and Robert Shimabukuro Sadamu, *Born in Seattle: The Campaign for Japanese American Redress* (Seattle: University of Washington Press, 2001).

26. Dale Minami, remarks at the Symposium on "Reparations for Slavery and Its Legacy," Boalt Hall School of Law, University of California, Berkeley, April 13, 2002.

27. Interview with John Tateishi, San Francisco, CA, March 3, 2003.

28. On the notion of constitutional patriotism, see Jürgen Habermas, "Geschichtsbewußtsein und posttraditionale Identität: Die Westorientierung der Bundesrepublik," in Habermas, *Eine Art Schadensabwicklung: Kleine politische Schriften VI* (Frankfurt am Main: Suhrkamp, 1987), p. 173.

29. Interview with Art Miki, Winnipeg, Manitoba, July 7, 2003.

30. Omatsu, *Bittersweet Passage*, p. 151.

31. Tomoko Makabe, *The Canadian Sansei* (Toronto: University of Toronto Press, 1998), p. 149.

32. Interview with Audrey Kobayashi, February 3, 2003.

33. Interview with Art Miki, Winnipeg, Manitoba, July 7, 2003.

34. Ibid.

35. Nagata, *Legacy of Injustice*, p. 181.

36. Reported in Lori Aratani, "As Their Numbers Shrink, Japanese American Heritage Thrives," *San Jose Mercury News*, July 6, 2001, available at *mercurynews.com*.

37. Makabe, *The Canadian Sansei*, p. 122.

38. Audrey Kobayashi, "The Japanese Canadian Redress Settlement and Its Implications for 'Race Relations'," *Canadian Ethnic Studies* 24, no. 1 (1992): 1–19.

39. See Maki et al., *Achieving the Impossible Dream*, pp. 182, 240.

40. The Commission on Wartime Relocation and Internment of Civilians envisaged in its recommendations that compensation would be due to "60,000 surviving persons excluded from their places of residence pursuant to Executive Order 9066"; see *Personal Justice Denied*, p. 463. By 1992, however, the Justice Department estimated that a total of 80,000 persons would be eligible for redress payments; see Maki et al., *Achieving the Impossible Dream*, p. 216.

41. See the Web site of the CLPEF at *www.momomedia.com*.

42. See its Web site at *www.crr.ca*.

43. Interview with Jim Matsuoka, Los Angeles, March 4, 2003.

44. For a discussion of the importance of honor in Japanese culture, see Ruth Benedict, *The Chrysanthemum and the Sword* (Boston: Mariner Books, 1989 [1946]).

45. Interview with John Tateishi, San Francisco, CA, March 3, 2003.

46. Interview with Haru Kuromiya, Los Angeles, March 4, 2003.

47. Interview with Art Miki, Winnipeg, Manitoba, July 7, 2003.

48. Interview with Keiko Miki, president of National Association of Japanese Canadians, Winnipeg, Manitoba, July 7, 2003.

49. Interview with Frank Kamiya, Japanese Canadian National Museum, Burnaby, British Columbia, August 6, 2003.

50. Interview with Art Miki, Winnipeg, Manitoba, July 7, 2003.

51. Omatsu, *Bittersweet Passage*, p. 171.

52. Interview with Keiko Miki, Winnipeg, Manitoba, July 7, 2003.

53. Omatsu, *Bittersweet Passage,* p. 171.

54. See John Torpey, "Introduction: Politics and the Past," in Torpey, ed., *Politics and the Past,* p. 17.

55. For an insightful discussion, see Jürgen Habermas, "Excursus on Benjamin's Theses on the Philosophy of History," in *The Philosophical Discourse of Modernity: Twelve Lectures,* trans. Frederick Lawrence (Cambridge, MA: MIT Press, 1987), pp. 11–16.

56. *Personal Justice Denied: Report of the Commission on Wartime Relocation and Internment of Civilians* (Seattle: University of Washington Press, 1997 [1983]), p. 460.

57. See Minow, *Between Vengeance and Forgiveness,* p. 103.

58. Senator Daniel Inouye, a key congressional supporter of the redress effort, eventually dissuaded him from this approach.

59. Interview with Frank Kitamoto, Bainbridge Island, WA, February 15, 2003.

60. On the distinction between these two types of reparations claims, see John Torpey, "'Making Whole What Has Been Smashed': Reflections on Reparations," *Journal of Modern History* 73, no. 2 (June 2001): 333–358.

61. Interview with John Tateishi, San Francisco, CA, March 3, 2003.

62. Interview with Art Miki, Winnipeg, Manitoba, July 7, 2003.

63. See Jürgen Habermas, *The Theory of Communicative Action,* vol. 2: *Lifeworld and System: A Critique of Functionalist Reason,* trans. Thomas McCarthy (Boston: Beacon Press, 1981), pp. 356–373; see also Sarah Lyall, "Britain's Stiff Upper Lip Is Being Twisted into a Snarl," *New York Times,* July 13, 2004, p. A3. A number of Canadians have suggested to me informally that the shift toward American-style litigiousness that is described in this *New York Times* article has been taking place in Canada as well.

64. Interview with Art Miki, Winnipeg, Manitoba, July 7, 2003.

65. Interview with John Tateishi, San Francisco, CA, March 3, 2003.

66. See Yasuko Takezawa, *Breaking the Silence: Redress and Japanese American Ethnicity* (Ithaca, NY: Cornell University Press, 1995), p. 197.

67. Interview with Jim Matsuoka, Los Angeles, March 4, 2003.

68. See Roy L. Brooks, "The Age of Apology," in Brooks, ed., *When Sorry Isn't Enough: The Controversy over Apologies and Reparations for Human Injustice* (New York: New York University Press, 1999), pp. 3–11.

69. For example, members of the National Coalition on Redress and Reconciliation, whose ideology was clearly more left-wing than that of the Japanese American Citizens League, were relatively critical of the standpoint of the Japanese American National Museum (JANM). It is worth noting that during July 1–August 15, 2004, the JANM hosted the Smithsonian Institution's exhibition, "September 11: Bearing Witness to History." Such an arguably nationalistic exhibition would not likely have been organized under the leadership of members of the NCRR.

70. Takezawa, *Breaking the Silence,* p. 210.

71. See Kobayashi, "The Japanese Canadian Redress Settlement," p. 4.

72. Interview with Art Miki, Winnipeg, Manitoba, July 7, 2003. As suggested by the lower figure quoted above from the work of Makabe, the actual rate of intermarriage is probably rather lower—though still fairly high.

73. Interview with Audrey Kobayashi, Vancouver, British Columbia, February 3, 2003.

74. Interview with Frank Kamiya, Japanese Canadian National Museum, Burnaby, British Columbia, August 6, 2003.

75. Interview with John Tateishi, San Francisco, CA, March 3, 2003.

76. Maier, "Overcoming the Past?" p. 296.

77. See Roger Daniels, "Relocation, Redress and the Report: A Historical Approach," in Brooks, ed., *When Sorry Isn't Enough*, p. 184.

78. Mark Selden, "Confronting World War II: The Atomic Bombing and the Internment of Japanese-Americans in U.S. History Textbooks," in Andrew Horvat and Gebhard Hielscher, eds., *Sharing the Burden of the Past: Legacies of War in Europe, America, and Asia* (Tokyo: The Asia Foundation/Friedrich-Ebert-Stiftung, 2003), p. 65.

79. For a suggestive discussion, see Jean Comaroff, "The End of History, Again: Pursuing the Past in the Postcolony," in S. Kaul et al., eds., *Postcolonial Studies and Beyond* (Durham, NC: Duke University Press, forthcoming).

80. See Ivan Karpf, "Culture and Representation," in I. Karpf and S. Lavine, eds., *Exhibiting Cultures: The Poetics and Politics of Museum Display* (Washington, DC: Smithsonian Institution Press, 1991).

81. To borrow the title of Pierre Nora, ed., *Les Lieux de mémoire* (7 vols.) (Paris: Edition Gallimard, 1984–1992); for an English version of some of this work, see Pierre Nora, ed., *Realms of Memory: Rethinking the French Past* (New York: Columbia University Press, 1992).

82. See Selden, "Confronting World War II," p. 66.

83. Although this discussion is informed by Bourdieu's stress on the importance in various social practices of "disinterestedness," my understanding of "symbolic capital" differs from his rendering in *Outline of a Theory of Practice*, trans. Richard Nice (New York: Cambridge University Press, 1977 [1972]), pp. 171–183.

84. See Carol Duncan, "Art Museums and the Ritual of Citizenship," in Karpf and Lavine, eds., *Exhibiting Cultures*, p. 93.

85. See Arthur Miki, *The Japanese Canadian Redress Legacy: A Community Revitalized* (Winnipeg: National Association of Japanese Canadians, 2003).

86. Interview with Audrey Kobayashi, Vancouver, British Columbia, February 3, 2003.

87. Tom Shomaya's address at the opening ceremony, cited in Miki, *The Japanese Canadian Redress Legacy*, p. 75.

88. See Susan Crane, "On Museums and Memory," in Crane, ed., *Museums and Memory* (Stanford, CA: Stanford University Press, 2000), p. 3.

89. See Christine Mullen, "Defining Communities Through Exhibiting and Col-

lecting," in I. Karpf, C. Mullen, and S. Lavine, eds., *Museums and Communities* (Washington, DC: Smithsonian Institution Press, 1992), p. 371.

90. See Novick, *The Holocaust in American Life.* The phrase "lachrymose conception of Jewish history" was coined by the great historian Salo Wittmayer Baron, who said it "treats Judaism as a sheer succession of miseries and persecutions."

91. Interview with Frank Kitamoto, Bainbridge Island, WA, February 15, 2003.

92. See Mary Waters, *Ethnic Options: Choosing Identities in America* (Berkeley: University of California Press, 1990), p. 4.

93. See *www.janm.org.*

94. Stan Fukawa, "JCNM President's Report 2000–2002," *Nikkei Images Newsletter* (Winter 2001): 14.

95. Interview with Frank Kamiya, Burnaby, British Columbia, August 6, 2003.

96. Ibid.

97. Evelyn Hu-DeHart, "Constructions of Asians in the Americas," lecture in the Green College Thematic Lecture Series "Reckoning with Race," University of British Columbia, Vancouver, British Columbia, January 2003.

98. Interview with Frank Kitamoto, Bainbridge Island, WA, February 15, 2003.

99. Interview with John Tateishi, San Francisco, CA, March 3, 2003.

100. *Banner* [NCRR Newsletter], Winter 2003.

101. See Balint, "Law's Constitutive Possibilities," p. 147.

102. Quoted in Florangela Davila, "Japanese Americans Know How It Feels to Be 'the Enemy'," *Seattle Times,* October 3, 2001, available at *www.seattletimes.nwsource.com.*

103. See Annie Nakao, "Japanese Americans Can Feel Muslims' Pain," *San Francisco Chronicle,* August 7, 2003, available at *www.sfgate.com.*

104. Internet media notice by the NAJC, March 31, 2003.

105. Interview with Art Miki, Winnipeg, Manitoba, July 7, 2003.

106. See John Biles and Humera Ibrahim, "Testing 'the Canadian Model': Hate, Bias and Fear After September 11th," *Canadian Issues* (Ottawa) (September 2002): 58.

107. Interview with Frank Kamiya, Burnaby, British Columbia, August 6, 2003.

108. Kobayashi, "The Japanese Canadian Redress Settlement," pp. 13–14.

109. For a discussion of the RCAP report, see Alan Cairns, "Coming to Terms with the Past," in Torpey, ed., *Politics and the Past,* pp. 77–80.

110. See Balint, "Law's Constitutive Possibilities," p. 145.

111. Daniels, "Relocation, Redress and the Report," p. 189.

112. Interview with John Tateishi, San Francisco, CA, March 3, 2003.

113. See Biles and Ibrahim, "Testing 'The Canadian Model' "; for a more skeptical view of Canadian multiculturalism emphasizing its nationalist and anti-American features, see Will Kymlicka, "Being Canadian," *Government and Opposition* 38, no. 3 (July 2003): 357–385.

114. See Minow, *Between Vengeance and Forgiveness,* p. 106.

4. Forty Acres

1. "Suits Ask Slavery Reparations," *Chicago Tribune*, March 27, 2002, Section 1, p. 9; the suit itself can be found online at *news.findlaw.com*. For further developments in the case, see Lori Rotenberk, "A Stern Judge Presides as Reparations Fight Begins," *Boston Sunday Globe*, August 24, 2003, p. A17.

2. See his oft-quoted observation, "There is almost no political question in the United States that is not resolved sooner or later into a judicial question." Alexis de Tocqueville, *Democracy in America*, trans. Harvey Mansfield and Delba Winthrop (Chicago: University of Chicago Press, 2000 [1835]), p. 257.

3. Linda Greenhouse, "Judges Back Rule Changes for Handling Class Actions," *New York Times*, September 25, 2002, p. A16.

4. John Locke, *Two Treatises of Government*, ed. Peter Laslett (New York: Mentor, 1965), Treatise II.

5. For a spectrum of views concerning the progress of the black population in the United States see above, p. 174n68.

6. Richard J. Herrnstein and Charles Murray, *The Bell Curve: Intelligence and Class Structure in American Life* (New York: Simon & Schuster, 1996). For a refutation of the biological arguments, see Joseph L. Graves Jr., *The Emperor's New Clothes: Biological Theories of Race at the Millennium* (New Brunswick, NJ: Rutgers University Press, 2001).

7. See Hugh Davis Graham, *Collision Course: The Strange Convergence of Affirmative Action and Immigration Policy in America* (New York: Oxford University Press, 2002) and Wilson, *The Bridge over the Racial Divide*. Also noteworthy are Robert Blauner's reflections on affirmative action in *Still the Big News: Racial Oppression in America*, rev. and exp. ed. (Philadelphia: Temple University Press, 2001), pp. 191–192.

8. Robert Westley, "Many Billions Gone: Is It Time to Reconsider the Case for Black Reparations?" *Boston College Law Review* 40, no. 1 (December 1998): 429, 432.

9. For a detailed discussion of these claims up until World War I, see John David Smith, "Historicizing the Slave Reparations Debate," paper presented at the conference "Historical Justice in International Perspective: How Societies Are Trying to Right the Wrongs of the Past," German Historical Institute, Washington, DC, March 2003. Smith is working on a history of the idea of reparations among blacks in the United States. Two examples of such claims are discussed in J. Clay Smith Jr., *Emancipation: The Making of the Black Lawyer, 1844–1944* (Philadelphia: University of Pennsylvania Press, 1993): the "Cotton Tax" suit claiming $68 million for slave-generated revenue from 1859 to 1868 (pp. 294–295, 303) and the protests against the recission of Special Field Order 15 authorizing black land settlement (pp. 191–192). Black lawyers led both movements.

10. Eric Foner, *A Short History of Reconstruction* (New York: Harper & Row, 1990), pp. 32, 71–72. For a discussion of the failures of the Freedmen's Bureau, see

W. E. B. Du Bois, *The Souls of Black Folk* (New York: Dover, 1994 [1903]), ch. 2, "Of the Dawn of Freedom," and, on the consequences of its failures, Jacqueline Jones, *The Dispossessed: America's Underclasses from the Civil War to the Present* (New York: Basic Books, 1992). John David Smith argues that the land was "probably" leased to the freedmen, but that the order was misconstrued by blacks as "conveying outright titles to the property." See Smith, "Historicizing the Slave Reparations Debate," p. 7.

11. On the significance of the 442d Regiment in the Japanese-American redress movement, see Mitchell Maki et al., *Achieving the Impossible Dream: How Japanese Americans Obtained Redress* (Urbana: University of Illinois Press, 1999), p. 153.

12. See the analysis in Robert Blauner's pathbreaking *Racial Oppression in America* (New York: Prentice-Hall, 1972), insightfully revised and updated in Blauner, *Still the Big News.*

13. See John David Skrentny, *The Minority Rights Revolution* (Cambridge, MA: Harvard University Press, 2002) and Graham, *Collision Course.*

14. Quoted in Harvard Sitkoff, *The Struggle for Black Equality, 1954–1980* (New York: Hill and Wang, 1981), p. 228.

15. See Robin D. G. Kelley, *Freedom Dreams: The Black Radical Imagination* (Boston: Beacon Press, 2002), pp. 118–120; Charles Ogletree, "Reparations, A Fundamental Issue of Social Justice," *The Black Collegian Online,* undated, *www.black-collegian.com;* and Arthur Serota, *Ending Apartheid in America: The Need for a Black Political Party and Reparations Now!* (Evanston, IL: Troubadour Press, 1996), Acknowledgments.

16. James Forman, *The Making of Black Revolutionaries* (Seattle: University of Washington Press, 1997 [1972]), pp. 545, 547; for the Manifesto itself, see Arnold Schuchter, *Reparations: The Black Manifesto and Its Challenge to White America* (Philadelphia: Lippincott, 1970); see also Rhonda Magee, "The Master's Tools, From the Bottom Up: Responses to African-American Reparations Theory in Mainstream and Outsider Remedies Discourse," *Virginia Law Review* 79, no. 4 (1993): 882–884; and Dawson, *Black Visions,* p. 119.

17. Charles Willie, "The Black Manifesto: Prophetic or Preposterous?" *The Episcopalian* (September 1969), quoted in Schuchter, *Reparations,* p. 11.

18. Dawson, *Black Visions,* p. 206.

19. Maki et al., *Achieving the Impossible Dream,* pp. 71, 252n35. For what it's worth, the idea of reparations goes without mention in the recent book by Roger Wilkins, Roy Wilkins's prominent nephew, *Jefferson's Pillow: The Founding Fathers and the Dilemma of Black Patriotism* (Boston: Beacon Press, 2001).

20. See Forman, *The Making of Black Revolutionaries,* p. 549.

21. See Michael Dawson's discussion of the tensions between black nationalists and the churches in *Black Visions,* pp. 107–108.

22. Alan Feuer, "Bitter Reparations Fight Reignited over Settlement," *New York Times,* November 21, 2000, p. A22; Joseph B. Treaster, "2 Holocaust Survivors

to Sue Group Set Up to Collect Insurance," *New York Times,* September 25, 2003, p. A16; William Glaberson, "Judge Rebuffs U.S. Holocaust Survivors on Distribution of a Fund," *New York Times,* November 22, 2003, p. A14.

23. Boris Bittker, *The Case for Black Reparations* (New York: Random House, 1973). Around the same time, R. S. Browne also published "The Economic Case for Reparations to Black America," *American Economic Review* 62, no. 1/2 (1972): 39–46.

24. A brief discussion of Bittker's book and some contemporary updating of his proposals can be found in Darrell L. Pugh, "Collective Rehabilitation," in Roy Brooks, ed., *When Sorry Isn't Enough: The Controversy over Apologies and Reparations for Human Injustice* (New York: New York University Press, 1999), pp. 372–373.

25. The story is recounted in Derrick A. Bell, *Confronting Authority: Reflections of an Ardent Protester* (Boston: Beacon Press, 1994).

26. See Derrick A. Bell, *And We Are Not Saved: The Elusive Quest for Racial Justice* (New York: Basic Books, 1987) and *Faces at the Bottom of the Well: The Permanence of Racism* (New York: Basic Books, 1992).

27. Derrick A. Bell, Jr., "Dissection of a Dream," *Harvard Civil Rights–Civil Liberties Law Review* 9, no. 1 (1974): 165.

28. Roy Brooks has sought to update Bittker's analysis of the constitutional obstacles confronting reparations claims in Boris I. Bittker and Roy L. Brooks, "The Constitutionality of Black Reparations," in Brooks, ed., *When Sorry Isn't Enough,* pp. 374–389.

29. Magee, "The Master's Tools, From the Bottom Up," p. 903.

30. See Lynette Clemetson, "Long Quest, Unlikely Allies: Black Museum Nears Reality," *New York Times,* June 29, 2003, pp. A1, A24, and Lynette Clemetson, "Bush Authorizes Black History Museum," *New York Times,* December 17, 2003, p. A32.

31. This interpretation is advanced by Dennis C. Sweet III, an attorney in Jackson, Mississippi who won a major settlement in the "fen-phen" diet drug case, in "Forum: Making the Case for Racial Reparations," *Harper's* (November 2000): 51. On the other hand, John Tateishi, a redress activist and now president of the Japanese American Citizens League, insisted in an interview with the author (San Francisco, CA, March 3, 2003) that the achievement of redress legislation was anything but a foregone conclusion.

32. See Joe R. Feagin and Eileen O'Brien, "The Growing Movement for Reparations," in Roy Brooks, ed., *When Sorry Isn't Enough,* p. 343.

33. The *Philadelphia Inquirer* ran two full-page editorials endorsing the idea of a study commission on May 20 and 21, 2001, generating hundreds of letters from readers.

34. Interview with Congressman Conyers, Washington, DC, March 27, 2003.

35. Conrad W. Worrill, "Millions for Reparations Rally: It's Our Turn," *The Black World Today,* April 1, 2002, available online at *www.encobra.com.*

36. Salim Muwakkil, "Time to Redress Slavery's Damage," *Chicago Sun-Times,* February 27, 1994, p. 45.

37. "The Business of Slavery and Penitence," *New York Times,* May 25, 2003, "Week in Review," p. 4.

38. Randall Robinson, *The Debt: What America Owes to Blacks* (New York: Dutton, 2000).

39. The meeting took place on January 11, 2000; see *www.transafricaforum.org;* a transcript is available at *www.transafricaforum.org.*

40. See *www.transafricaforum.org.*

41. "Six Meetings Before Lunch" aired April 4, 2000; quotations are taken from the script provided to me by NBC. For a superb discussion of the reasons men took part in the Civil War, see James M. McPherson, *For Cause & Comrades: Why Men Fought in the Civil War* (New York: Oxford University Press, 1997). McPherson argues that relatively few Union soldiers fought chiefly to end slavery, although this became an increasingly important motivation toward the end of the war.

42. "Forum: Making the Case for Racial Reparations," *Harper's* (November 2000): 37–51.

43. See *www.dir.salon.com.*

44. See Diana Jean Schemo, "An Ad Provokes Campus Protests and Pushes Limits of Expression," *New York Times,* March 21, 2001, pp. A1, A17; see also "Rhode Island: Debate Canceled," *New York Times,* April 4, 2001, p. A15.

45. For an overview of the controversy, see *www.murchisoncenter.org.*

46. A videotape of Horowitz's debate with N'COBRA representative Dorothy Lewis on April 4, 2001 at MIT is available from C-SPAN under the title, "Black Reparations Debate." See Horowitz's followup piece in *Salon.com,* "My 15 Minutes," at *www.dir.salon.com/.*

47. See the Web site of Horowitz's publication "Frontpage Magazine.Com," *www .frontpagemag.com.*

48. John McWhorter, "Against Reparations," *The New Republic* (July 23, 2001), pp. 32–38.

49. The document, dated July 19, 2001, can be found at *www.hrw.org.*

50. Jack E. White, "Don't Waste Your Breath," *Time,* April 2, 2001, p. 27.

51. See Adolph L. Reed Jr., "Class Notes: The Case Against Reparations," *The Progressive* (December 2000), available at *www.progressive.org.*

52. Here Reed refers to Daryl Michael Scott, *Contempt and Pity: Social Policy and the Image of the Damaged Black Psyche, 1880–1996* (Chapel Hill: University of North Carolina Press, 1997).

53. Quoted in Danny Postel, "The Awful Truth," *Chronicle of Higher Education,* July 12, 2002, p. A14; also available at *www.chronicle.com.*

54. See Mahmood Mamdani, "Degrees of Reconciliation and Forms of Justice: Making Sense of the African Experience," paper presented at the conference "Justice or Reconciliation?" at the Center for International Studies, University of Chicago, April 25–26, 1997, p. 6; quoted in Priscilla Hayner, *Unspeakable Truths: Confronting State Terror and Atrocity* (New York: Routledge, 2001), p. 164, and Mahmood Mamdani, "A Diminished Truth," in Wilmot James and Linda van de Vijver, eds., *After the TRC: Reflections on Truth and Reconciliation in*

South Africa (Athens: Ohio University Press, 2001 [2000]), p. 59. The distinction between commemorative and anti-systemic reparations that I made in "'Making Whole What Has Been Smashed': Reflections on Reparations" is analogous.

55. See Kenneth B. Nunn, "Rosewood," in Brooks, ed., *When Sorry Isn't Enough,* pp. 435–437 and Ross E. Milloy, "Panel Calls for Reparations in Tulsa Race Riot," *New York Times,* March 1, 2001, p. A12. The final report of the Oklahoma Commission to Study the Tulsa Race Riot of 1921 can be found at *www.ok-history.mus.ok.us;* see also Alfred L. Brophy, *Reconstructing the Dreamland: The Tulsa Race Riot of 1921* (New York: Oxford University Press, 2002) and James S. Hirsch, *Riot and Remembrance: The Tulsa Race War and Its Legacy* (Boston: Houghton Mifflin, 2002).

56. See Lyle Denniston, "Judge Dismisses Riots Reparations Suit," *Boston.com,* March 23, 2004, available at *www.boston.com.*

57. Ben Dalby, "Slavery and the Question of Reparations," *International Socialist Review,* no. 26 (November–December 2002): 74–80.

58. See the evident frustration in Charles Ogletree Jr., *All Deliberate Speed: Reflections on the First Half Century of* Brown v. Board of Education (New York: Norton, 2004).

59. Charles J. Ogletree Jr., "Litigating the Legacy of Slavery," *New York Times,* March 31, 2002, p. 9.

60. The statement can be found online at *www.ag-east.org.*

61. Barry Meier, "Lawyer in Holocaust Case Faces Litany of Complaints," *New York Times,* September 8, 2000, pp. A1, A21.

62. See Chapter 5.

63. Interview with Charles Ogletree, Oak Bluffs, MA, August 21, 2002.

64. Dated on April 16, 2002, the document is available online at *www.encobra.com,* in the author's possession.

65. Adamma Ince, "No Masses, No Movement: Black Boomers Shout Reparations in the Court—But Go Silent in the 'Hood," *Village Voice,* May 22–28, 2002; available online at *www.villagevoice.com.*

66. See the announcement online at *www.thedrammehinstitute.org.*

67. Interview with Charles Ogletree, Oak Bluffs, MA, August 21, 2002; see also "Slavery Reparations Advocates Voice Demands in Washington," *New York Times,* August 18, 2002, p. 23. In a telephone interview with the author on March 23, 2003, Bill Fletcher, a former trade unionist who is now the president of TransAfrica Forum and a supportive realist about the reparations movement, referred to the August event ironically as the "Dozens for Reparations Rally."

68. For an unflattering portrayal of the New Black Panther Party and its conflicts with the original group bearing that name, see Dean E. Murphy, "Black Panthers, Gone Gray, Fight Rival Group," *New York Times,* October 8, 2002, pp. A1, A21.

69. See the announcements of these various organizations, available online at *www.nbufront.org* and *www.ag-east.org.*

70. Dawson, *Black Visions*, p. 308. On Garvey and Garveyism, see Judith Stein, *Marcus Garvey: Race and Class in Modern Society* (Baton Rouge: Louisiana State University Press, 1986).

71. Ibid., p. 60.

72. See Ince, "No Masses, No Movement." The scene in the movie *Barbershop* in which reparations is discussed suggests that the idea is familiar, but it generates little enthusiasm.

73. According to Feagin and O'Brien, however, the NAACP has come out in support of the idea; see "The Growing Movement for Reparations," p. 343. At an NAACP-sponsored event in which I participated in Oak Bluffs, Massachusetts on August 26, 2002, however, NAACP Legal Defense Fund lawyer Ted Shaw stated that the organization had not endorsed the quest for reparations.

74. See *www.naacp.org*, accessed July 20, 2004.

75. On this point, see Felicia R. Lee, "Hip-Hop Is Enlisted in Social Causes," *New York Times*, June 22, 2002, pp. A13, A15.

76. On the deceptiveness of the apparent somnolescence of the 1950s, see Todd Gitlin, *The Sixties: Years of Hope, Days of Rage* (New York: Bantam, 1987), ch. 1, "Cornucopia and Its Discontents."

77. See, for example, William H. Chafe, *Civilities and Civil Rights: Greensboro, North Carolina and the Black Struggle for Freedom* (New York: Oxford University Press, 1980), pp. 13, 42–44; and Harvard Sitkoff, *The Struggle for Black Equality, 1954–1980* (New York: Hill and Wang, 1981), *passim*.

78. On these points, see Gerald N. Rosenberg, *The Hollow Hope: Can Courts Bring about Social Change?* (Chicago: University of Chicago Press, 1991), Part I.

79. Charles Ogletree suggested the latter interpretation in my interview with him on August 21, 2002.

80. Charles Ogletree, one of the lead lawyers in the case, stated that the judgment would be appealed and that "this has always been viewed as a marathon, not a sprint. There is a lot of fight left in our clients." Lyle Denniston, "Judge Dismisses Riots Reparations Suit," *Boston.com*, March 23, 2004.

81. See Dalton Conley, "Calculating Slavery Reparations: Numbers, Theory, and Implications," in John Torpey, ed., *Politics and the Past: On Repairing Historical Injustices* (Lanham, MD: Rowman & Littlefield, 2003), pp. 117–125.

82. Charles J. Ogletree, Jr., *All Deliberate Speed*, pp. 292–293; see also Ogletree, "The Case for Reparations," *USA Weekend*, August 18, 2002, available at *www.usaweekend.com*.

83. Ogletree, *All Deliberate Speed*, p. 290.

84. Chris Burrell, "Forum Explores Issue of Reparations," *(Martha's) Vineyard Gazette*, September 4, 2002.

85. Comments at the Oak Bluffs NAACP event on reparations, August 26, 2002.

86. Jennifer Hochschild, "The Price of Reparations," *Contexts* 1, no. 4 (Fall/Winter 2002): 4.

87. Carol Swain, *The New White Nationalism in America: Its Challenge to Integration* (New York: Cambridge University Press, 2002), p. 181.

88. An example of the kind of argument I am making is Wilson, *The Bridge over*

the Racial Divide. See also the report of the American Political Science Associa-tion's Task Force on Inequality and American Democracy, *American Democracy in an Age of Inequality,* released June 2004, available at *www.apsanet.org.*

89. See Diana Jean Schemo, "U. of Michigan Draws a New Type of Recruit," *New York Times,* February 21, 2003, p. A18 and Diana Jean Schemo, "Doctors, Sol-diers, and Others Weigh in on Campus Diversity," *New York Times,* February 23, 2003, "Week in Review," p. 7.

90. See Nicholas Lemann, "A Decision that Universities Can Relate To," *New York Times,* "Week in Review," June 29, 2003, p. 14.

91. See Michael T. Martin and Marilyn Yaquinto, "Reparations for 'America's Ho-locaust': Activism for Global Justice," *Race & Class* 45, no. 4 (April–June 2004): 1–25, and Sam Anderson and Muntu Matsimela, "The Reparations Movement: An Assessment of Recent and Current Activism," *Socialism & Democracy* 17, no. 1 (2003): 270–273.

5. Post-Colonial Reparations

1. Document in author's possession.

2. See Jan-Bart Gewald, *Herero Heroes: A Socio-Political History of the Herero of Na-mibia, 1890–1923* (Athens: Ohio University Press, 1999), pp. 141–171. Journal-istic accounts typically claim that the German assault was provoked by a planned Herero revolt. According to Gewald, a leading historian of the region, however, "The Herero-German war was not the result of a premeditated Herero insurrection against German colonial governance. Ideas of a nation-wide insurrection existed solely in German colonial minds . . . The Herero-German war broke out as the result of settler paranoia coupled with the in-competence and panic of a German officer" (p. 191).

3. Casper W. Erichsen, "A Forgotten History," *Mail & Guardian* (Johannesburg), August 17, 2001.

4. AFP, "Germany Expresses 'Regret' over Genocide in Colonial Africa," January 12, 2004, available at *www.channelnewsasia.com.*

5. The South African government, which took over control of Namibia from the Germans during World War I, has also been called upon to pay reparations, but this demand has been largely ignored. See Jeremy Sarkin, "Holding Multi-national Corporations Accountable for Human Rights and Humanitarian Law Violations Committed During Colonialism and Apartheid," in Eva Brems, ed., *In Bedrijven en Mensenrechten* (Maklu, 2003), p. 30n148; and Warren Buford and Hugo van der Merwe, "Reparation in Southern Africa," *Cahiers d'études af-ricaines* 44, no. 1–2 (2004); manuscript pp. 33–41. I am grateful to Hugo van der Merwe of the Centre for the Study of Violence and Reconciliation (CSVR) for supplying me the manuscript of this article and to CSVR researcher Nahla Valji for making the connection between us.

6. Interview with Herero Paramount Chief Kuaima Riruako, Windhoek, Namibia, January 3, 2003.

7. Gewald, *Herero Heroes*, p. 288.

8. Sidney Harring, "The Legal Claim for German Reparations to the Herero Nation," available at *www.academic.udayton.edu;* excerpted from Sidney Harring, "German Reparations to the Herero Nation: An Assertion of Herero Nationhood in the Path of Namibian Development?" *West Virginia Law Review* 104 (Winter 2002).

9. Accordingly, local descendants of the German colonists are less concerned about reparations payments coming from the German government. Their fear is that the Herero could make inroads on the millions of acres of ranches they own in the country.

10. See F. Bridgland, "Germany's Genocide Rehearsal," *The Scotsman,* September 26, 2001, and T. Bensman, "Tribe Demands Holocaust Reparations: Germany's Genocidal War Against Namibia's Herero Was Rehearsal for World War II Atrocities," *The Salt Lake Tribune*, March 18, 1999; both cited in Sarkin, "Holding Multinational Corporations Accountable," p. 31n152 and p. 34n164.

11. Interview with Herero Paramount Chief Kuaima Riruako, Windhoek, Namibia, January 3, 2003. The relevant portion of von Trotha's order reads as follows: "The Herero people must . . . leave the land. If the populace does not do this I will force them with the *Groot Rohr* [cannon]. Within the German borders every Herero, with or without a gun, with or without cattle, will be shot. I will no longer accept women and children, I will drive them back to their people or I will let them be shot at." Quoted in Gewald, *Herero Heroes,* pp. 172–173.

12. For a good synopsis of the process, see Francis Jennings, "Appendix: The Formative Period of a Large Society: A Comparative Approach," in his *The Invasion of America: Indians, Colonialism, and the Cant of Conquest* (New York: Norton, 1976), pp. 327–335.

13. On the historiographical problem of the missing order to carry out the genocide against the Jews, see Michael Marrus, *The Holocaust in History* (New York: Meridian, 1987), pp. 32–34.

14. Frank Chalk, "The Implementation of the Persecution of the Jews, the 'Gypsies' (Sinti and Roma), People of Color and Others in Germany, 1933–1940," available at *www.google.de.* See also Michael Burleigh and Wolfgang Wippermann, *The Racial State: Germany, 1933–1945* (New York: Cambridge University Press, 1991), pp. 38, 52. For Fischer's work, see Eugen Fischer, *Die Rehobother Bastards und das Bastardierungsproblem beim Menschen* (Jena: Gustav Fischer, 1913). In one of the many ironies of Namibian history, the "Basters" of the Rehoboth area still go by this name and apparently do not regard it with shame despite the fact that the word is essentially the equivalent of the cognate English term.

15. Hannah Arendt, *The Origins of Totalitarianism* (New York: Harcourt, Brace, 1973 [1951]), Part II, "Imperialism."

16. These horrors have now been presented in harrowing fictionalized form in André Brink, *The Other Side of Silence* (London: Secker & Warburg, 2002).

17. Donald G. McNeil Jr., "Its Past on Its Sleeve, Tribe Seeks Bonn's Apology," *New York Times* (West Coast edition), May 31, 1998, p. A3.

18. Susanne Bittorf, "Fischer verspricht Namibia Hilfe," *Süddeutsche Zeitung,* October 30, 2003, p. 7. Fischer's exact words were that he would "keine Äusserung vornehmen, die entschädigungsrelevant wäre."

19. AFP, "Germany Expresses 'Regret' over Genocide in Colonial Africa." See also "Namibia: Germany Regrets Colonial Massacre," *New York Times,* "World Briefing," January 13, 2004, p. A15.

20. BBC News, "Germany Avoids Herero Reparations," July 18, 2004; available at *www.news.bbc.co.uk.*

21. Interview with Professor Mburumba Kerina, Windhoek, Namibia, January 3, 2003.

22. See "Namibia: Tensions Revealed in Swapo," *SouthScan* 19, no. 11 (May 28, 2004): 6.

23. Interview with Professor Mburumba Kerina, Windhoek, Namibia, January 3, 2003.

24. See Warren Buford and Hugo van der Merwe, "Reparation in Southern Africa," *Cahiers d'études africaines* 44, no. 1–2 (2004): manuscript pp. 33–41. The quotations are from p. 40.

25. Quoted in Bittorf, "Fischer verspricht Namibia Hilfe," p. 7.

26. Interview with Herero Paramount Chief Kuaima Riruako, Windhoek, Namibia, January 3, 2003.

27. Harring, "The Legal Claim for German Reparations to the Herero Nation."

28. See Ludolf Herbst and Constantin Goschler, *Wiedergutmachung in der Bundesrepublik Deutschland* (München: R. Oldenbourg, 1989).

29. See McNeil, "Its Past on Its Sleeve, Tribe Seeks Bonn's Apology," p. A3.

30. Telephone interview with Philip Musolino, September 6, 2002.

31. Superior Court of the District of Columbia, Civil Division, Case No. 01–0004447, September 18, 2001, p. 21.

32. J. R. Paul, "Holding Multi-National Corporations Responsible Under International Law," *Hastings International and Comparative Law Review* (Spring 2001), quoted in Sarkin, "Holding Multinational Corporations Accountable," p. 9.

33. U.N. Integrated Regional Information Networks, "Hereros Claim Against Berlin," September 21, 2001, available at *www.namibia.de.*

34. Quoted in Sarkin, "Holding Multinational Corporations Accountable," p. 32.

35. AFP, "Germany Expresses 'Regret' over Genocide in Colonial Africa."

36. Interview with John Tateishi, President, Japanese American Citizens League, San Francisco, CA, March 3, 2003.

37. "Namibia: A Century Later, Tribe Sues," *New York Times,* September 7, 2001, p. A8.

38. B. Stephens, "Translating *Filartiga:* A Comparative and International Law Analysis of Domestic Remedies for International Human Rights Violations," vol. 27 (2002), p. 1; quoted in Sarkin, "Holding Multinational Corporations Accountable," p. 20.

39. Sarkin, "Holding Multinational Corporations Accountable," pp. 16–17. See Sarkin for an extended analysis of the legal background to the centrality of U.S. courts in this kind of litigation.

40. "'Historische Verantwortung'," *Frankfurter Allgemeine Zeitung,* October 31, 2003, p. 6.

41. Harring, "The Legal Claim for German Reparations to the Herero Nation."

42. "Brandenburg schließt Vertrag mit dem Vatikan," *Süddeutsche Zeitung,* November 6, 2003, p. 8. My translation and emphasis.

43. See Erichsen, "A Forgotten History."

44. The point here is not to condemn "outside agitators" but to understand the process of diffusion of the idea of reparations.

45. Christopher J. Colvin, *Overview of the Reparations Programme in South Africa* (Centre for the Study of Violence and Reconciliation, n.p. [Cape Town?], n.d. [2003]), p. 29.

46. Arthur Serota, *Ending Apartheid in America: The Need for a Black Political Party and Reparations Now* (Evanston, IL: Troubadour Press, 1996).

47. See Sitkoff, *The Struggle for Black Equality, 1954–1980* (New York: Hill and Wang, 1981) and Fredrickson, *Black Liberation: A Comparative History of Black Ideologies in the United States and South Africa* (New York: Oxford University Press, 1995).

48. On the spread of truth commissions generally, see Priscilla Hayner, *Unspeakable Truths: Confronting State Terror and Atrocity* (New York: Routledge, 2001).

49. For critical views of the TRC, see Heribert Adam, "The Presence of the Past: South Africa's Truth Commission as a Model?" in A. Tayob and W. Weisse, eds., *Religion and Politics in South Africa* (Muenster: Waxmann, 2000), pp. 140–158; and Richard Wilson, *The Politics of Truth and Reconciliation in South Africa: Legitimating the Post-Apartheid State* (New York: Cambridge University Press, 2001).

50. Mahmood Mamdani, "A Diminished Truth," in Wilmot James and Linda van de Vijver, eds., *After the TRC: Reflections on Truth and Reconciliation in South Africa* (Athens: Ohio University Press, 2001), pp. 58–61.

51. Colvin, *Overview,* p. 29.

52. Ibid., p. 1.

53. Interview with Mary Burton, Cape Town, South Africa, January 8, 2003; Interview with George Dor, General Secretary, Jubilee South Africa, Johannesburg, South Africa, January 16, 2003. Buford and van der Merwe state that the urgent interim reparations were in the amount of R2000–R7500; see "Reparation in Southern Africa," manuscript p. 13.

54. Colvin, *Overview,* p. 21.

55. Interview with Reverend Michael Lapsley, Director, Institute for the Healing of Memories, Cape Town, January 9, 2003. On this point, see Heribert Adam, Frederik Van Zyl Slabbert, and Kogila Moodley, *Comrades in Business: Post-Liberation Politics in South Africa* (Cape Town: Tafelberg, 1997).

56. Interview with Mary Burton, Cape Town, South Africa, January 8, 2003.

57. The Soweto uprising began as a protest against government efforts to impose Afrikaans as an official language of instruction; hence, schoolchildren were at the heart of events. As a testament to the boy's memory, the Hector Petersen Apartheid Museum in Soweto opened in 2002.

58. Quoted in Sarkin, "Holding Multinational Corporations Accountable," p. 36.

59. See BBC News, "Apartheid Victims File Suit," June 19, 2002, available at *www .news.bbc.co.uk.*

60. See their background report, Jubilee 2000 South Africa, "Apartheid-Caused Debt: The Role of German and Swiss Finance," available online at *aidc.org.za* or from Aktion Finanzplatz Schweiz, *www.aktionfinanzplatz.ch;* authored by Mascha Madörin and Gottfried Wellmer, with a contribution by Martine Egil and originally published in German by Bread for the World, Stuttgart, in February 1999.

61. Nacha Cattan, "Restitution Attorneys Plan Lawsuits Backing 3rd World Debt Relief," *The Forward,* November 30, 2001, available online at *www.forward.com.*

62. Gail Appleson, "Apartheid Victims Sue Citigroup, Others," *Reuters,* June 19, 2002, available at *www.siliconvalley.com.* The suit that Hausfeld was preparing, in conjunction with the Khulumani Support Group and Jubilee 2000 South Africa, was filed on November 12, 2002; see below and *www.google.ca.*

63. "Reparations Cases May Reopen Macro-Economic Debate," *SouthScan* 18, no. 22 (October 31, 2003): 6.

64. Hlengiwe Mkhize, "Reparation Issue Needs Political Solution," *Sunday Times* (Johannesburg), July 7, 2002, available at *www.suntimes.co.za.*

65. Colvin, *Overview, passim;* see the Khulumani Support Group Web site at *www .khulumani.net.*

66. Quoted in *SouthScan* 17, no. 23 (November 15, 2002): 8.

67. Interview with George Dor, General Secretary, Jubilee South Africa, Johannesburg, South Africa, January 16, 2003.

68. See the "Briefing on the Apartheid Debt and Reparations Campaign," n.d. [November 12, 2002], and Apartheid Debt and Reparations Campaign, "Media Statement," November 12, 2002, both in the author's possession.

69. "Swiss Corporations Manoeuvre to Avoid Apartheid Compensation Claims," *SouthScan* 17, no. 23 (November 15, 2002): 8.

70. Interview with George Dor, General Secretary, Jubilee South Africa, Johannesburg, South Africa, January 16, 2003.

71. For a discussion of some of the complexities facing the South African government concerning reparations lawsuits, see "Reparations Action May Throw Spanner in the NEPAD Works," *Southscan* 17, no. 13 (June 28, 2002): 1–2, and "Swiss Corporations Manoeuvre to Avoid Apartheid Compensation Claims," *Southscan* 17, no. 23 (November 15, 2002): 6–7.

72. See Christelle Terreblanche, "Nobel Laureate Endorses Apartheid Reparations," *Independent On Line* (Johannesburg), August 13, 2003, available at *www.iol.co .za.*

73. Buford and van der Merwe, "Reparation in Southern Africa," manuscript p. 4;

the quotation is from Ginger Thompson, "South Africa to Pay Reparations to Victims of Apartheid Crimes," *New York Times,* April 16, 2003, p. A7.

74. "Reparations Cases May Reopen Macro-Economic Debate," *SouthScan* 18, no. 22 (October 31, 2003): 6.

75. "Government Dismisses Tutu's Reparations Support," *Southscan* 19, no. 3 (February 6, 2004): 7.

76. Interview with Frelimo Phaka, General Secretary, South African Reparations Movement (SARM), Johannesburg, January 15, 2003.

77. SARM, "Summary of Recent Activities," n.d. [December 2002], in the author's possession.

78. SARM material in the author's possession.

79. Interview with George Dor, General Secretary, Jubilee South Africa, Johannesburg, South Africa, January 16, 2003. Biko's death in the custody of police officers in the jail at Port Elizabeth in 1977 was commemorated in Peter Gabriel's haunting elegy, "Biko" (from "Peter Gabriel," Geffen Records, 1980).

80. See Ronald Niezen, *The Origins of Indigenism: Human Rights and the Politics of Identity* (Berkeley: University of California Press, 2003).

81. Anne M. Simmons, "A Tribe Makes a Waterfront Claim," *Los Angeles Times,* October 14, 2001.

82. See Sharon LaFraniere and Michael Wines, "Africa Puzzle: Landless Blacks and White Farms," *New York Times,* January 6, 2004, pp. A1, A10.

83. Interview with Frelimo Phaka, General Secretary, South African Reparations Movement (SARM), Johannesburg, January 15, 2003.

84. SARM, "Summary of Recent Activities," n.d. [December 2002], in the author's possession.

85. Interview with Frelimo Phaka, General Secretary, South African Reparations Movement (SARM), Johannesburg, January 15, 2003.

86. Mike Cohen, "Indigenous S. Africans Demand Rights," *Associated Press,* April 1, 2001. Presumably the idea here is to emulate the "indigenous" people of Canada, who have had themselves declared the "First Nations" of that country in an effort to undermine the founding mythology that ascribed the country's founding to "two nations," the English and the French.

87. Simmons, "A Tribe Makes a Waterfront Claim."

88. "Richtersveld Case Highlights Racial Discrimination in Botswana," News Release, Survival International, October 30, 2003.

89. "Bushmen's Court Case Against Botswana to Be Heard," News Release, Survival International, January 24, 2003.

90. Sharon LaFraniere and Michael Wines, "Africa Puzzle: Landless Blacks and White Farms," *New York Times,* January 6, 2004, p. A10.

91. *SouthScan* 19, no. 11 (May 28, 2004): 8.

92. Interview with Reverend Michael Lapsley, Director, Institute for the Healing of Memories, Cape Town, January 9, 2003.

93. Interview with George Dor, General Secretary, Jubilee South Africa, Johannesburg, South Africa, January 16, 2003.

Conclusion

1. On this point, see Carol Gluck, "The 'End' of the Postwar: Japan at the Turn of the Millennium," in Jeffrey K. Olick, ed., *States of Memory: Continuities, Conflicts, and Transformations in National Retrospection* (Durham, NC: Duke University Press, 2003), p. 312; see also Wendy Brown, *Politics Out of History* (Princeton, NJ: Princeton University Press, 2001).

2. Robert Hughes, *The Culture of Complaint: The Fraying of America* (New York: Oxford University Press, 1993) and Jean-Michel Chaumont, *La concurrence des victimes: Génocide, identité, reconnaissance* (Paris: Éditions La Decouverte, 1997).

3. David Garland, *The Culture of Control: Crime and Social Order in Contemporary Society* (Chicago: University of Chicago Press, 2001), pp. 11–12.

4. For a suggestive discussion, see Jean Comaroff, "The End of History, Again: Pursuing the Past in the Postcolony," in S. Kaul et al., eds., *Postcolonial Studies and Beyond* (Durham, NC: Duke University Press, 2005).

5. Charles S. Maier, *The Unmasterable Past: History, Holocaust, and German National Identity* (Cambridge, MA: Harvard University Press, 1997 [1988], p. 32.

6. See Todd Gitlin, *The Twilight of Common Dreams: Why America Is Wracked by Culture Wars* (New York: Metropolitan Books, 1995).

7. This is the chief argument of Peter Novick, *The Holocaust in American Life* (Boston: Houghton Mifflin, 1999). See the critical remarks on Novick in Jeffrey Alexander, "On the Social Construction of Moral Universals: The Holocaust from War Crime to Trauma Drama," *European Journal of Social Theory* 5, no. 1 (February 2002): 5–85.

8. See Joshua Fogel, "Introduction: The Nanjing Massacre in History," in Fogel, ed., *The Nanjing Massacre in History and Historiography* (Berkeley: University of California Press, 2000), pp. 3–4, and Ian Buruma, "Commentary," in Andrew Horvat and Gebhard Hielscher, eds., *Sharing the Burden of the Past: Legacies of War in Europe, America, and Asia* (Tokyo: The Asia Foundation/Friedrich-Ebert-Stiftung, 2003), p. 139.

9. See, for example, William Kornhauser, *The Politics of Mass Society* (Glencoe, IL: Free Press, 1959) and Richard Hofstadter, *Anti-Intellectualism in American Life* (New York: Vintage, 1962).

10. Immediately after the "Republican Revolution" that brought a Republican Congress to power in 1994, U.S. government agencies such as the United States Institute of Peace, where I then worked, were compelled to introduce into their informational literature language regarding our "customer service."

11. Perhaps the canonical version of this argument is Will Kymlicka, *Multicultural Citizenship: A Liberal Theory of Minority Rights* (New York: Oxford University Press, 1995).

12. See the Report of the American Political Science Assocation Task Force on Inequality and American Democracy, *American Democracy in an Age of Rising Inequality*, issued June 2004, available at *www.apsanet.org*.

13. On the question of whether we have become more civilized, I want to thank

Andy Markovits for a suggestive discussion of the transformation of the contemporary circus; with regard to the morality of eating animals, I have in mind the writings of Peter Singer, *Animal Liberation* (New York: Ecco, 2001 [1975]). On the whole problem, see Ariel Colonomos and John Torpey, eds., "World Civility?" special issue of *Journal of Human Rights* 3, no. 2 (2004).

14. Adam Liptak, "Court Dismisses Claims of Slave Laborers: California Law Allowing World War II Reparations Is Struck Down," *New York Times*, January 22, 2003, p. A12.

15. Linda Greenhouse, "Justices Take Case on Nazi-Looted Art," *New York Times*, October 1, 2003, p. A20.

16. See Linda Greenhouse, "Reviewing Foreigners' Use of Federal Courts," *New York Times*, December 2, 2003, p. A22.

17. Linda Greenhouse, "Human Rights Abuses Worldwide Are Held to Fall Under U.S. Courts," *New York Times*, June 30, 2004, p. A19.

18. The "Basic Principles and Guidelines" can be found at *www.unhchr.ch*. See also Stephan Parmentier et al., eds., *Reparation for Victims of Gross and Systematic Human Rights Violations* (Antwerp: Intersentia, 2006).

19. Quoted from a 1937 letter to Walter Benjamin in Rolf Tiedemann, *Dialektik im Stillstand: Versuche zum Spätwerk Walter Benjamins* (Frankfurt: Suhrkamp, 1983), p. 107. My translation.

Index